T0301620

Environmental Transition in Nordic and Baltic Countries

NEW HORIZONS IN ENVIRONMENTAL ECONOMICS

General Editor: Wallace E. Oates, *Professor of Economics, University of Maryland*

This important series is designed to make a significant contribution to the development of the principles and practices of environmental economics. It includes both theoretical and empirical work. International in scope, it addresses issues of current and future concern in both East and West and in developed and developing countries.

The main purpose of the series is to create a forum for the publication of high quality work and to show how economic analysis can make a contribution to understanding and resolving the environmental problems confronting the world in the late twentieth century.

Recent titles in the series include:

Environmental Transition in Nordic and Baltic Countries

Edited by

Hans Aage

Professor of Economics, University of Roskilde, Denmark

NEW HORIZONS IN ENVIRONMENTAL ECONOMICS

Edward Elgar

Cheltenham, UK • Northampton, MA, USA

Published by
Edward Elgar Publishing Limited
Glensanda House
Montpellier Parade
Cheltenham
Glos GL50 1UA
UK

Edward Elgar Publishing, Inc.
6 Market Street
Northampton
Massachusetts 01060
USA

A catalogue record for this book
is available from the British Library

Library of Congress Cataloguing in Publication Data

Environmental transition in Nordic and Baltic countries / edited by
   Hans Aage
      (New horizons in environmental economics)
      Includes bibliographical references.
         1. Scandinavia—Environmental conditions. 2. Baltic States-
   -Environmental conditions. 3. Environmental policy—Scandinavia.
   4. Environmental policy—Baltic States. 5. Conservation of
   natural resources—Economic aspects—Scandinavia. 6. Conservation of
   natural resources—Economic aspects—Baltic States. I. Aage, Hans.
   II. Series.
   GE160.S34E58   1998
   363.7'00948—dc21   98–28490
                                                       CIP

ISBN 1 85898 629 X

Printed and bound in Great Britain by
Biddles Ltd, Guildford and King's Lynn

Contents

v

PART FOUR: INTERNATIONAL CO-OPERATION

Tables

Contributors

Hans Aage, Professor of Economics, Dr.Polit., Department of Social Sciences, Roskilde University.

Asbjørn Aaheim, Senior Research Fellow, Centre for International Climate and Environmental Research, University of Oslo.

Sigridur Benediktsdottir, Research Assistant, Institute of Economic Studies, University of Iceland.

Linas Čekanavičius, Head of Department, Ph.D., Department of Economic Systems Analysis, Vilnius University.

Raimonds Ernšteins, Assistant Professor, Director, Ph.D., Centre for Environmental Science and Management Studies, University of Latvia.

Anders Christian Hansen, Assistant Professor, Department of Social Sciences, Roskilde University.

Tryggvi Thor Herbertsson, Director, Institute of Economic Studies, University of Iceland.

Anni Huhtala, Senior Research Fellow, Ph.D., Finnish Forest Research Institute, Academy of Finland

Jesper Jespersen, Professor, Ph.D., Department of Social Sciences, Roskilde University.

Tiit Kallaste, Acting Director, Ph.D., The Stockholm Environment Institute, Tallinn Centre.

Ivars Kudreņickis, Senior Specialist, Centre for Environmental Science and Management Studies, University of Latvia.

Karl-Göran Mäler, Professor of Economics, Director, Ph.D., The Beijer International Institute of Ecological Economics, The Royal Swedish Academy of Sciences.

Valdis Mežapuķe, Senior Research Fellow, Dr.Econ., Institute of Economics, Latvian Academy of Sciences.

Eva Samakovlis, Research Fellow, Department of Economics, Umeå University.

Vytautas Snieška, Head of Department, Ph.D., Department of Economics, Kaunas University of Technology.

Erik Terk, Director, Ph.D., The Estonian Institute of Future Studies.

PART ONE

Introduction

1. Environmental Transition: A Comparative View

Hans Aage

1.1 Historical and Global Perspectives

In a historical and global perspective the similarities between Eastern and Western Europe figure more prominently than the differences. Long-term growth paths in Eastern Europe and Russia resemble those of Western Europe (cf. Table 1.1). In the late 1980s the former planned economies of Eastern Europe and the USSR, excluding Albania and Romania, belonged to the top 27 per cent of the world population concerning GDP per capita, and to the top 24 per cent concerning the human development index (cf. Table 1.2).

Table 1.2 shows that with respect to consumption of resources Eastern Europe and the Soviet Union did achieve a level which is on a par with that of the rich western economies. In 1989 energy consumption was relatively high, and very high if energy consumption is computed per unit GDP instead of per capita, but consumption of fertilizer and pesticides were closer to the average. The main differences are that they used resources relatively inefficiently, that progress was small from 1973 to 1989, that they polluted more than western countries – approximately as western countries did 20–30 years before – and furthermore that pollution was more concentrated in a few heavily polluted areas. As regards the more global, less visible and more serious types of pollution, for example the emission of greenhouse gases, Eastern Europe and the former USSR did not contribute more than average (cf. Feshbach and Friendly, 1992, pp. 50, 164; Ponting, 1991, pp. 260–2).

Concerning energy consumption several studies show that Eastern Europe and the former USSR used 50–150 per cent more energy per unit output than the OECD average (Moe, 1995; OECD and IEA, 1990). This is not explained by differences in production structure and climatic conditions. The comparison between the Soviet Union and Canada is particularly interesting because of climatic as well as some structural similarities, as both countries exported energy corresponding to to some 20 per cent of total energy output in the late

Table 1.1   *Annual growth rates of GDP per capita in selected countries, 1400–1989*

per cent annual growth		1400 –1820	1820 –1870	1870 –1913	1913 –1950	1950 –1973	1973 –1989	GDP per capita 1989
1.	Japan	..	0.1	1.4	0.9	8.0	3.0	81.5
2.	Norway	..	0.5	1.3	2.1	3.2	3.1	76.6
3.	USA	..	1.3	1.8	1.6	2.4	1.7	100.0
4.	Sweden	..	0.7	1.5	2.1	3.1	1.7	80.8
5.	United Kingdom	0.3	1.3	1.0	0.8	2.5	1.9	74.8
6.	Iceland	..	..	..	..	4.2	1.8	79.5
7.	Germany	..	1.1	1.6	0.3	5.0	2.0	82.7
8.	Finland	..	0.8	1.4	1.9	4.3	2.8	76.6
9.	Denmark	..	0.9	1.6	1.6	3.1	1.7	80.9
10.	Ireland	..	1.3	1.0	0.7	3.1	2.4	47.2
11.	Greece	..	..	..	0.5	6.2	1.7	47.1
12.	Czechoslovakia	..	0.6	1.4	1.4	3.1	1.4	40.1
13.	Lithuania	..	..	..	..	3.4	1.0	35.0
14.	Estonia	..	..	..	..	3.4	1.0	37.5
15.	Latvia	..	..	..	..	3.4	1.0	36.3
16.	USSR	..	0.6	0.9	1.8	3.4	1.0	32.5
17.	Korea, Republic of	..	..	..	-0.2	5.3	6.9	38.1
18.	Argentina	..	..	2.5	0.7	2.1	-1.1	30.6
19.	Brazil	..	0.2	0.3	1.9	3.8	1.7	23.6
20.	Thailand	..	..	0.4	0.0	3.2	5.0	17.5
21.	China	0.0	0.0	0.6	-0.3	2.9	5.2	12.2
22.	Indonesia	..	0.1	0.8	-0.1	2.5	2.8	11.0
23.	Ghana	..	..	..	1.7	0.2	-1.7	4.4
24.	India	..	0.1	0.4	-0.3	1.6	2.7	6.0
25.	Nigeria	..	..	..	..	3.2	-0.3	4.9
	Western countries	0.2	1.1	1.6	1.3	3.2	1.9	87.6

Notes: Countries are ranked in the same order as in Table 1.2. Changing borders of countries have been taken into account, but differ from those in Table 1.2. Early growth rates are very uncertain, and the oldest numbers are rough estimates for orders of magnitude. Growth rates for the Baltic countries are simply assumed to equal those of the USSR. GDP per capita for 1989 is expressed as an index with USA equal to 100. Western countries include Western Europe, except Ireland and Southern Europe, and USA, Canada, Australia and New Zealand.
Sources: Maddison, 1995, pp. 142, 194–206, 212, 217; Maddison, 1991, p. 10; Persson, 1988, p. 139.

80s (OECD and IEA, 1990), and countries, which possess large energy reserves, also in general tend to consume large quantities of energy. Soviet overall energy intensity was about 50 per cent higher than the Canadian in 1988. This is only partly due to structural differences and mainly to higher energy intensities in most sectors, especially in energy production itself. The marginal costs of Soviet oil extraction have soared – thus it increased 10 times from 1974–82 and average costs doubled – even to the point where increasing oil extraction produced a negative net energy output. The reason is first of all increasing transport distances and depletion of high quality deposits. Therefore investment in energy conservation became extremely profitable. It is difficult to understand why opportunities like these were not exploited. Although energy efficiency has improved considerably in western industrial countries especially since 1973, there are, however, also large profitable possibilities for energy savings which remain unexploited, mainly because investors in energy savings require very high returns, often recoupment periods of three years or less (Aage, 1994, p. 30).

This raises some doubt concerning the ever recurring explanation, that is lack of market institutions, which are also regarded as the panacea for all ecological problems (Feshbach and Friendly, 1992; OECD and IEA, 1990). This could possibly be relevant for minimizing costs of oil production, and price increases are an important means of saving energy, but it presents a paradox for everybody trained in the economic theory of externalities. So far marketization has entailed imports of hazardous waste in Eastern Europe, logging in Russian national parks, and systematic poaching in wildlife reserves for endangered species, and marketization and liberalization of foreign trade might entail harmful effects for the environment. But it is nevertheless true that 'simply freeing the market will help clean Eastern Europe's dirt' (The Economist, 17 February 1991, p. 34), namely by closing down 20–40 per cent of industry as happened after 1989 also in the Baltic countries.

The basic fact of Table 1.2 is the similarity of performance of eastern and western countries and the difference between rich and poor countries. The ecological crisis is not caused by any economic system, but by our common wish for economic growth which is also completely dominating in Eastern Europe and Russia: 'For all the apparent gulf between the market-dominated economies of the West and the centrally planned economies of the communist world, when it comes to attitudes to the natural world their outlook turns out to be remarkably similar' (Ponting, 1991, p. 153). This seems to counter the prevailing view: 'Ecocide in the USSR stems from the force, not the failure, of utopian ambitions'. And, 'The Soviet economic and political system, in any case, insured a low level of priority for environmental protection' (Feshbach and Friendly, 1992, pp. 1, 11, 29, 44). But it is more representative of empirical fact.

Energy consumption is stagnating in the western countries, but in the growing economies in Asia it is strongly increasing; from 1980 to 1994 energy consumption increased at an annual rate of 9.5 per cent in South Korea, 5.0 per cent in China, 6.6 per cent in India, and domestic oil production in many of these countries is stagnating or declining. Energy and raw

Table 1.2   *Production, consumption of resources, and human development*
in selected countries, 1989

	Human development index	Population million	GDP per capita	Energy consumption per capita	Energy consumption per unit GDP
1. Japan	.981	123.1	81.5	44.2	54.2
2. Norway	.978	4.2	76.6	77.8	101.6
3. USA	.976	248.8	100.0	100.0	100.0
4. Sweden	.976	8.5	80.8	70.6	87.4
5. United Kingdom	.962	57.2	74.8	46.8	62.6
6. Iceland	.958	0.3	79.5	118.3	148.8
7. Germany, Fed. Republic	.955	62.0	82.7	56.0	67.7
8. Finland	.953	5.0	76.6	82.7	108.0
9. Denmark	.953	5.1	80.9	47.0	58.1
10. Ireland	.921	3.5	47.2	38.9	82.4
11. Greece	.901	10.0	47.1	27.0	57.3
12. Czechoslovakia	.897	15.6	40.1	60.2	150.1
13. Lithuania	.883	3.7	35.0	50.0	142.9
14. Estonia	.882	1.6	37.5	57.6	153.6
15. Latvia	.880	2.7	36.3	33.9	93.3
16. USSR	.873	281.1	32.5	64.3	197.9
17. Korea, Republic of	.871	42.4	38.1	26.2	68.8
18. Argentina	.833	31.9	30.6	20.0	65.4
19. Brazil	.739	147.3	23.6	15.4	65.3
20. Thailand	.685	55.4	17.5	9.1	52.0
21. China	.612	1113.9	12.2	8.0	65.6
22. Indonesia	.491	178.2	11.0	4.9	44.6
23. Ghana	.310	14.4	4.4	5.1	115.9
24. India	.297	832.5	6.0	4.0	66.7
25. Nigeria	.241	113.8	4.9	4.3	87.8

Notes and sources: All data except population and the human development index are expressed relative to the numbers for the USA which are set equal to 100. The Human Development Index refers to 1990, most other data to 1989, but in some cases data from earlier years have been used, notably for countries outside the OECD area.

Human Development Index 1990: UNDP, 1992, pp. 127–9. The index combines life expectancy at birth, adult literacy, mean years of schooling, and GDP per capita assuming decreasing utility of income as expressed by the Atkinson index. For Estonia, Latvia and Lithuania figures were not available until 1994, and these figures have been used for interpolation, cf. UNDP, Human Development Report 1994, p. 129.

Population: World Bank, 1991, pp. 204–5; UNDP, 1992, pp. 98–100.

Table 1.2   *(continued)*

	CO_2 emis- sions per capita	CO_2 emis- sions per unit GDP	SO_2 emis- sions per capita	SO_2 emis- sions per unit GDP	NO_x emis- sions per capita	NO_x emis- sions per unit GDP	Ferti- lizer use per area unit	Pesti- cide use per area unit
1.	43.0	52.8	8.6	10.6	13.8	16.9	419.3	759.8
2.	55.7	72.7	16.9	22.1	64.4	84.1	243.0	60.3
3.	100.0	100.0	100.0	100.0	100.0	100.0	100.0	100.0
4.	35.3	43.7	22.7	28.1	56.7	70.2	123.1	41.8
5.	50.5	67.5	78.3	104.7	60.3	80.6	377.5	253.4
6.	39.1	49.1	40.0	50.3	93.4	117.5	144.4	..
7.	52.6	63.6	18.3	22.1	40.9	49.5	289.2	182.8
8.	52.2	68.2	58.7	76.6	71.7	92.8	211.4	46.7
9.	46.9	58.0	45.1	55.7	64.6	79.6	256.3	115.3
10.	42.7	90.5	55.7	118.0	42.9	90.9	743.6	101.7
11.	36.1	76.7	42.4	90.0	39.9	84.7	176.6	106.6
12.	73.8	184.0	198.4	494.8	86.8	216.5	286.2	146.4
13.	47.2	134.9	69.5	198.6	56.4	161.1	327.0	108.0
14.	114.7	305.9	203.4	542.4	84.2	224.5	206.3	64.8
15.	24.9	68.6	31.8	87.6	36.4	100.3	256.6	126.0
16.	68.8	211.7	37.5	115.4	18.3	56.3	122.6	117.1
17.	26.5	69.6	41.1	107.9	31.3	82.2	434.7	558.5
18.	18.8	61.4	..	..	..	..	5.3	21.0
19.	40.0	169.5	..	..	..	..	48.4	30.7
20.	33.8	193.1	..	..	..	..	34.7	56.6
21.	10.9	89.3	..	..	..	..	268.4	83.5
22.	28.8	261.8	..	..	..	..	119.0	39.2
23.	12.2	277.3	..	..	..	..	4.2	..
24.	4.7	78.3	..	..	..	..	65.3	16.0
25.	15.6	318.4	..	..	..	..	10.5	6.5

GDP per capita: Table 1.1; Aage, 1991.

Energy consumption: OECD, 1997a, p. 187; World Resources Institute, 1993, pp. 316–7; World Bank, 1991, pp. 212–3; Salay et. al., 1993, p. 183. For energy consumption per unit GDP other studies suggest considerably higher figures for the Baltic countries and the USSR, particularly for Latvia, cf. Chap. 10, p. 145.

CO_2 emissions: World Resources Institute, 1993, pp. 346–9. Net additions to atmospheric concentration of green house gases by carbon dioxide emissions from fossil fuels use, cement production, and land use changes; OECD, 1997a, p. 46; Salay et.al., 1993, p. 198.

SO_2 and NO_x emissions, and fertilizer and pesticide use: OECD, 1997a, pp. 19–28, 241–45; World Resources Institute, 1993, p. 351; World Resources Institute, 1997, p. 330; Salay et. al., 1993, pp. 194, 196; Ministry of Economic Affairs, 1996, p. 228; Halsnæs and Sørensen, 1993.

materials prices are expected to follow a long-term increasing trend because of increasing demand due to economic growth. For 1980–95 China holds the record for economic growth with an annual rate of 11.1 per cent for GDP per capita, followed by Taiwan, Thailand, Botswana and South Korea with 8–9 per cent. Some developing countries had growth rates of 4–6 per cent, including Indonesia, Chile, Egypt, India, Malaysia and Turkey, whereas growth amounted to 1–3 per cent in Argentina, Brazil, Mexico, Saudi Arabia and Zimbabwe and was still lower in a number of countries in Africa (World Bank, 1997).

The main cultural, political and economic challenges of our time are related to global problems of distribution and global problems of environment and resources (cf. Aage, 1984). Thus, competition for resources and markets is likely to be intense in the global economic environment, where the Baltic countries attempt to recover from economic depression and to reach a standard of living comparable to that of the Nordic countries, which on their part strive to improve their production and income levels even further.

1.2 Resources, Environment and Growth in Nordic and Baltic Countries

The Nordic and Baltic countries all face a tremendous task of environmental transition. Changing conditions for economic activity necessitate restructuring of production and consumption because problems related to resource availability, effects upon natural assets, and environmental impacts upon welfare are becoming still more perceptible and severe. Basic methodological issues of accounting for environmental welfare impacts, including costs of policies, changes in human, physical and natural capital, transboundary effects and impacts over time and across generations, are addressed in Chapter 2 by Karl-Göran Mäler. The following eleven chapters provide comparable reviews for five Nordic and three Baltic countries concerning resource development and consumption, environmental conditions, and economic growth, as well as resource and environmental policies and instruments and the role of environmental problems in the political debate. The remaining two chapters deal with transboundary environmental problems in the Baltic Sea region and international co-operation and assistance.[1]

The Nordic countries are more richly endowed with natural resources than the Baltic countries, and the resource base is more important for the Nordic economies. In the Nordic countries renewable resources include Atlantic fish stocks and geothermal energy resources in Iceland, hydroelectric power in Norway and Sweden, and forests in Norway, Sweden and Finland. There are also considerable exhaustible resources including oil in the Norwegian and Danish parts of the North Sea and mineral resources in Sweden. In the Baltic countries the main natural resources consist of agricultural lands and fresh water resources, but in addition there are large deposits of oil-shale and some other mineral resources in Estonia, and in all three Baltic countries there are forests, peat and also hydroelectric power resources.

Recent records of economic growth also differ sharply between Nordic and Baltic countries. From 1989 to 1995 levels of output in the Nordic countries were retained or improved, most in Norway by 20 per cent, albeit Sweden and Finland both experienced temporary set-backs with negative growth in the early 90s. In contrast, the Baltic countries went through major transition crises, and GDP declined by 35 per cent in Estonia, 49 per cent in Latvia and 61 per cent in Lithuania (cf. Table 1.3). Taking initial differences into account (cf. Table 1.2) this means that the order of magnitude of GDP per capita levels in the Baltic countries are now 20–30 per cent of the Nordic levels.

Table 1.3   Economic growth, energy consumption, and pollution in Nordic and Baltic countries, 1989–95

index for 1995 with 1989=100	GDP	Energy consump-tion	CO_2 emis-sions	SO_2 emis-sions	NO_x emis-sions	Ferti-lizer use
Iceland	104.6	103.1	108.6	96.2	111.4	105.0
Finland	96.7	102.2	98.2	39.3	87.4	74.6
Norway	120.9	106.1	103.0	59.3	96.9	95.8
Sweden	103.4	106.7	100.0	58.8	88.7	89.3
Denmark	111.9	118.2	117.2	77.5	89.0	71.3
Estonia	65.0	64.4	..	52.3	61.1	..
Latvia	50.5	49.6	51.3	67.7	66.3	5.5
Lithuania	38.7	54.0	50.1	42.4	78.3	..

Notes: Nordic countries: Anthropogenic CO_2 emissions include emissions from energy use only; emissions in Denmark have been almost unchanged since 1980, but in 1989 CO_2 emissions were exceptionally low. The index for fertilizer use is for 1994 with 1989=100.
Baltic countries: Data comparability is limited. In several cases data refer to the years 1990 and 1994; energy consumption data are incomplete; thus, for Estonia only energy from oil-shale is included, and pollution data cover only parts of the country.
Sources: OECD, 1997a; various tables and data from this volume.

Changes in energy consumption and carbon dioxide emissions largely follow the pattern of GDP developments in all eight countries. Levels of energy consumption per unit GDP were high and close to the Soviet average in 1989 in Estonia and Lithuania, which both produced and exported energy made from oil-shale and nuclear power, respectively, but lower in Latvia (cf. Table 1.2). Air pollution from sulphur oxide and nitrogen oxide emissions has declined in the Nordic as well as in the Baltic countries, but for widely different reasons. In the Baltic countries the decline is explained by the economic recession, and levels of sulphur oxide pollution per unit GDP is very high, notably in Estonia due to oil-shale use. Lower levels of sulphur oxide pollution in the Nordic countries is the result of environmental policies beginning in the 70s. Concerning reduction of pollution from fertilizer use in agriculture the Nordic countries have been less successful.

Currently growth rates are positive in the Baltic as well as in the Nordic countries, but the conditions for environmental and resource policy differ. The Baltic countries face an enormous dual task of economic and environmental transition, and transition to a market economy is likely to affect the environment in several ways. Production recovery will have immediate negative environmental impacts, but other aspect of transition will also influence environmental policies. Restructuring towards a larger share of services in output tends to reduce energy consumption and pollution; economic accounting under market conditions will improve resource efficiency; privatization of production and resource ownership may change the conditions for environmental policies; and aspirations for EU membership will induce more ambitious policies in order to comply with EU environmental standards.

1.3 Policies and Instruments

Despite the evident differences between Nordic and Baltic countries concerning the state of the economy and the environment, there are several similarities and many common problems for environmental and resource policy.

A common task for energy policy is to improve efficiency and to adjust to expected higher costs of energy consumption. This is one among many areas where the Baltic countries have had to free themselves from the Soviet legacy, namely to remove subsidies and increase energy prices from the very low Soviet levels to world market prices, and this has been a difficult task with consequences for social policy as well as for business competitiveness. Another common endeavour is to substitute less polluting and possibly renewable resources for oil. The Baltic countries in particular want to reduce their dependency upon Russian oil, but in this as in many other respects economic considerations have taken priority. Nuclear power is important in Sweden and Lithuania and also used in Finland. Sweden has decided to phase out nuclear power, but the time schedule is still subject to debate. In Lithuania proposals in the early 90s for closing down the Ignalina nuclear power plant has been suspended for economic reasons, and efforts are concentrated on improving nuclear safety with assistance from international, including Swedish and Danish, experts (Fennhan, 1994).

Resource management is becoming an issue particularly in some of the Nordic countries. In Iceland overfishing of stocks has occurred in the recent past, and it proved difficult to gain support for the more strict policies now pursued. In the Faroe Islands, which enjoy home rule within the Danish kingdom, an overfishing crisis caused a collapse of the economy in the early 90s. Oil resources in the Norwegian and Danish parts of the North Sea are being depleted at rather fast rates of exploitation since the temporary increase of world market prices for oil in the 70s, and the fast rates persist despite the current low oil prices. Utilization of forest resources are regulated by the governments. In Estonia exploitation of oil-shale has been reduced in recent years, and mining of phosphorite for fertilizer was discontinued in 1991, both because of severe environmental impacts.

Environmental policies concerning air pollution in the Nordic countries started in the 70s, and effects have been considerable in reducing notably sulphur dioxide emissions, but also other types of emissions including pollution from motor cars and in recent years carbon dioxide emissions. Water pollution originating in agriculture, households and industry has also been reduced, but in Denmark the outcome of an expensive water purification programme has been disappointing mainly because of economic consequences for agriculture. In the Baltic countries environmental policies were less strict in the Soviet period, when norms were often stringent but enforcement lenient, and during the transition period economic growth has been an overwhelming concern. But now environmental policies are being initiated. Due to the small size of the economies environmental problems are correspondingly less acute, except in specific areas where pollution is concentrated. This also implies that environmental improvements can be achieved at relatively low costs in the Baltic countries (cf. Eckerberg et.al., 1994).

In all eight countries long run sustainability is the declared ambition of environmental and resource policy, but except for fisheries and forest management policies are mostly in a research and preparation stage. Research is carried out concerning accounting and substitutability between man-made physical and human capital on the one hand and natural capital on the other hand, and technological development of renewable resources is supported. But the general conclusion is that much remains to be done before sustainability can be achieved.

Despite all the differences concerning initial economic conditions, resource and environmental situations and policy problems, when it comes to the choice of policy instruments there are many similarities and common experiences. In all eight countries it is acknowledged that governmental regulation of environment and resources is badly needed. Four types of instruments are generally under consideration: administrative regulation, taxation, transferable quotas and permits, and public investment and subsidies. So far administrative regulation has been most extensively used, but there is a common trend to prefer economic incentives, and they are increasingly introduced. Transferable catch quotas have been used in the Icelandic fisheries management since the

80s, and systems of environmental taxation are increasingly used in all eight countries, but in many cases, particularly in the Baltic countries, rates of taxation are still low. The most elaborate system of taxation seems to be in effect in Sweden.

Although notably transferable quotas and permits are usually refered to as market oriented, all four types of instruments are basically incentive mechanisms for centrally decided policies, as total amounts of resource use and pollution are set politically and market allocation is limited to the distribution of the totals between various uses. Differences could easily be overrated. Even administrative regulation becomes a purely economic incentive in terms of fines, if the criminality of offending regulations is ignored by the public. Also taxation and transferable permits have similar effects in many respects. However, there are several merits related to strong economic incentives and the polluter pays principle, including the possibility of providing funding for public enviromental investments (OECD, 1997b, 1997c).

Common to all policy instruments is the serious problem of monitoring and the related problem of communicating environmental policies to the public. In all eight countries schemes for co-operation between government, local governments and organizations are being developed for these purposes. Like monetary policy, environmental policy is an area where politicians may be tempted to disregard long-term costs in the pursuit of short-term gains, and hence there is an argument for delegating environmental decisions to independent bodies as is the case for monetary authorities, in other words to create 'environmental boards' in analogy with the 'currency boards' now established in the Baltic countries. An example of this kind of independent body exists in Scandinavian countries, namely the so-called Water Courts which are entitled with certain discretionary powers. Thus, construction of hydropower plants and some other types of constructions including the bridge across the Sound between Sweden and Denmark require permission from the Swedish Water Court (Vattendomstolen) (Lundquist, 1996, pp. 281, 309).

1.4 International Co-operation

Environmental problems are international. Due to the prevailing western winds Sweden and Norway are net importers of pollution, and Denmark, Finland and the Baltic countries are net exporters, but the transboundary pollution between the two regions are small. However, the Baltic Sea is a common concern, and co-operation dates back to the signing of the Helsinki Convention in 1974 and the creation of the Helsinki Commission (HELCOM). Since then environmental monitoring of the Baltic Sea area has been intensified, and one outcome is a listing of pollution hot spots in the Baltic Sea area accompanied by an elaborate and costly programme of investments required for removing them.

Only a small part of the programme has been carried out due to lack of finance. The Baltic states, Russia and Poland contribute significantly to the pollution of the Baltic Sea, although not more than the Nordic countries, and in the 90s the pollution load has decreased as a consequence of the falling production in the Baltic states and Russia.

Although environmental problems are not generally more severe in the Baltic than in the Nordic countries, reduction of pollution is often cost-efficient in the Baltic countries, because pollution there is more concentrated to certain types and places, and the Nordic countries provide significant environmental assistance to the Baltic countries. International co-operation is gaining increasing importance for the Baltic countries, as they receive assistance from various international financial institutions, and the Baltic states are ratifying an increasing number of international environmental conventions.

1.5 Policy Debates

In the late 80s environmental problems came to the fore of the public debate in the Baltic countries. This was an area where public debate was possible, and the green movement played a significant role in the liberation from Soviet rule. However, during the transition the green parties lost momentum, and concurrently with the deepening of the economic recession environmental problems were crowded out from the policy debate by acute economic concerns. This is also reflected in public opinion polls.

In the Nordic countries a public debate on environmental problems has been going on with varying intensity during three decades, and there are green organizations with large memberships and also some political influence. The two sides in the debate are often environmentalist on the one side and representatives for economic interests like fisheries or agriculture on the other. A third party is scientists, and a fourth is the economics profession. Although the economists were not very active in fostering the environmental debate, in recent years they have tried hard to convince the public of the merits of economic incentives in environmental policy. Large parts of the green movements have regarded these economic policy instruments as suspect or even unethical in relation to environmental problems. Thus it appears that even economists have a mission to accomplish in promoting the necessary resource and environmental policies.

NOTE

1. These papers were prepared as part of the Baltic Transition Programme initiated in 1992 and financed by the Nordic Economic Research Council. Another outcome of this programme is the research reports published by Haavisto (1997). Support from the Nordic Economic Research Council and supplementary financial support form the University of Roskilde for a workshop in Svaneke on the island of Bornholm in the Baltic Sea on 18–21 April 1996 is gratefully acknowledged by the contributors to this volume.

REFERENCES

Aage, H. (1984), 'Economic Arguments on the Sufficiency of Natural Resources', *Cambridge Journal of Economics*, **8** (1), 105–13.

Aage, H. (1991), 'The Baltic Republics', pp. 146–66 in R. Weichhardt (ed.), *The Soviet Economy under Gorbachev*, Bruxelles: NATO Economics Directorate.

Aage, H. (1994), 'Sustainable Transition', pp. 15–42 in R.W. Campbell (ed.), *The Postcommunist Economic Transformation. Essays in Honor of Gregory Grossman*, Boulder: Westview Press.

Eckerberg, K., P.K. Mydske, A. Niemi-Iilahti and K. Hilmer Pedersen (eds.) (1994), *Comparing Nordic and Baltic Countries – Environmental Problems and Policies in Agriculture and Forestry*, TemaNord 1994, (572), Copenhagen: Nordic Council of Ministers.

Fennhan, J. (1994), 'Energy Strategies for the Baltic Countries', in J. Birk Mortensen (ed.), *Environmental Economics and the Baltic Region*, Copenhagen: Copenhagen University, Institute of Economics.

Feshbach, M. and A. Friendly (1992), *Ecocide in the USSR*, New York: Basic Books.

Haavisto, T. (ed.) (1997), *The Transition to a Market Economy. Transformation and Reform in the Baltic States*, Cheltenham: Edward Elgar.

Halsnæs, K. and L. Sørensen (1993), 'Perspectives of Regional Coordinated Energy and Environmental Planning', *Nordiske Seminar- og Arbejdsrapporter* (640), Copenhagen: Nordic Council of Ministers.

Lundquist, L.J. (1996): 'Sweden', in P.M. Christiansen (ed.), *Governing the Environment. Politics, Policy and Organization in the Nordic Countries* (Nord 1996:5), Copenhagen: Nordic Council of Ministers.

Maddison, A. (1991), *Dynamic Forces in Capitalist Development, A Long-Run Comparative View*, Oxford: Oxford University Press.

Maddison, A. (1995), *Monitoring the World Economy 1820–1982*, Paris: OECD.

Mäler, K.-G. (1990), 'International Environmental Problems', *Oxford Review of Economic Policy*, **6** (1), 80–108.

Ministry of Economic Affairs (1996), *Enlargement of the EU Towards the East – Economic Perspectives* (in Danish), Copenhagen: Ministry of Economic Affairs.

Moe, M. (1995), *Environmental Administration in Denmark*, Copenhagen: Ministry of the Environment.

OECD (1997a), *OECD Environmental Data, Compendium 1997*, Paris: OECD.

OECD (1997b), *Environment Taxes and Green Tax Reform*, Paris: OECD.

OECD (1997c), *Evaluating Economic Instruments for Environmental Policy*, Paris: OECD.

OECD and IEA (1990), *Energy Efficiency in the USSR*, Note by the Secretariat of the Ad Hoc Group on International Energy Relations, Paris: OECD.

Persson, K.G. (1988), *Pre-Industrial Economic Growth*, Oxford: Basil Blackwell.

Ponting, C. (1991), *A Green History of the World*, Harmondsworth: Penguin.

Salay, J., J. Fenhann, K. Jaanimägi and L. Kristoferson (1993), 'Energy and Environment in the Baltic States', *Annual Review of Energy and Environment* (18), 169–216.

UNDP (1992), *Human Development Report 1992*, Oxford: Oxford University Press.

World Bank (1991), *World Development Report 1991: The Challenge of Development*, Oxford: Oxford University Press.

World Bank (1997), *World Development Report 1997: The State in a Changing World*, Oxford: Oxford University Press.

World Resources Institute (1993), *World Resources 1992–93*, Oxford: Oxford University Press.

World Resources Institute (1997), *World Resources 1996–97*, Oxford: Oxford University Press.

2. Welfare Indices and the Environmental Resource Base

Karl-Göran Mäler

2.1 Introduction

Man has always relied upon natural resources. The whole economic system could be seen as a machine that feeds upon raw material and energy in order to produce the well-being of man. The economics of these is now well understood, but there are many other resources, perhaps more subtle but even more important. These include all the life supporting services provided by the ecosystem, such as control of micro climate, hydrological control, recycling of nutrients and carbon, as well as providing food, recreation and other welfare enhancing functions. The economics of these renewable goods is much less known. There are two main reasons for this.

The first has to do with the fact that these goods or resources are dynamic in the following sense. The ecological systems develop according to internal dynamic laws and according to the stress they are exposed to from external disturbances. The major disturbance is obviously the intervention of man. Because the dynamics are complex and not well known, it may be difficult or even impossible to predict the future behaviour of an ecosystem. It is now well known that some systems may change the stability domain completely if the disturbance is large enough. This happens if the resilience of the system is exhausted. Often this change of stability domains is irreversible. However, because we do not know the underlying system, it may be impossible to predict exactly how much we can perturb the system without experiencing irreversible changes. It is also well known that some systems are chaotic, which implies that it is impossible to predict with any precision their future states. How do we carry out economic analyses of such systems? This question has only been researched during the last couple of years, and it is too early to report on any major breakthroughs.

The second reason for the difficulties in analysing these ecological services is that very often property rights to these goods are not well defined. This

16

implies that most often, they cannot be bought or sold on markets and therefore they are not visible to either the individual, the firm or the state. This in turn implies that they are overused, because no one is accountable for their maintenance. Furthermore, the non-visibility implies that they will not be accounted for in the traditional national accounts. This is the problem that will be discussed in this chapter.

The gross national product – GNP – has today become commonly used as an index of welfare in a country. If GNP increases, then this is assumed to be a sign that the average welfare in the country increases, and if GNP in one country is greater than GNP in another country, then the first country is thought to have a higher welfare. This notion that GNP is a measure of material well-being is very common. However, one of the conclusions of this chapter is that GNP is a bad measure of well-being. But the focus on the GNP has shown without doubt that a single and simple measure of well-being will be used, in spite of all its shortcomings. There is therefore a legitimate question whether it is possible to improve the existing measure – GNP – in order to get a more reliable measure of well-being.

The purpose of this chapter is to discuss the theoretical basis for using a national product concept as an index of well-being and the assumptions that are needed for making such an interpretation. However, it should be stressed that national income accounts have other, probably more important purposes, than to measure well-being.[1]

Economic theory guarantees that if a few technical assumptions (like convexity of production possibilities and preferences) are valid, then there is a linear index that can be used for evaluating small projects, that is, that can be used for establishing whether a small project will enhance human well-being or not. The notion of a project should be interpreted in the broadest sense. A project is simply any change in the organization of the economy that effects present and future consumption streams. It covers the investment in a pulp and paper plant as well as the aggregate of all changes in the economy during a year! A project is small if it does not affect prices. Projects must be small in order to enable us to construct linear indices. If prices do not remain constant, then any index must necessarily be non-linear, because one would then have to include changes in consumers' and producers' surpluses.[2] The established notion of GNP is a notion of a linear index, that is the sum of constant prices times quantities. In our efforts to extend the GNP measure to something more appropriate and at the same time preserve its linearity, it is thus necessary to restrict the analysis to small projects.

The index we are looking for is obviously a marginal social cost-benefit rule, that is a rule that tells us whether a project is socially desirable or not, and how to rank the social desirability of projects. However, it should be obvious that such a social cost-benefit rule will be dependent on the conse-

quences for income distribution. Established national product concepts do not
include distributional impacts and we will therefore disregard them in this
chapter, although there are no theoretical reasons why distributional impacts
should be neglected in the construction of an index.

The social desirability of different projects can be represented in many
different but consistent ways in the form of an index. Basically, the different
but consistent indices will differ from each other in the choice of base prices.
In particular, the future of the economy is very important in determining the
appropriate prices. Perhaps the most natural choice is based on the use of
future optimal growth as a benchmark. One index can therefore be based on
prices along an optimal growth path. Another index can be based on local
prices, that is the prices the households are facing when they make their
consumption decisions. One could also construct an index based on the local
prices for the current period and on optimal prices for the future; this resem-
bles the standard interpretation of current computations of national product,
and it is in fact perhaps the most natural approach (Mäler, 1991).

These ideas can be illustrated in a simple economy with two consumer
goods and with one individual. In the optimum production point, where an
indifference curve is tangent to the production possibility frontier, the optimal
prices are given by the slope of the common tangent. One index the national
product could be defined as is as follows:

$$NP = p_x X + p_y Y, \tag{2.1}$$

where X and Y are amounts produced and the two p's the respective prices.
Often the optimal prices can also be used to indicate the direction of change
in well-being when the economy changes from one non-optimum point to
another.

Another index can also be used, namely one based on local prices which
are given as the slope of the tangent to the indifference curve through the
actual, non-optimal point of production. The national product calculated with
these current marginal consumer valuations is an appropriate index for a
marginal social cost-benefit rule.

This latter index has also the advantage that – if the production possibilities
and the preferences are convex – that if the economy is undergoing a series
of changes that all improve the national product, then the allocation will
ultimately converge towards the optimal allocation. This follows from results
on the gradient process. This is a mathematical procedure searching for a
maximum. The idea can be compared to climbing a hill by choosing the
steepest path. By following such a path, one can be assured that one is
following the shortest way to the top.

The rather simple ideas expounded above will now be used to develop a framework for the construction of an index for a much more complicated economy than that we have discussed so far. However, note that some of the restrictions we have used are really of no interest. The restriction to two commodities is in fact more general than we need, so we will limit ourselves to one consumer good without restricting the generality of the analysis. We will also maintain the assumption of only one individual, so as to enable us to bypass distributional issues. The issues we will consider are as follows: 1) labour as a factor of production, 2) non-market flows of services including environmental damage, 3) capital stocks, 4) valuation issues.

2.2 Labour

Above, we have assumed the existence of a production possibility frontier. The existence of such a frontier depends on the existence of factors of production and institutions that allocate these factors between alternative uses. Let us assume, for the time being, that there is only one factor of production – labour. Let us also assume that there is a perfect market for labour that is in equilibrium at each point of time.

If the supply of labour is completely inelastic, we could stop the story here, because any marginal project would not change the supply of labour, and labour would then not be relevant for the index we are trying to construct. So let us assume that the labour supply is elastic. But that implies implicitly that labour time has an alternative use, namely leisure. On the margin, the individual will value one hour of labour time, which equals the wage rate, as much as one more hour of leisure. On the margin, the individual is therefore indifferent between working one more hour or having one more hour for leisure. But as we are only trying to evaluate marginal projects, this has as a consequence that wage income should not be part of our index. A constant returns to scale project that would increase employment and thereby reduce leisure time and which only uses labour as a factor of production would not increase (or decrease) well-being because the gains from increased production of consumer goods is completely offset by the cost from reductions in leisure. Thus, with perfect, equilibrating labour markets, labour income should not be included in the national product measure.

This is a rather startling conclusion, and we shall shortly modify it. In view of the historical fact that national income measures were constructed to help designing economic policies for demand management in the Keynesean spirit, one could argue that labour income is perhaps the most central part of the national product. This would imply that the national product measure may have at least two different uses, and the appropriate concept for one use will in general be quite different from the concept apropriate for another use! It is therefore necessary to distinguish between different concepts of national products, and preferably, we should give the different concepts different names. In spite of this we will in this chapter continue to use national product as the generic name for our index for evaluating marginal projects.

Our conclusion is based on a number of implicit assumptions. The most obvious assumption is of course that labour markets equilibrate. We are too familiar with unemployment to accept the proposition that labour markets are in equilibrium. But still, we can construct an index as if they are in equilibrium as was demonstrated in the introduction. Or we can use local prices, that is the workers marginal reservation price for taking a job. Assume for simplicity that the reservation price is zero, that is the worker is willing to take a job as long as he gets something above zero. Then the accounting price for labour would be zero, and the wage bill, evaluated at this price, would still be zero. This also boils down to the exclusion of labour income from the national product measure.

This last discussion has some important implications for the discussion on how to treat defensive expenditures, that is expenditures for cleaning up environments that have already been damaged. It has been proposed that conventional national income accounts would register an increase in GNP because of damage to the environment due to pollution. The reason is that households or the governments will hire labour to clean up and that increase in the employment will show up as an increase in GNP. Therefore, it is argued, the defensive expenditures should be deducted from GNP. This conclusion is obviously wrong. If the economy is in full employment, then the hiring of people doing the clean up will be offset by a reduction in production somewhere else in the economy. If the economy is not in full employment, then (assuming local prices equal to zero) the wage bill should be zero, and there will be no increase in GNP. Thus the defensive expenditures should be excluded from GNP provided we value labour employment correctly.

The main assumption behind the conclusion that labour income should not matter, is, however, a different one. We have assumed above that labour time and leisure are substitutes. However, usually the workers are trained and therefore carrying human capital. Part of their salaries is therefore a return on that capital. That part cannot be regarded as a substitute to leisure. Only that part of their salaries that corresponds to raw labour will on the margin be valued at the same rate as leisure. The return on their human capital should therefore be included in our index. However, this may create severe practical problems. How do we separate out the returns on human capital from the reward of raw labour? So far, there are no reasonable ways of doing that. In the rest of this chapter we will neglect valuation of labour and leisure and instead focus on environmental resources.

2.3 Flow of Goods and Services

So far we have assumed that welfare is determined only by the goods consumed and that these goods can be bought and sold on markets. However, human welfare is also dependent on many non-market goods and services. A few of these are already included in the Standard National Accounts. For example, the production in the public sector is in general not marketed but included in GNP. However, there are many other goods and services that are neglected. In fact, human life depends crucially on services provided by fundamental ecological systems, and many of these services are not provided through markets. The inclusion of these services changes the national accounts in two ways: it changes the current flow of goods and services and it changes the future flow of goods and services through current changes in the resource base. We will in this section limit ourselves to a discussion of the current flow of services and return to the issue of changes in the stocks later.

The current flow of services from natural capital can affect human well-being in two ways. The services can directly affect human well-being, as exemplified by clean air, recreational opportunities, direct food gathering etc. The services can also affect human well-being indirectly through their uses as inputs in production units. We will assume that the value of production in these units is already included the national accounts. But that means that changes in these services are measured by the conventional GNP; a change in the quantity of one service will affect the operating surplus or perhaps the use of other inputs – that is the profit or the expenditures for substitutes – and the operating surplus is accounted for in the value added of the production unit. However, the direct use of these services is not accounted for in SNA.

There is a considerable confusion (which I myself have contributed to) on how to include the direct services. The confusion has to do with our definition of the direct services. One example may illustrate the point. Assume an individual lives close to a highway. The project we are considering is an increase in the traffic, which will increase the noise and therefore reduce the well-being of the individual. As a consequence, the individual will invest in three pane windows and increased insulation in order to reduce the indoor noise. Should these defensive expenditures be subtracted in order to reach a more appropriate national product index? That depends on the way we are measuring the environmental damage! Let N be the outdoor noise level. As a result of the increased traffic, the noise level increases from N' to N''. The original indoor noise level was M', and because of the defensive expenditures, that level is maintained. Let $D(N)$ be the damage function (the willingness to pay for a quiet neighbourhood). One correct way of adjusting the national product index is to subtract

$$D'(N')*(N'' - N') = D(N'') - D(N') \tag{2.2}$$

from the conventional national product. Here $D'(N)$ is the marginal damage, which is used because we are studying a marginal change. Note that this implies that we are using local prices, that is the marginal willingness to pay for noise reduction in the actual situation (where noise is N'). In this case, we should ensure that all prices used in computing the index are reflecting the actual marginal willingness to pay for the goods and services. We could also have made use of the optimal prices. If $N*$ is the optimal noise level, then the adjustment would have been $D'(N*)(N'' - N')$. In this case, all accounting prices should reflect the optimal accounting prices.

However, sometimes one sees a different formulation, where the damage function is $D(M)$. Because of the defensive expenditures the indoor noise level is unchanged and the adjustment should therefore be made by subtracting these expenditures. This is correct, if the defensive expenditures are approximately equal to (2.2). But there is no reason to assume that defensive expenditures always are a good approximation of the true environmental damage. In fact, one can imagine cases where environmental damage is negatively correlated with the defensive expenditures. It may therefore be dangerous to use defensive expenditures uncritically as a measure of the environmental damage.

But if we cannot use routinely the defensive expenditures as an index of environmental damage, how should one go about approximating environmental damage? During the last twenty years or so, the techniques for estimating environmental damages in monetary terms have developed considerably (cf. Freeman, 1993). However, these techniques have been developed for use in particular situations where a cost-benefit analysis is needed for making decisions and not for routine production of national product estimates. If these rather sophisticated techniques were to be used, the cost for adjusting the national product measures might be prohibitive. Therefore, simple, robust methods of approximation are needed. The conventional way of including the public sector in SNA may give some clues. Output from the public sector is in general not marketed, and therefore there is no way of assessing the value of that output directly. SNA has solved the problem by looking at the cost of production in the public sector. This is a correct approach if the public output corresponds to the demand. In fact, if our politicians are able to make correct decisions on the size and composition of the public sector, then the cost of production in the public sector would exactly correspond to the value of the output. Probably no one would argue that our politicians are that wise, but still this approximation of the value of the public output seems to work. Why not use the same basic idea when approximating the value of environmental damage?

That idea would require that there are politically determined targets for environmental policies – ambient standards, emissions targets etc. The cost of achieving the target emission reduction is, although not perfect, an approximation of the environmental damage. If the political system has determined explicit targets for environmental policies, then one could use the costs of achieving these targets as approximations when reducing the conventional national product concepts for the flow of environmental services. However, politicians very seldom determine specific targets in environmental policies, and the scope of this approach to evaluating environmental damage is therefore limited.

Similarly, if the political bodies have determined emission taxes instead of quantity targets, these taxes could be interpreted as proxies for the social marginal damage from further pollution. In Sweden, the emission tax on sulphur is 30 000 SEK per ton. This reveals implicitly that society values the damage from one more ton as 30 000 SEK. Note that this is very much related to a revealed preference approach, that is from observed behaviour draw conclusions on the preferences of the decision maker.

However, there are very few such emission taxes and in most countries there are no environmental taxes at all. Thus, the revealed preference approach seems to be limited in establishing good environmental adjustments of the national product, simply because governments have not been explicit either on environmental targets or introducing environmental taxes.

Irrespective of the difficulties in finding methods for estimating environmental damages, one should keep in mind that almost any arbitrary choice of a reasonable estimator will improve the conventional GNP as a marginal social cost-benefit rule.

The discussion has so far focussed on the situation in one country and not included the relations between this country and the rest of the world. These relations include trade and capital movements. However, they also include transboundary pollution. Some of the environmental damage at home is due to pollution in other countries and some of the domestic emissions will create environmental problems in other countries. How should these transboundary effects be included?

Returning to the purpose of environmentally adjusted national product, we need to decide whose well–being should be considered. Should we consider the global population or should we limit ourselves to the citizens of the own country? Assume that we are interested in a marginal cost-benefit rule for projects in our own country and that rule should include the impact on the well-being of all individuals, both in the home country and in all the other relevant countries. Then we should deduct the environmental damage our projects give rise to, irrespective in which country. Thus, export of pollution should be counted negatively. Furthermore, as the cost-benefit rule in this case applies to domestic projects only, the import of pollution should not be accounted for. Thus, if the objective is to create an index measuring the impact on global well-being from projects in one country, then environmentally damaging activities in other countries should not be included. If all countries base their accounts on this objective, all accounts would be consistent with each other and it would make sense adding them. In fact the global national product calculated in this way would give the same result as the result from a calculation in which we considered the whole globe as one country.

Another way of doing the calculations would be to base them on a cost-benefit rule that considers all changes on earth as the project, but to limit the consequences to citizens in the own country. This is an equally valid starting point, and will in general give a different answer. If all countries apply the same rule, we would once again have consistent system. The difference between the two approaches is similar to the difference between gross domestic product and gross national product, the difference being the treatment of factor payment across national borders.

2.4   Environmental Assets

The analysis in the previous section dealt only with current flows of goods and services. That discussion is relevant if we are only interested in the well-being in one particular time period. However, projects during that period will in general have effects on future well-being, through the accumulation and decumulation of productive assets. The oppportunities for the well-being of future generations are given by the stock of such assets which the current generation is leaving to the future. If we are – and we should be if we take the concept of sustainable development seriously – interested in the well-being of the current as well as of all future generations, we should obviously include the net changes in the productive assets in the accounts (Solow, 1986).

In current Standard National Accounts (SNA) changes in only two such assets are included: real man-made capital and human capital. In the gross national product, GNP, gross investments in real capital are included. From the point of view of a marginal cost-benefit rule that relates to the well-being of future generations, this is irrelevant. What is interesting is the net change in the stock of real capital and therefore in the net national product, NNP, in which depreciation of the stock of real capital has been deducted. It is obvious that investments that are completely or partially offset by depreciation of the capital stock due to obsolence, wear and tear, etc, will not contribute to higher future well-being (cf. Hartwick, 1990; Repetto et. al., 1989).

Changes in human capital are consequences of education, research and development. Some of the costs for these activities are included in the standard GNP measure, but classified mainly as public consumption. It seems reasonable to reclassify expenditures that increase human capital from consumption to investment. The total investment costs in human capital are composed of the costs of teachers, buildings, teaching materials and, perhaps most important, the opportunity costs for the time the students allocate to their studies. This latter component is not included in SNA. It seems reasonable that they should be part of the gross capital formation. On the other hand, it seems extremely difficult to define in a theoretically correct way the depreciation charges needed for the calculation of the net change in the stock of human capital.

However, of more interest in this connection is the fact that changes in many stocks of natural resources are not included in SNA. As many of these resources generate essential life supporting services, their exclusion may severely distort the net national product estimates. It should be of highest priority to try to include changes in the complete asset base in the accounts. How changes in these assets should be included in the national accounts is still controversial, although it should not be. Once again, starting with the objective of creating a marginal social cost-benefit rule, we have to decide what the impacts on well-being will be from current projects. In order to do that we must make some assumptions on how the future will look in order to derive the appropriate shadow prices, and the simplest and most practical assumption is to assume that the economy will follow an optimal path from now on. In section 2.1 we concluded that we could use the optimal prices even if the economy is not at the optimum. The same is true in this dynamic setting. We use the optimal path as a vehicle to compute accounting prices which then are used to value the current changes in resource stocks. Basically, these prices will reflect the present value of the future stream of welfare from one more unit of the resource today. Having computed these accounting prices, it follows that we should add to the conventional national product the value of changes of resource stocks at these prices (cf. Weitzman, 1976).

This conclusion has some important implications. One is that we include the price times the change in the resource stock. The change in the accounting price is not included, that is, we do not consider capital gains or losses. Another one is that for exhaustible resources, the change will be negative unless new discoveries are being made. If the discoveries are deterministic – perhaps not very likely – in that one can predict with some certainty that new reserves will be found if investment is made in exploration, then the net stock may increase. On the other hand, if discoveries are completely random, then changes in the stock should be valued with accounting prices that take into account the possible but uncertain future discoveries (cf. Dasgupta and Mäler, 1991). These are known as contingent claims prices. However, this is probably only a theoretical speculation as such prices will be extremely difficult to estimate. Furthermore, the so-called El Serafy model (Ahmad et. al., 1989) for computing the depreciation charges for exhaustible resources is basically wrong, because it is based on a completely arbitrary prediction of the future – a prediction which is not self-consistent. El Serafy considers the case when a resource has a fixed lifespan and will generate a constant revenue for each of the remaining years. He then transforms this revenue into consumption charges that can go on for ever, which enables him to compute the depreciation charge. However, as the assumptions are arbitrary, the computed depreciation charge will also be arbitrary.

For many of the resources included in the stock of natural capital, the same problems will arise as for the flow of services discussed in the previous section. This is exemplified by the stock of biodiversity. There are no market prices for such an asset because it is not traded. Instead, one has to follow the same rather ad hoc approaches that were discussed in connection with the valuation of environmental services in the previous section. However, there are important resources for which there are market prices. Most of the exhaustible resources are traded on markets and the established market prices could be used as a first approximation in computing the appropriate depreciation charges.

2.5   Net National Product

Let us summarize the findings so far. We have developed a marginal, that is a linear, index that will show whether the performance of the economy during a specific time period has been improving the present value of current and future well-being or not. Such an index should look like the following:

> *Net national product =*
>   + consumption of marketed goods + public expenditures
>   + the value of the net change of real capital
>   – wage bill for raw labour
>   + opportunity costs for students
>   – flow of environmental damages
>   + the value of the net change in the environmental resource base.

It is possible to show that this net national product concept has some rather interesting properties (Mäler, 1991; Dasgupta and Mäler, 1991):

> i) NNP will approximately be the return on the total wealth in the economy, that is the sum of the values of real capital, human capital and natural capital.

ii) NNP will, approximately, be the maximum constant well-being that, in the absence of non-anticipated technical progress, is feasible. A higher well-being today than NNP will reduce well-being in the future.

The NNP is a linear measure. In fact it is, if we are following an optimal path, a linear approximation to the optimal present value of future welfare. It can be shown that this optimal present value of future welfare will exactly correspond to the return on the total wealth. However, we may not be following an optimal path. That is the reason why the two propositions above must contain the adjective approximately. NNP can thus be viewed, not only as an index for marginal cost-benefit analysis but also as an index for whether the development is sustainable or not.

2.6 An Accounting System

The theoretical arguments put forward in the previous sections are obviously far different from the basic idea underlying the Standard National Accounts. Furthermore, they are also quite different from the ideas underlying the United Nations' (1993) system of Integrated Environmental and Economic Accounting. Obviously, the ideas expounded in this paper will be very difficult to implement, particularly because of the inherent difficulties of valuing environmental services. However, it is possible to embed the arguments above in an accounting framework, similar to SNA. A brief presentation of such a framework is illustrated in the Social Accounting Matrix in Table 2.1. It does not take into account the conclusion that wages for raw labour should not be included. It does not include international relations, and it does not include the input-output structure of the economy. Furthermore, it would be desirable to include a finer classification of institutions, including the public sector, instead of having households as the only institutions.

The economy has been divided into seven different accounts: households, two factors of production, one for production, one for abatement (or for expenditures for environmental improvements in general), one for savings and investment and one for the environment. Each row corresponds to incomes for the corresponding account, while the columns correspond to the outgoings. The households have thus incomes that correspond to wages, profits and an implicit rent on the environmental assets. These incomes are spent on purchases of consumer goods, savings (including savings in the form of net additions to the environmental assets), and the imputed value of the environmental services consumed by the households. In a corresponding way, the ingoings to the production account are the incomes from sales to household, the sales to firms for investment goods and from the sales to the account for abatement. The total gross savings in the economy consist of households' savings and

Table 2.1   A Social Accounting Matrix with environmental accounts

	House-holds	Labour	Capital	Produc-tion	Abate-ment	Savings Invest-ment	Envi-ron-ment
House-holds		wages	profits				rent
Labour				wages	wages		
Capital				profits	profits		
Produc-tion	con-sump-tion				inputs	gross invest-ment	
Abate-ment				abate-ment			
Savings Invest-ment	house-hold savings			depre-ciation	depre-ciation		
Envi-ron-ment	envi-ron-mental services			envi-ron-mental dam-ages	envi-ron-mental dam-ages	net change of re-sources	

depreciation of capital stocks. Thus savings corresponds to investment in real capital and net additions to the stock of natural capital.

The net national product is given as the sum in the first column, that is the value of consumption plus net savings less the reduction in environmental services, that is environmental damages. The net national income is given in the usual way as the sum in the first row, that is wages plus profits plus the return on environmental capital.

NOTES

1. The SNA was created to enable governments to manage effective demand according to Keynes' economic theories. It was not created to give a measure of well-being. GNP is an appropriate measure for the former objective but not for the latter.
2. Producer's surplus is simply the profit of the producer. The consumer's surplus is more complicated. It is essentially the difference between the maximum amount an individual is willing pay for a bundle of goods and services he is consuming and the amount he actually

is paying. It tries to catch the property that an individual may put a higher value on the first units of a commodity he is consuming than the last (and this is the source of non-linearity).

REFERENCES

Ahmad, Y.J., S. El Serafy and E. Lutz (1989), *Environmental Accounting for Sustainable Development*, Washington, D.C.: The World Bank.

Dasgupta, P. and K.-G. Mäler (1991), *Environment and Emerging Development Issues*, Oxford: Clarendon.

Freeman, A.M. (1993), *The Measurement of Environmental and Resource Values: Theory and Methods*, Washington, D.C.: Resources For the Future.

Hartwick, J.M. (1990), 'Natural Resources, National Accounting and Economic Depreciation', *Journal of Public Economics*, **43** (3), 291–304.

Mäler, K.-G. (1991), 'National Accounts and Environmental Resources', *Environmental and Resource Economics*, **1** (1), 1–15.

Repetto, R., W. Magrath, M. Wells, C. Beer and F. Rossini (1989), *Wasting Assets and Natural Resources in the National Income Accounts*, Washington, D.C.: World Resources Institute.

Solow, R. (1986), 'On the Intergenerational Allocation of Natural Resources', *Scandinavian Journal of Economics*, **88** (1), 141–49.

United Nations (1993), *Handbook of National Accounting: Integrated Environmental and Economic Accounting*, Series F (61), Department of Economic and Social Information and Policy Analysis, Statistical Division, New York: United Nations.

Weitzman, M. (1976), 'On the Welfare Significance of National Product in a Dynamic Economy', *Quarterly Journal of Economics*, **90** (1), 156–62.

PART TWO

Nordic Countries

3. Iceland: Fish Stocks, Geothermal Power, and Desertification

Tryggvi Thor Herbertsson and Sigridur Benediktsdottir

3.1 Economic Growth and Renewable Resources

The Icelandic economy relies on exploiting renewable resources, in particular the fish stocks, and as a result sustainable growth is of paramount importance. The basic concern here is intergenerational equity and the role of supra-national policy makers. Natural developments which affect the country's natural resources are directly reflected in the standards of living in Iceland. Consequently, understanding of the necessity for preservation and management of resources is high.

Economic growth in Iceland from 1946 to 1993 was on average 4.7 per cent per year or 2.8 per cent per working individual. Since the 1950s growth rates have declined, and during the period 1986–93 GDP growth was 2.46 per cent or 1.10 per cent per worker (National Economic Institute Iceland, 1995). This corresponds well to the so-called productivity slowdown of the OECD countries and to the convergence hypothesis (cf. Barro and Sala-i-Martin, 1995). However, given the importance of the resource base for the Icelandic economy, overutilization of fish stocks, particularly the cod stock, and unfavourable environmental conditions could be significant parts of the explanation (Herbertsson and Magnusson, 1995b).

3.2 Exploitation and Management of Fish Stocks

Marine-product exports account for nearly 80 per cent of the commodity exports in Iceland or 50 per cent of the foreign exchange earnings, which indicates the importance of the fishing resources for the Icelanders. Cod, haddock and saithe are the most valuable species.

At the end of World War II **the cod stock** was practically a virgin stock, weighing more than 2.5 million tons, as almost no fishing took place in

Icelandic waters during the war. The subsequent decrease of the stock was reversed by the extension of the fisheries zone in 1974 to 200 nautical miles until 1980, when overutilization and harsh biological conditions caused it to decrease to less than 0.6 million tons in 1993. Since then it has recovered to the current size of 0.9 million tons in 1997.

Table 3.1   Fishable stocks, catches, and total allowable catches for cod, haddock, and saithe in Icelandic waters, 1980–96

1000 tons		1980	1985	1990	1996
Cod	stock	1548	920	841	694
	catches	429	323	333	181
	TAC	300	200	250	186
Haddock	stock	293	150	210	162
	catches	48	50	66	56
	TAC	60	45	60	45
Saithe	stock	306	280	449	123
	catches	52	55	95	40
	TAC	60	60	90	50

Notes: Total allowable catches (TAC) are recommended by the Marine Research Institution (MRI) based on estimates of the total biomass and the optimum stock size defined as the size with maximum sustainable yield.
Source: MRI, Iceland; Herbertsson and Magnusson, 1994a, 1994b, 1995a.

In order to manage the cod fisheries, the Icelandic government has adopted a catch rule enforced from the start of the 1995–96 fishing year. According to this management scheme, catches will be limited to 25 per cent of the average fishable stock biomass, however, with a minimum catch level of 155 thousand tons. This would allow the spawning stock biomass to increase by some 10 per cent in 1998 and would lead to a marked reduction in fishing mortality. Moreover, if this catch rule is applied it has been estimated that the probability of a stock collapse in the long term is less than 1 per cent (Baldursson et. al., 1996). Therefore, this newly adopted management framework would appear to lead to rational utilization of the cod stock and the MRI recommends its implementation (Bardarson and Herbertson, 1995).

The MRI did not begin to measure the haddock stock size until 1962. It appears as if the stock has been around the optimal fishable stock size, especially since 1977 (cf. Table 3.1). In general the fishable haddock stock is in good condition, and if its current management is maintained the resource rent from it can be collected in the future under an efficient fisheries management system. The saithe stock is of a different nature than the cod and haddock stocks, since it is a highly migratory stock, which renders assessments of local, optimal stock sizes essentially meaningless. Since 1975 the saithe stock has been stable compared to the other two stocks, and it is in reasonably good shape. This also applies to other fish stocks apart from the cod stock, if we disregard the spawning stock size.

The fisheries management system was simple up to 1984: anyone owning a boat could enter the fisheries. The only restrictions were temporary closings and a limit to the number of days during which a fisherman was allowed to utilize a certain stock. This caused overinvestment of capital in the fisheries. In 1984, an individual vessel transferable quota (ITQ) management system was introduced in the fisheries for major species, and it was made more uniform in 1988 (Arnason, 1995).[1] According to this system each vessel is issued an annual catch quota, which is simply a multiple of the total allowable catch for the year in question and the vessel's calculated share thereof. A particular vessel may hold quota shares for many different species. The TAC is determined by the Ministry of Fisheries on the basis of recommendations from the Marine Research Institute.

The Ministry of Fisheries has some autonomy in the annual allocation of quotas and is not entirely bound by the rule described earlier. Thus, according to previous practice of the Ministry, proven seaworthiness and some minimal fishing activity of the vessel seems to be a prerequisite for receiving a quota. Quotas may be revoked at any time if the vessel in question is deemed to have violated the fishing regulations laid down by the Ministry of Fisheries.

TAC shares can be officially modified by a permanent transfer between vessels. The allocated vessel quotas or any fraction thereof are transferable subject to some restrictions. As quotas are only issued for a certain period of time, transfers of future quotas, although by no means prohibited, are really only feasible on a contingency basis. The only way for an individual to enter the fisheries is by purchasing quotas from vessels already participating in the fisheries. This has made entrance almost impossible in practice.

Although the system is economically efficient it has invoked considerable political debate in Iceland with respect to fairness and equity, and it is now being evaluated with an eye to potential changes. Its opponents argue that the resource rent only goes to the chosen few, who were lucky enough to be already engaged in fisheries when the current system was imposed. Theoretically, a green tax system would give results equivalent to the currently used system. The difference is that the resource rent would end up as government revenue instead of profits for private firms. Opponents of green taxes point at the distortionary effect of taxes but often ignore the 'double dividend' nature of environmental taxes, as the tax not only raises government revenue and distortions, but also decreases distortions from the common property problem in fisheries so the total effect is probably positive.

If a taxation scheme, whether Pigou's or Coase's, were adopted, new problems would arise. The first is an information problem, since for any tax to work properly in fisheries the government would have to know all of the fishermen's cost functions. The tax should affect the fishing firms to a varying extent, with the smaller firms paying a higher rate than the larger firms. Another problem that arises is the knowledge problem. How would the government decide on the correct taxes? As demonstrated by Hayek the market solves the knowledge problem through the price mechanism provided that property rights are established, which will minimize the commons problem, for example in fisheries. An ITQ system is a form of property rights system, and it is a better solution than any taxing scheme.

The principal benefits of property rights based systems are the small information requirements they involve. The flip side of the coin is that this might accelerate unequal income distribution and social unrest, and the economy, if dependent enough on the resource, might be infected by the Dutch disease (cf. Sachs and Warner, 1995, and Gylfason et. al., 1998). Taxing the harvesting sector optimally, on the other hand, requires costly information on each agent utilizing the resource, implying costs that might be greater than the actual benefits. If, on the other hand, a sufficiently simple tax rule could be found that would enable the realization of a sufficiently large proportion of the resource rent, the income distribution would be unchanged and Dutch disease regimes avoided. The economy could get huge benefits in terms of increased welfare, although from a theoretical point of view it is a second-best solution, with optimal taxes or property rights as the first best solution (Herbertsson and Sørensen, 1998).

Due to the problem of the commons in fisheries **utilization of stocks** must be managed by the government or a coalition of firms operating in the fisheries.[2] The way in which the Icelanders manage their resources is to give the state the greatest authority. The government allocates TACs to the fisheries and, in an ideal setting, the TAC issued by the government and the TAC recommended by the MRI should be approximately equal. This is, however, not always the case. In the period 1976–94 landings did exceed recommended TACs 17 times out of 19 for cod, 10 times out of 17 for haddock and 7 times out of 16 for saithe. The average annual percentage by which cod catches exceeded the recommended from MRI was 24 per cent. These figures show that advice from specialists has not been taken very seriously, resulting in poor management of the fish stocks.

3.3 Energy Consumption and Efficiency

No matter how important the fishing industry is for the Icelandic economy, it has been obvious for a number of years that it cannot by itself sustain economic growth much longer. More attention has, therefore, been shifted to the exploitation of the second major resource base of the country, the power potential of its rivers and geothermal areas, as a major source upon which to build further economic growth.

Shortly after World War II increased attention was given to utilizing the water-power resources to diversify the economy. Ever since one of the main objectives of most governments has been to attract foreign investors in power-intensive industries. This has been partly successful, and the energy-intensive industries now play an increasing role in the economic development of Iceland.[3] At the same time private consumption of energy has been rising rapidly, and Iceland is now among the countries with the highest per capita consumption of energy in the world (cf. Table 1.2). Increasing utilization of geothermal and hydroelectric energy has reduced coal consumption to less than 3 per cent in recent years and, more importantly, oil now provides only about 30 per cent of the primary energy used in Iceland (cf. Table 3.2).

Table 3.2   Energy consumption by source in Iceland, 1940–96

	1940		1960		1980		1990		1996	
	kTOE	per cent	kTOE	per cent	kTOE	per cent	kTOE	per cent	kTOE	per cent
Hydroelectric	4	3	45	8	263	18	357	17	410	17
Geothermal	13	9	106	19	639	43	1039	49	1205	51
Peat	4	3	0	0	0	0	0	0	0	0
Coal	92	67	16	3	21	1	68	3	63	3
Oil	25	18	381	70	570	38	675	32	679	29
Total	138	100	548	100	1493	100	2139	100	2357	100

Note: Energy is measured in thousand tons of oil equivalent (kTOE); 1 PJ = 23.9 kTOE.
Source: National Energy Authority, Iceland.

The large share of hydroelectric and geothermal power is of great importance for the environment since hydroelectric and geothermal power production is essentially non-polluting and to a large extent renewable. There are, however, other environmental effects.

The technically harnessable **hydroelectric energy** potential in Iceland has been estimated at approximately 64 000 GWh of electricity per year. According to current assessments, some 50 per cent of this can be exploited after economical and ecological considerations have been taken into account, whereas only 14 per cent has been utilized until now. The harnessing of hydroelectric power energy involves large structures and distribution systems such as generating stations, roads and high-voltage pylons and transmission lines which exclude alternative use of land, and can alter or destroy the beauty of the landscape. Changes of waterways affect the ecological balance and biodiversity by altering river courses, waterfalls and ground water levels, and by flooding extensive land areas for reservoirs which also increases risks of erosion. The amount of land required for all economically feasible hydroelectric powerplants in Iceland, is estimated at 1100 km², or just over 1 per cent of the country's area. According to existing plans 300–400 km² of this area are covered by continuous vegetation, an area corresponding to 1.5 per cent of the country's entire ground cover, and 300 km² are rivers and lakes. In addition, in 1990 high-voltage pylons and power transmission lines excluded alternative use of 270 km² of land.

Assessments of the environmental impact of hydroelectric power development projects were introduced in 1971 and extended in 1993. They have resulted in the increased use of tunnels to convey water. The aim of the 1993 law is to set clear rules as to what should be assessed and what environmental effects should be considered in the assessment, and the law states that those options which will prove most efficient in the long term should be chosen without exception.

Iceland is very rich in **geothermal resources**. The average regional heatflow within the country is two to four times the global average. Thermal areas are classified on the basis of the maximum subsurface temperature of the thermal water. In the low-temperature areas the maximum temperature at a depth of 1 km is less than 150°C, while hotter areas are classified as high-temperature areas. The low-temperature areas are characterized by hot-water springs with temperatures at or near the surface ranging from slightly above ambient temperature to 100°C and with relatively low amounts of dissolved chemicals. The hot springs are common all over the country except in the east and southeast. About 1000 hot-spring localities have been located and 19 high-temperature areas with steam fields.

The technically harnessable electric power from the geothermal resources is about 190 000 GWh/year for 100 years. Of this only some 20 000 GWh/year, primarily from the hotter areas, have been estimated to be sufficiently profitable, if environmental effects are disregarded. At present only about 1.5 per cent of the economically harnessable geothermal energy has been exploited, primarily for space heating where it provides 85 per cent of the country's requirements.

Assessments of the environmental impact of geothermal development have been carried out for many years but are much more limited in scope than in the case of hydroelectric power development. Harnessing of geothermal energy may, however, in the long run have an even stronger impact than carefully planned hydroelectric energy utilization. These effects include the exhaustion of natural hot springs and changes to other visible features of geothermal areas. Development of high-temperature fields also causes air pollution and pollution of surface and ground water. Plant effluents having different chemical composition from the surface water at the site affect the soil and fragile vegetation.

These factors have not been considered sufficiently with regard to the development of the geothermal industry; some consideration has been given to the effects on ground water used for human consumption, but the effect on soil and vegetation around the geothermal reservoirs has not been considered adequately. It is now clear that many of the harnessable heat sources will never be utilized because of their importance for tourism, not to mention their importance to the Icelandic people who are increasingly conscious of the vulnerable natural beauty of their land.

The exhaustion of natural hot springs is more a local problem than a problem for the geothermal industry in Iceland as whole. This is due to the active volcanism through which depleted geothermal reservoirs are periodically replaced by new ones, although often at different locations.

Air pollution resulting from utilization of high-temperature fields is composed of carbon dioxide, hydrogen sulphide, hydrogen, methane, nitrogen and argon, with the first two produced in the largest volumes. Nitrogen and argon are considered harmless. Geothermal energy sources emit much less carbon dioxide than fossil fuel, up to ten times less. Hydrogen sulphide is a poisonous gas and corrodes metal. The gas rarifies quickly so the damage is restricted to the immediate area around the geothermal plants. How much of the hydrogen sulphide decomposes into sulphur is a matter of debate.

Effluent water from geothermal plants can be disposed of in several ways. The most harmless method is to reinject the water into the geothermal reservoirs, but unfortunately this is also the most expensive method in the short run, and it has not been used in Iceland to date. It is quite common to collect the effluent water in lagoons, as in the Blue Lagoon, which diminishes heat pollution but also entails danger of ground water pollution and siliceous formation. The cheapest way to get rid of effluent water is to pump it directly into the sea. This method is the most expensive in the long run because of the resulting chemical and heat pollution. Although the chemicals in the effluent are far from being hazardous in the short run, they could accumulate in the long run. The effects on the biosphere could be devastating.

3.4 Air Pollution

Overall legislation on environmental issues has not been adopted in Iceland. Nonetheless, most aspects of environmental issues are covered by existing laws and regulations, administered by The Ministry for the Environment which was established in 1990

Ambient concentration levels in Iceland are low and practically negligible due to the small population and low population density, the low level of industrialization, the heavy reliance on less-polluting renewable energy resources, that is hydroelectric and geothermal energy, and the limited crop production and use of pesticides and fertilizers. It also reflects the ability of strong winds and ocean currents to disperse pollutants. But local pollution problems do exist. Increased urbanization in the Reykjavík area and rapid growth in the number of motor vehicles result in occasional periods of smog.

Table 3.3   Air pollution in Iceland by source, 1988–96

1000 tons	1988	1990	1992	1993	1994	1995	1996
Sulphur oxide (SO_2)	8.56	8.22	8.14	8.69	8.02	8.12	8.38
Carbon dioxide (CO_2)	2117	2147	2197	2302	2265	2282	2323
Nitrogen oxide (NO_2)	24.92	26.27	28.44	29.34	29.20	28.41	28.74
Lead	.012	.013	.007	.005	.005	.004	.001
Chlorofluorocarbons	-	.142	.070	.067	.032	.000	.008

Note: Data for 1996 are preliminary.
Source: Statistics Iceland.

Concentrations of **polluting substances** such as SO_2, NO_X and heavy metals in the ambient air of the rural areas of Iceland are very low compared to corresponding levels in other European countries. However, per capita emissions of NO_X are very high, and concerning CO_2 and SO_2 they are about average (OECD, 1994; cf. Tables 3.3 and 1.2).

The growing fishing fleet with high fuel combustion is the major cause of this. This must, however, be viewed with caution, because of the low population density of Iceland. These concentrations do not seem to cause ecological damage even though the ecosystem is very fragile.

Air pollution is to a great extent of foreign origin, and Iceland can be seen as an importing country. The quantities imported are relatively small but far exceed the quantities generated in Iceland. For instance, the amount of sulphur deposition in Iceland of foreign origin is 25 times the amount of national origin. Iceland is also exporting sulphur but there are 5 times more imports than exports.

The total anthropogenic emission of SO_2 was 8.38 tons during 1996, of which 65 per cent was from geothermal power plants. The original form of the emission in the geothermal areas is natural and anthropogenic sulphur emission (H_2S); due to possible oxidation it is accounted for in the statistics for SO_2 emission. It is nevertheless uncertain how rapidly and fully natural and anthropogenic sulphur emission oxidates to form SO_2. In recent years the total anthropogenic emission of SO_2 has not increased as much as the combustion of fossil fuels because the major increase has been in fuels with low sulphur content. Because of the geographical location and limited emissions of pollutants in Iceland, the absolute level of acid deposition over Iceland is very small, that is at least five times less than in any other European country.

The total anthropogenic emission of CO_2 from Icelandic sources during 1996 was 2.3 million tons or 8.8 tons CO_2 per capita, of which 79 per cent was due to combustion of light fuel. On account of growing domestic fossil fuel combustion, the main increase being in light fuel oil, the emission of CO_2 has been growing in Iceland for the last few years, mostly because of the rapidly growing fishing fleet. In 1994 approximately 35 per cent of emissions originated from the fishing fleet, whereas the share was less than 30 per cent before 1990. Domestic transportation is the second largest source of CO_2 emissions with a 28 per cent share, which has been growing in the recent years. Icelandic CO_2 emissions per capita are not negligible compared to other countries. However, the two largest sources of emissions are in sectors where substitution is very difficult and this has caused problems with regards to international commitments on stabilizing and possibly reducing CO_2 emissions in Iceland.

Of the total NO_x emission of 28.74 thousand tons from fossil fuel combustion fishing vessels accounted for 80 per cent and road transportation only for 8 per cent, and the increase in emissions of nitrogen oxide of 1.8 per cent annually during the last eight years is solely due to increased emission from fishing vessels. Emission from other sources has almost without exception been decreasing, most notably in road transport where the increased use of three-way catalytic converters in passenger vehicles, compulsory since 1992 for new passenger cars, has decreased the NO_x emission considerably.

Lead pollution from motor cars has also fallen appreciably in the last few years. Although no overall goals have been adopted towards reducing pollution from motor vehicles, some policy measures have been implemented. The lead content of petrol was reduced from 0.4 g/litre in 1987 to 0.04 g/litre in 1994. In 1988 importation of lead-free gasoline began and reached a market share of 84.2 per cent in 1994 because of price differentials in favour of unleaded gasoline – an example of successfully applied economic instruments.

The addition of man-made **greenhouse gases** to the earth's atmospheric system, leading to a potential increase in the temperature at the earth's surface, could affect the Icelandic economy considerably because of its dependence on natural resources. CO_2, CFC, CH_4 and halon are major contributors to the global warming potential.

Emission of CH_4 is negligible in Iceland (only around 21 000 tons), and emission of chlorofluorocarbons has decreased in recent years. According to the Montreal Protocol on substances that deplete the ozone layer of 1987, Iceland is committed to reducing the use of CFCs by 50 per cent of the 1986 level by 1995, and by 15 per cent more by 1997, and furthermore to discontinuing the use of all CFCs by 2000. As a result of these measures, production of CFCs in Iceland has already declined from 200 tons in 1986 to 28 tons in 1994, which fulfils commitments many times over. The halon production also declined from 14.6 tons in 1986 to 0.4 tons in 1994.

The stratospheric ozone layer above Iceland in the summer has become thinner at a rate of 0.5 per cent per year between 1979–90. This is probably due to movement of air. No significant change in the ozone layer was found during the winter. Recent measurements do not confirm that the thinning of the ozone layer is continuing in the years after 1990.

Problems of coordinating **local and international actions** are apparent in Iceland, where air pollution has not decreased in recent years, except concerning emissions of lead and chlorofluorocarbons. This does not, however, give a clear picture of the achievements of the Icelandic authorities. The rapidly increasing share of geothermal and hydroelectric power in Iceland's energy use after World War II decreased pollution from fossil fuel burning enormously. Fossil fuel is now almost solely used in transportation where substitution is nearly impossible for the time being. This means that reducing CO_2 emissions compared to 1990 emission levels may be particularly difficult to obtain in Iceland.

According to Icelandic policy, the Protocols to the Geneva Convention ought to be revised to incorporate the concept of critical load, that is the highest level of depositions or concentration at which harmful effects on the ecosystem are not expected. If international commitments had due regard for these concepts, there would be no need to reduce the emissions in areas which are exposed to a very small concentration of biodegradable pollutants.

Although Iceland is not seriously polluted by foreign sources, it would benefit from a reduction in emission of air pollutants in Europe. With this aim in mind, Iceland may find itself in the position of having to reduce its own emissions to be in accord with international agreements or as a result of being a party to the Nordic Council or the EEA; this could entail economically inefficient pollution abatement measures in Iceland.

3.5   Waste

The Ministry for the Environment has developed a national strategy to respond to what it admits to be 'the urgent need for improvements in waste management' (OECD, 1993). In Iceland as in other western countries there has been an awakening interest around the country in the need for improvement in waste management. However, limited financial resources of local authorities and the absence of severe pollution problems have limited concrete actions in this area.

The total generation of waste in Iceland is 185 000 tons per year, in addition to 6400 tons of hazardous waste. Households generates 43 per cent of the waste and other municipal sources another 34 per cent. Local authorities are responsible for the collection and disposal of municipal and household solid waste. They are also responsible for operating satisfactory facilities for disposal of other solid waste, while industries generating the waste are responsible for transporting it to the appropriate disposal facilities. Only in the Reykjavík area has a modern centre been established for receiving and handling household and industrial solid waste. It serves close to 60 per cent of the population of Iceland. In most outlying areas local household and industrial waste is primarily disposed of in landfills. Of household and municipal waste 10 per cent is recycled or prepared for recycling abroad, 73 per cent is disposed of in landfills and 17 per cent in incineration plants.

Recycling is promoted by several economic instruments, including fees on single-use plastic shopping bags, charges on commercial enterprises for waste collection on the basis of nature and quantity, and return fees on beverage containers with a rate of return above 75 per cent, the highest in Europe. A deposit on new motor vehicles is required by law; it is refunded once vehicles have been disposed of in an environmentally sound manner.

Such incentives do not apply to households, which pay a flat fee for the collection of waste. Thus collection of batteries is only about 12 per cent, because no fine has to be paid for throwing them away with other household waste. Returns of paper and cardboard have also been far from adequate, because too few households sort their refuse. High inspection cost is one of the excuses for having a flat fee on household collection of waste, but in a world with increasing prices for example for paper and plastic material it is only a question of time until it will pay to introduce a service-connected fee.

Hazardous waste constitutes about 3.3 per cent of waste generated in Iceland including waste mineral oils (78 per cent), medical waste (11 per cent), waste from small enterprises and households (11 per cent) and only 1 tonne of PCB (polychlorinated biphenyls) and similar waste materials. In 1991 a modern reception centre for sorting and packing hazardous waste materials was opened in Reykjavík. Iceland also has a programme for the systematic collection of PCBs. Once collected, PCBs are exported for disposal in recognized hazardous waste treatment facilities abroad. A bill on general fees for hazardous chemicals is being debated in the Althing.

3.6 Water Pollution and Resources

Iceland is a party to a number of important international agreements and has played a very active role at international level in protecting the ocean against **pollution**, which is considered the greatest threat to sustainable development of the marine resources, and the country is committed to protection of the marine environment against all types of pollution. This policy is economically justified by the heavy dependence upon fisheries of the Icelandic economy.

Danger of pollution does not only stem from Icelandic sources so the Icelandic authorities are greatly concerned about activities in other regions of the world which could lead to the release of radioactive or persistent organic substances into the sea, even though such substances would be very strongly diluted before they reach Iceland. The economic consequences of a significant pollution release in the North Atlantic at some distance from Iceland could be dramatic, while the chances of full compensation for the damage suffered by Iceland would be fairly small under present international law. Present radioactivity levels of Icelandic waters are, in fact, among the lowest in Europe. Concentrations of other pollution substances such as trace metals and chlorinated hydrocarbons are also very low.

In addition to pollution from vessels, discharge of waste water is a major source of marine pollution. Currently, only 6 per cent of the population of Iceland is connected to secondary waste water treatment plants, a very low share compared to other countries. As a result there is occasional visible and olfactory pollution, although strong ocean currents tend to mask this pollution.

Fresh water resources in Iceland are abundant and generally of high quality. Although the level of demand for fresh water per capita in Iceland is now among the highest in the world, still the annual water withdrawal is far below available quantities: only 0.1 per cent as compared to 1.8 per cent in Sweden and 20 per cent in the UK. The fresh water sources for human consumption in Iceland are mostly restricted to ground water.

Pollution of surface and ground water is minimal. In agriculture, the limited crop production and low use of fertilizers and pesticides pose few pollution pressures. In addition, lava acts as a natural filter of pollution in many parts of the country. However, some localized pollution of surface and ground water exists, and pollution threats are increasing. Rapidly increasing tourism, outdoor activities and the building of summer residences pose increasing diffuse pollution threats.

3.7 Soil Erosion

Soil conservation and afforestation are the greatest environmental tasks in Iceland at the moment besides managing the fish stocks. Volcanic eruptions are frequent and volcanic ash deposits are widespread.

When Iceland was settled in the ninth century rapid population growth and introduction of grazing animals led to intense use of the fragile ecosystem. In the ninth century forests covered 40 per cent of all land, as compared to only 1 per cent at present, and 60 per cent of all land was usable for agriculture;

at present approximately 30 per cent of all land in Iceland is cultivable. The deforestation and desertification is due to three independent factors, volcanic activity, climate changes and human activities, with the last factor probably being the most important one.

Degradation was severe and erosion accelerated significantly soon after the settlement, leading to a substantial reduction in the population with social unrest and poverty. Evidence for vegetation changes is provided by historical records, the Icelandic Sagas, annals, old farm surveys, old place names and current vegetation remnants, tephrocronology (dating with the help of volcanic ash layers), and pollen analyses. Changes include both composition changes, due to grazing and wood cutting, and reduction in vegetation cover and formation of deserts. Decreased vegetation vigour lead to increased cryoturbation and solifluction processes that accelerate erosion.

Now, more than 37 per cent of the country is barren desert with an additional 10–15 per cent of disturbed areas with limited plant production, some of which is caused by volcanic activity. At the time of settlement, Icelandic deserts were only 5–15 per cent, and vegetated areas were much more vigorous than now. The barren surfaces are very sandy with grains consisting of volcanic glass, tephra and crystalline materials that are basaltic, giving the surfaces a dark and often almost black colour. These soils are infertile, mostly due to a lack of organic matter and nitrogen. Only 0.5–5 per cent vegetation cover can be sustained on these surfaces.

The climate in Iceland became gradually cooler during the 11th century, which made vegetation less resistant and ecosystems more vulnerable to erosion than before. Glaciers started to advance because of the cooler climate, and they currently cover about 10 per cent of the country. During volcanic eruptions rapid cooling of magma by glacial meltwater resulted in increased tephra production. The glaciers developed vast outwash plains that provided sand feeding drift areas. Eruptions under glaciers cause large scale floods that build vast sand deposits on the glacial plains and along rivers. Some glacially covered thermal areas also result in floods at regular intervals. These factors, intensified by land use, have resulted in almost total desertification of 5000 km^2 in northeast Iceland, which is perhaps the world's longest sand-sea outside of arid areas.

Soil erosion in Iceland is characterized by a total removal of the fertile soil resource, leaving behind infertile barren surfaces. Icelanders have been battling desertification processes for a long time. In the 1880s severe sand encroachment threatened the existence of important agricultural areas in the southern lowlands. As a result of reclamation experiments in that area, the Icelandic Soil Conservation and Reclamation Service was established in 1907. It is possibly the world's oldest operating soil conservation institute. Soil erosion still continues on Icelandic grazing lands and is considered the most severe environmental problem in Iceland, according to several public opinion polls.

3.8   Resource and Environmental Costs as Constraints on Growth

Today, Iceland is a diversified, affluent industrial society, where services are far the most important occupation in terms of numbers. But the mechanization of the fishing industry was accompanied by serious overfishing and excessive, unprofitable investment in the fishing industry, which in turn was fuelled by high inflation and excessive borrowing abroad in the 1970s and 1980s. One of the most important problems facing the government of Iceland in the 1990s is, therefore, to enforce an efficient fisheries management system and to stimulate reduction of the fishing fleet to a size that is commensurate with the maximum sustainable catch of fish. The required reforms must at the same time diversify the economy and stimulate economic growth (Gylfason, 1997). It is of utmost importance to stop the desertification and deforestation of the island in a manner compatible with the needs of tourism and agriculture. Tourism now provides 25 per cent of total foreign exchange earnings. To safeguard the vulnerable natural beauty of the landscape in Iceland and to further strengthen the tourist industry soil erosion has to be stopped.

NOTES

1. The system is, however, not a true ITQ system, as the politicans left a loophole. A fisherman on a certain type of small boat is allowed to fish as much as he can as long as he uses hand- or long-line. The fisherman with the best boat and the most effort will recive the largest share of the overall catch quota placed on these boats. Such 'fisheries Olympics' call for *capital stuffing*. The number of small boats fishing under this system increased from 1150 in 1984 to 2000 in 1991, and their share of the cod catch, the most valuable catch excluding crustaceans, from 6 per cent in 1984 to 14 per cent in 1992.
2. The theory predicts that under a competitive fisheries management system fishermen will overinvest in capital and use too much labour in their search for higher profits. The resource rent will be dissipated and overutilization of the fish stocks will result. This outcome is also referred to as the 'tragedy of the commons' (cf. Gordon, 1954; Harding, 1968; Clark, 1990).
3. The enlargement of the Alusuisse aluminium smelter, which was agreed upon at the end of 1995, has changed growth forecasts for the year 1996 considerably. Instead of the previously forecast 2 per cent growth the National Economic Institute now forecasts 2.7 per cent growth for 1996.

REFERENCES

Arnason, R. (1995), *The Icelandic Fishing Industry: Evolution and Management of a Fishing Industry*, Cambridge: Fishing News Books.

Baldursson, F., A. Danielsson and G. Stefansson (1996), 'On the Rational Utilization of the Icelandic Cod Stock', *ICES Journal of Marine Resources* (forthcoming).

Bardarson, H. and T.T. Herbertsson (1995), 'The Icelandic Fisheries Management System: Prospects for the Future' (in Icelandic), *mimeo*, Department of Economics, University of Iceland.

Barro, R. and X. Sala-i-Martin (1995), *Economic Growth*, New York: McGraw-Hill.

Clark, C.W. (1990), *Mathematical Bioeconomics. The Optimal Management of Renewable Resources*, 2nd ed., New York: Wiley-Interscience Publications.

Gordon, H.S. (1954), 'The Economic Theory of a Common Property Resource – The Fisheries', *Journal of Political Economy,* **62** (2), 124–42.

Gylfason, T. (1997), 'Iceland', *Collier's Encyclopedia*, Vol. 12, London: Collier-Macmillan.

Gylfason, T., T.T. Herbertsson and G. Zoega (1998), 'Mixed Blessing: Natural Resources and Economic Growth', *Macroeconomic Dynamics* (forthcoming).

Harding, G. (1968), 'The Tragedy of the Commons', *Science*, 162, 1243–47.

Herbertsson, T.T. and G. Magnusson (1994a), *The Icelandic and Faroese Economies: A Comparison of the Fishing Sector*, Report to a committee appointed by the Prime Minister of Denmark, Department of Economics, University of Iceland, Report no. 3, July.

Herbertsson, T.T. and G. Magnusson (1994b), 'The Economic Situation in the Faroe Islands' (in Icelandic), *Financial Bulletin of the Central Bank of Iceland*, **XLI** (2), 178–91.

Herbertsson, T.T. and G. Magnusson (1995a), 'Autonomy and Fisheries Management: Iceland and the Faroe Islands', *mimeo*, Department of Economics, University of Iceland.

Herbertsson, T.T. and G. Magnusson (1995b), 'Accounting for Growth in the Five Nordic Countries, 1971–1992', *Working Papers*, **W96** (10), Department of Economics, University of Iceland.

Herbertsson, T.T. and A. Sørensen (1998), 'Policy Rules for Exploitation of Renewable Resources: A Macroeconomic Perspective', *Environmental and Resource Economics* (forthcoming).

National Economic Institute Iceland (1995), *National Accounts 1945-1992*, Reykjavík: Statistics Iceland.

OECD (1993), 'Iceland', *OECD Environmental Performance Reviews*, Paris: OECD.

OECD (1994), *Environmental Indicators*, Paris: OECD.

Sachs, J. and A. Warner (1995), 'Natural Resource Abundance and Economic Growth', *NBER Working Paper Series*, **5398**, December.

4. Finland: Forestry, Energy Policy, and Restructuring

Anni Huhtala

4.1 The Economic Basis for Environmental Policy

During the past few years Finland has gone through its worst recession in the post-war period. From 1990 to 1993, the real GDP fell by almost 15 per cent, the unemployment rate rose from 3.5 to 19 per cent, and the central government debt increased from 10 per cent to 60 per cent of GDP. Before the recession the annual change of GDP had been positive for 13 consecutive years, on average 3–4 per cent.

The origins of the recession lie in several unlucky internal and external coincidences: high debt ratios ultimately causing a banking crisis; collapse of trade with the Soviet Union and a simultaneous slowdown in the traditional western markets so that exports dropped from 30 to 22 per cent of GDP; weakening of Finland's international cost-competitiveness due to wage increases which were, however, covered by productivity growth and improvement in the terms of trade in the open sector.

The policy response has been a depreciation of the markka which was allowed to float in the fall of 1992, low rates of inflation, and a narrowing of long-term interest differentials *vis-à-vis* German rates. Economic policy aiming at low real interest rates and rapid growth has been motivated also by the attainment of ecological sustainability: capital replacement based on cleaner technology would be encouraged by the lowest possible interest rates (Ministry of the Environment, 1995, p. 19). Furthermore, as part of the policy of compliance with the EU Maastricht convergence criteria, there have been attempts to cut government spending, especially welfare expenditures, to reduce taxation, to improve labour market flexibility and to privatize state-owned companies. Individual proposals on selling state-owned forests have also been made.

The persistence of high unemployment is not unrelated to a well-known structural reform, which has been going on for decades. Since 1960 working hours per unit of real product have declined to a fifth while the use of electricity per unit has increased by half. It has been claimed that a restructuring of the Finnish economy may also be induced by a growth in the productivity of natural resources. The share of the heavy basic industry would shrink due to increased natural resource productivity, which would in turn decrease the capital, energy and emissions intensity of the economy. This would release resources from investment for consumption.

4.2 Energy: Consumption, Efficiency and Policy

The Finnish per capita **energy consumption** is the highest among the Scandinavian countries (cf. Table 1.2), and the share of domestic energy is 32 per cent, or 41 per cent if nuclear energy is included. The high energy intensity is only partly explained by cold climate and high demand for traffic and transport due to low population density and long distances in the country, as almost half of the total energy consumption was used in manufacturing, especially in the pulp and paper industry and metallurgy. Space heating, excluding industrial installations, accounted for 22 per cent and transport for 13 per cent of the total energy consumption.

Table 4.1   Energy consumption by source in Finland, 1970–94

	1970		1991		1992		1993		1994	
	kTOE	per cent	kTOE	per cent	kTOE	per cent	kTOE	per cent	kTOE	per cent
Imported energy and nuclear power:										
Coal	1826	10	3205	11	2618	9	3086	10	4113	13
Natural gas	11	0	2382	8	2470	8	2556	8	2822	9
Nuclear power	0	0	4600	15	4543	15	4700	16	4582	14
Electricity	132	1	1795	6	2059	7	1884	6	1520	5
Oil	10167	54	8995	30	8858	30	8469	28	8849	28
Domestic sources:										
Hydroelectric	2339	12	3270	11	3739	12	3336	11	2918	9
Black liquor	1420	7	1992	7	2056	7	2342	8	2570	8
Waste wood	498	3	811	3	807	3	994	3	1092	3
Fire wood	2271	12	850	3	850	3	845	3	844	3
Peat	22	0	1388	5	1361	5	1436	5	1621	5
Other sources	298	2	580	2	609	2	656	2	682	2
Total	18984	101	29868	101	29970	101	30304	100	31613	99

Notes: Energy is measured in thousand tons of oil equivalent (kTOE). Electricity includes only imports of electricity. Black liquor includes black and sulphite liquor. Because of rounding percentage numbers do not add to 100.
Source: Statistics Finland, 1994.

Manufacturing accounts also for the largest share of electricity consumption, over half of Finland's total consumption. The demand for electricity has grown considerably because of a tendency within industry to switch from fuels to electricity, and because of investment in the forest products industry in mechanical rather than chemical pulp-making. Consumption of electricity for space heating purposes has also increased.

The composition of **energy sources** has remained roughly the same for the past ten years; imported organic fuels satisfy half of Finland's primary energy demand (cf. Table 4.1). The high dependency upon oil, almost 80 per cent of which comes from North Sea, is related to the fact that most freight is transported by road vehicles. On the other hand, the forest industry has decreased oil consumption in favour of natural gas and nuclear power (Ministry of Trade and Industry, 1993, p. 18; Finnish Forest Industries Federation, 1993, p. 11). Even though Finland uses large amounts of imported energy, almost 36 per cent of energy consumption is used for exports, mainly pulp and paper and basic metal products. About 40 per cent of the energy used finds its way to households in the form of products and services.

The plans for the official **energy policy** in Finland are based on the negative stand adopted by parliament in the autumn of 1993 on the building of new nuclear power capacity. Energy policy must, however, address the expected increase in energy demand. Recently, the Finnish government has announced the intention to concentrate on measures affecting energy efficiency, usage of bioenergy and other renewable energy sources, the electricity market, energy taxation and promotion of energy technology.

Finland is one of the leading countries in the use of domestic biofuels. The share of wood derived fuels in the total primary energy needs is about 14 per cent and that of peat about 5 per cent. At present, 75 000 hectares of Finnish bogs are drained for energy production. The annual energy usage of peat is 1.6 MTOE (cf. Table 4.1), whereas the reserves have been estimated to be as great as 420 MTOE. The energy use of peat is not unproblematic. Bogs function as a carbon reservoir, but when burned, peat releases carbon dioxide. The carbon dioxide balance of draining bogs and planting trees on them is not straightforward to calculate.

The possibilities for increasing the use of biofuels are significant. New production methods for wood and peat fuels are being developed in order to decrease the production costs to the level of imported fuels. Also non-food production on fields withdrawn from farming is encouraged. The consumption of bioenergy is expected to increase by a quarter by 2005.

Use of hydropower has a long tradition in Finland. Today there are six major harnessed river systems, of which the northernmost, the river Kemijoki, produces 30 per cent of the domestic supply of hydroelectricity. Additional hydropower would come from the Vuotos basin and additional plants on the

Kemijoki river. The discussion of building the Vuotos basin started in the 1950s, and it has been the longest lasting environmental conflict in Finland involving local people, representatives for industry and environmentalists. The permit for building the basin is currently being considered in the Water Court. The rapids of another large river system in Finnish Lapland, the river Ounasjoki, are protected by law. Yet, as the unemployment rate in the province has always been among the highest in the country (currently at 17 per cent), hopes to dam this river for energy production are voiced from time to time. These plans conflict with ambitions for increasing (eco)tourism in the area.

Also wind power parks in Finland's archipelagos have raised conflicting interests mainly due to aesthetic deterioration of landscapes. Quite recently, however, optimistic scenarios about wind power capacity in Lapland's mountain areas have been presented. Public funding has been provided for studying wind power in Finland in the arctic areas where the theoretical energy potential could at maximum be about 14 TWh annually. In practice, wind power could provide 10 per cent of electricity consumption in Finland.

Despite the high energy intensity of Finnish industrial production, energy efficiency has improved considerably, following the oil crisis in the 1970s, and fuel consumption has since declined by 30 per cent. Even though fuels have been partly replaced by electricity, energy intensity in industry has declined. However, energy use in absolute terms has increased due to larger volumes of output. The amount of energy used for space heating in Finland has remained unchanged since the 1970s, although the volume of buildings requiring heating has greatly increased, as a result of improved thermal insulation and more efficient management of heat.

Inefficiencies in the use of energy are pronounced in parts of the service sector and in private households. Electricity consumption in the service sector has doubled in the past couple of decades due to new shopping malls, sports complexes, restaurants and other service facilities. Electricity consumption per household has increased by roughly 40 per cent during the past 15 years.

Since the middle of the 1980s investments in energy saving in the industry and service sector have been promoted by financial support. The costs of the savings measures undertaken have been low, but also the total energy savings achieved have been relatively small. Several new programmes have been launched to improve and develop energy technology. Total funding for the energy technology research programmes for the years 1993–98 is approximately 260 million ECU. Investments in research and development are supporting the government's energy saving programme which aims at reducing energy consumption by 10–15 per cent by 2010 compared to a situation where no new conservation measures are taken.

A recent major change has been the deregulation process which aims at promoting competition in the Finnish electricity market. A stock exchange for electricity started in August 1996. However, concern has arisen that competition will benefit major customers, whereas households end up paying a larger share of the energy bill in the future.

4.3   Domestic Resources: Forests and Lakes

Forests are overwhelmingly Finland's most abundant natural resource. Of the total land area about 60 per cent is forest land, and an additional 20 per cent consists of scrub, waste land and forest roads. The rest is cultivated land (8 per cent) and water areas (10 per cent) (Statistics Finland, 1995).

The forest industry accounts for about half of Finland's net export revenues which is the highest share in the industrialized countries. In 1992 the per capita export revenues earned by the forest industry were 1350 ECU, the largest in the world; in Sweden the figure was 950 (Finnish Forest Industries Federation, 1993, pp. 6, 10). However, the forests have a considerable non-commercial value, which is reflected in Finns' concerns about forests and their protection. Today the effects of monoculture, loss of biodiversity and acidification affect the image of the industry and hence also have indirect commercial value.

In recent years, the forest industry has used 45–55 million cubic metres of wood annually, of which on average 90 per cent has been domestic round-wood. The result of the intense commercial use of **forests resources** for raw material is that the age structure of trees has become more homogeneous in Finnish forests. This means that even though growth clearly exceeds the total drain, most of the growth is taking place in commercial forests. At the same time, genetically rich old growth forests are becoming scarce, and biodiversity in forests is declining.

Another environmental concern related to the current rapid forest growth is the deposition of airborne nitrogen. In the long run, nitrogen pollutants may no longer have only positive effects as fertilizers but make trees more prone to frosts and pest-spread diseases. Uncertain factors which also potentially weaken the renewable resource base are other air pollutants, halogenated hydrocarbon compounds and ozone, and climate change. The growth rate of forests has started decreasing in southern Finland.

Ownership of Finland's forests is private for 55 per cent of the commercial forest land. Even though companies own 8 per cent and the state 33 per cent of forest land, the commercial value of private forests is greater than these percentages might suggest. In the early 1990s, almost 75 per cent of the wood raw material used by the forest industry originated from private forests, most of which are situated in the best areas of southern Finland in terms of forest yield and diversity.

The structure of forest ownership is important in the sense that the private ownership of land and other property is strongly protected in the Finnish Constitution. In practice this has meant that when nature conservation areas are discussed, compensation to private landowners has often become the major issue. This has also been the case quite recently in the preparation of a comprehensive 'coastline protection programme'.

Sustainable use of forests has been regulated since as early as 1886 when 'laying waste forest land' was prohibited by law. The more modern acts concerning private forests have maintained the same principle in securing that forests will not be destroyed and that forest growth and regeneration will be taken care of. Felling and silvicultural practices have changed considerably over the years. Huge clear-cut areas, similar to those in the 1950s in northern Finland encompassing up to 1000 hectares, would be devastating for the reputation of Finnish forestry today. At present, less than 0.4 per cent of Finland's forested land is clear-cut annually (Statistics Finland, 1995, p. 15).

Forest taxation was reformed in 1993, and during a transition period of at most 13 years the tax will change from a site productivity (per hectare) tax to a yield (timber sales) tax. Excluding the potentially negative effects of the disincentives it contains for forest improvement efforts during the transition period, the new tax is expected to promote multiple use of forests; areas used for recreation and voluntary preservation are no longer taxed. When the forest owner harvests the forest, utility that non-owners derive from the forest is not taken into account. Accordingly, the yield tax could be used as a Pigouvian tax to internalize this externality (Koskela and Ollikainen, 1995).

The right of public access, 'everyman's right', has made the recreational use of forests possible for non-forest owners as well. Moreover, one of the new rights included in the Constitution is the right to a sound environment (Ministry of the Environment, 1995, p. 13; Joas, 1996). Sustaining nature, the environment and the cultural heritage is promoted also by a system of 27 nature parks and reserves. In addition, some virgin forests and peatland areas are protected. The main concern is that most of the protected areas are in the north, while forest reserves in the southern part of the country are small. Roughly 15 per cent of the productive forests of Finnish Lapland are situated in reserves, compared with only 0.3 per cent of the forest area of southern Finland. In practice, almost all protected old growth forests are on state owned land in northern Finland.

In addition to proper forest landscapes, a typical feature of Finnish nature is the great number of **wetlands**. Bogs once covered almost a third of the country but only half of the original bog area is left today. Bog drainage was particularly extensive in the late 1960s. Most of the drained bogs are now in forestry use (60 per cent), with a minor share being used for farming (7 per cent). About 30 per cent of drainage areas have been of no benefit to forestry, because of their low nutrient contents and exposure to wind. That is why completely new drains for forestry are hardly done any more.

Finns use about 260 litres of water per day per capita, of which 45 per cent is surface water and 55 per cent ground water. Thanks to Finland's cold climate, precipitation is far greater than evaporation, so that ground water is not easily depleted. *Eskers* and similar moraine formations have an especially large water storage capacity. However, their importance as water reservoirs has been threatened by other economic interests since they also contain valuable building materials, such as gravel and sand.

Despite the great number of lakes in Finland, fishing is mainly done by about 1.7 million recreational fishermen who catch about 47 000 tons. Commercial fishing is concentrated in the marine areas, and the annual catch is about 80 000 tons, mainly Baltic herring (90 per cent) used as feed in the fur industry. Even though fishing accounts only for 0.2 per cent of GDP, it has considerable local economic importance. The greatest current concern in fishery is that as a result of harnessing rivers and intensive marine fishing, natural reserves of salmon have declined. The so-called M–74 virus is endangering the salmon species in the two salmon rivers still left, the river Tornionjoki and the river Simojoki. As a result of the already alarming decline in the stock of salmon fry, a seasonal fishing moratorium in Finland's fishing zone has been implemented for 1996–97. Finland also stocks approximately 2 million one- and two-year-old salmon in the Baltic Sea annually (Finnish Game and Fisheries Research Institute, 1995). The Finnish catch makes up part of the EU's quota.

Reindeer husbandry is also of great local importance; it is a central part of the culture of the Sami people in Lapland. In recent years, the total reindeer stock has increased to such a high level that overgrazing has become a serious problem. Currently, the number of reindeer is more than 340 000, which greatly exceeds the number that can be sustained in the long run.

The most important **ore deposits** contain copper, nickel, chromium, iron and zinc. At the end of 1992 there were 32 ore, industrial mineral and limestone mines in operation in Finland. A great proportion of the known ore reserves have been exploited, but the geological prerequisites are said to be promising for the finding of new ore deposits (Statistics Finland, 1994, p. 61). For two years it has been possible also for multinational mining companies to make claims on the Finnish bedrock. According to the Mining Act mines require an environmental permit and are subject to environmental impact assessment procedures (Hermanson and Joas, 1996).

4.4   Environmental Effects and Policies

In general terms, the **air** in Finland is still relatively clean even though hazardous levels of impurities are occasionally reached locally (cf. Table 4.2).

Sulphur emissions result principally from fossil fuel combustion, whereas increased traffic accounts for the largest share of nitrogen oxide emissions. In order to prevent air pollution from causing direct danger to human health, the government has established ambient air quality standards and limit values also for other harmful emissions, such as levels of particulate matter and carbon monoxide. Moreover, levels of volatile organic compounds (VOC), ozone and toxic heavy metals are monitored and controlled.

Table 4.2   Pollution in Finland by source, 1970–2005

1000 tons	1970	1980	1990	1992	1993	1994	2005
Sulphur oxide (SO_2)	-	584	258	141	122	117	-
Nitrogen oxide (NO_2)	-	295	300	284	281	283	-
Carbon dioxide (CO_2)	-	-	93000	-	-	-	98000
BOD_7 (million tons)	519	-	105	74	55	51	21
Pesticides	1.36	-	2.05	1.43	1.28	1.32	-

Notes: Carbon dioxide includes other greenhouse gases; BOD_7 expresses water pollution in terms of Biological Oxygen Demand, originating mainly in the pulp and paper industry (72 per cent); figures for the year 2005 are proposed targets.
Source: Statistics Finland, 1995.

Finland's emissions of compounds causing acidification have been substantially reduced. Acidifying SO_2 emissions and BOD_7 have both declined by approximately 80 per cent over the last 15 years (Wahlström et. al., 1996, p. 214). But the country also imports acid rain from Western and Eastern Europe. It has been more cost-effective for the country to subsidize investments in environmental projects with Finnish business participation in the nearby regions of Russia and the Baltic States than to invest solely in the reduction of its own emissions (Statistics Finland, 1995, p. 23; Ministry of the Environment, 1995, p 95; Tahvonen et. al., 1993). The Ministry of the Environment has identified the most important environmental problems in the areas close to Finland, and has as the first western country applied debt-for-nature swaps for environment- and energy-saving investments in Poland.

Over half of the carbon dioxide emissions which contribute to the greenhouse effect come from power plants and boilers and 15 per cent from processes in forest industry. On the other hand, Finland's extensive forests and peatlands significantly counter the greenhouse effect. The country's forests and forest soils are estimated to contain about 2000 million tons of carbon, with the total increasing by about 7 million tons a year, which corresponds to 27 million tons of carbon dioxide. Bogs are estimated to contain 625 million tons of carbon with a rate of increase of 0.8 million tons a year or 2.9 million tons of carbon dioxide equivalent.

Due to dispersed community structure, large acreage and a remote location, Finland's need for traffic and transportation is high. Traffic and transportation account for 15 per cent of Finland's total energy consumption and about 40 per cent of its oil consumption. The sector generates annually about one fifth of all emissions of carbon dioxide, almost all carbon monoxide, about half of nitrogen oxides and volatile hydrocarbon compounds (VOC), and one third of particulates. These emissions are released very near to the ground and hence do not disperse into the ambient air as efficiently as flue gas emissions from high stacks (Ministry of Trade and Industry, 1993, pp. 13–14).

While the **water pollution** load caused by municipalities and industry has been reduced considerably in the past decades, control of nutrient runoff from agriculture has not been as successful. The environmental impact of agriculture on the eutrophication of water courses is significant, since the majority of farms are located by water courses. Due to intensive fertilization, agriculture accounts for 44 per cent of the nitrogen load and 62 per cent of the phosphorus load in the water. Compared to other EU countries the nitrogen and phosphorus surpluses in Finnish agriculture are, however, relatively small. Also, the total amount of pesticides used is low, and the resulting residues in food are negligible (Statistics Finland, 1995, p. 31). Nearly all ammonia emissions in Finland are of agricultural origin.

Every tenth of the species of organisms found in Finland are classified as threatened. Forestry is the greatest single threat to Finnish flora and fauna, since more than 40 per cent of the endangered species live in forests. Forest ecosystems that are rich in biological diversity are also better equipped to cope with climatic change and other stress factors (Ministry of the Environment, 1995, pp 91–93).

The total amount of **waste** generated in Finland is currently about 85–90 million tons a year, including by-products from mining (39 per cent), industry (17 per cent), and agriculture and forestry (33 per cent) that are not defined as waste in many other countries. The amount of waste generated by municipalities or human settlements is 2.1 million tons annually, of which some 30 per cent is recovered. The recovery rate for industry is about 60 per cent. A considerable amount of waste still ends up in landfills, for example about 32 million tons in 1992. Another concern is soil contamination in old landfills and industrial sites; some 1200 sites will need restoration by 2015. So far, nuclear waste from two of the four reactors in Finland has been transported back to the Russian supplier, and the rest has been placed in interim storage. Utility companies are investigating possibilities for the disposal of waste in the Finnish bedrock starting from 2020. Several Russian nuclear power plants located near the Finnish border are another potential risk.

A characteristic of Finnish **environmental policies** is that there are many individual acts or secondary decrees and rules, but no specific and comprehensive environmental act of law. The Ministry of the Environment was not founded until 1983. Although the use of economic instruments and incentives is gaining popularity among politicians, environmental policy in practice is still mainly based on legal regulations. The most common regulation mechanisms are environmental permit and acknowledgement procedures, self-control on the part of polluting industries in combination with general emission level guidelines, mandatory rules and supervision by authorities (Joas, 1996). The Environmental Damage Act of 1995 makes legal subjects, for example companies, liable for compensation or fines if the environment is damaged (Joas, 1996; Ministry of the Environment, 1995, p 134).

Table 4.3   Green taxes in Finland, 1993–97

million FIM	1993	1994	1995	1996	1997
Drink carton tax	35	64	102	106	106
Fertilizer tax	516	267	-	-	-
Pesticide fee	6	6	6	6	6
Electricity tax	656	56	-	-	-
Energy tax	8 404	9 815	11 628	13 550	14 100
Oil pollution fees	55	50	55	54	54
Motor vehicle taxes	2 494	3 516	4 399	5 500	5 740
Tax on charter flights	111	80	-	-	-
Water protection fee	2	2	3	2	2
State waste duty	-	-	-	80	300
Total	12 279	13 856	16 194	19 298	20 308
Total, per cent of total tax revenue	10	11	11	12	12

Notes: Figures for 1996 and 1997 are budget figures; The total tax revenue used in the bottom row does not include social security payments; 1 FIM equals .17 ECU.
Source: Statistics Finland, 1995.

Green taxes are to be considered the most important economic instruments for the future (cf. Table 4.3). There are, however, at least two sides in the greening of a tax coin: on the one hand, the taxes are important for fiscal reasons; on the other, they affect the international competitiveness of industry and have ultimately been introduced in a less radical form than that planned before the economic recession (Statistics Finland, 1995, p. 7).

Energy taxation is generally lower for industry than for households. Tax on light fuel oil, for example, has been almost three times higher for households than for industry. Until recently, there was a political intention to tax energy production directly for environmental policy reasons. The tax based on energy content was 0.60 ECU per megawatt hour and the carbon tax 6.60 ECU per ton of carbon dioxide in 1995 (Statistics Finland, 1995, p. 24). In

1990, Finland was the first country in the World to impose a CO_2 charge, but since early 1997 energy taxation is increasingly based on the consumption of electricity, not so much on the production of CO_2 content as before. The argument for this policy change was the reluctance of other countries to impose similar non-exempt CO_2 charges on their industries. Taxes on electricity have, however, been criticized, since they would weaken the role of energy taxes as an instrument of environmental policy. Moreover, the Finnish environment-based energy taxes were not found to be particularly high compared to those in the other Nordic countries (Malaska et. al., 1996).

The most important instrument concerning air pollution is legal regulation, and particularly the Act on Environmental Permits and the Environmental Impact Assessment. In practice, this means that production facilities are subject to prior notification and environmental permit procedures. To reduce air pollution from transportation, emission limits have been tightened concurrently with the introduction of new technology, like catalytic converters and unleaded petrol. In addition, environment-related taxes and fees have been imposed so that the use of cars is relatively expensive in Finland. The tax on petrol is the third highest in Western Europe (Statistics Finland, 1995, p. 29).

The present level of sulphur dioxide emissions is already below the 80 per cent reduction target from the 1980 level, but cutting nitrogen oxides emissions by 30 per cent from the 1980 level by 1998 seems hard to achieve; a reduction of 15 per cent is a more realistic goal. Finland's scenario for the trend in greenhouse gas emissions looks gloomy, since emissions are expected to increase by about 30 per cent by 2000 (Statistics Finland, 1995, pp. 19-21).

Water pollution control in agriculture has mainly been based on administrative regulations and voluntary efforts. In 1990, however, an environmental tax was introduced on phosphorus, and two years later a tax on nitrogen as well as set-aside obligations which also reduced the use of fertilizers. The fertilizer taxes were, however, abolished upon Finland's accession into the EU in 1995; the mandatory set-aside regulations were also relaxed.

So-called environmental management contracts are a new economic instrument launched in 1995. All farms making a contract will receive basic environmental support. The contracts restrict the use of fertilizers and pesticides, require that a minimum of 30 per cent of the arable land on a farm should have vegetation coverage outside the growing season, and stipulate that filter strips be used along main ditches and water courses. If farms commit to longer-term environmental contracts, for example, by establishing riparian zones for 20 years or by totally giving up conventional intensive cultivation and starting 'organic' farming, special environmental support is paid. These measures are expected to reduce nutrient loads on water courses and the risks of the leaching of pesticides by 30–50 per cent in the next 5–10 years.

A main instrument for nature conservation is funding for compensating landowners. Finland's Nature Conservation Act dates back to 1923, and the current reform of the act has proved difficult due to lack of funding. There are already 200 000 hectares of private land, with a purchase value of over 350 million ECU, for which protection has been approved but not implemented due to lack of funding (Statistics Finland, 1995, p. 17). As a result, conservation has been financially easier on state land, so that conservation areas have been concentrated in northern Finland. Several forms of funding have been suggested to protect valuable forests on private land: forest/nature conservation bonds, 'forest user fees', taxes on summer residences, etc. However, biodiversity protection also requires that the practices of treating commercial forests should be renewed.

The leading principle in waste management will be to prevent problems and to increase producer responsibility. In September 1996 a national waste tax was imposed on waste delivered to landfills (Statistics Finland, 1995, p. 6) in order to limit the generation of waste and to encourage recycling and other recovery of waste.

4.5 Resources, Environmental Costs, and Economic Growth

Finnish **industry** is now taking the environmental concerns of its customers abroad more seriously. Environmentally sound production technology is seen as an important component of competitiveness. Environmentally friendly exports amount to about 20 per cent of the total, and the absolute amount is expected to increase fivefold by 2010 (Statistics Finland, 1995, p. 10). In 1993, industrial environmental investment totalled 275 million ECU or 10 per cent of total industrial investment, of which 63 per cent was for pollution control and 3 per cent for water protection. Environmental operating expenditures amounted to 260 million ECU; the total costs of industrial environmental protection were thus 0.75 per cent of GDP. The most recent water protection programme will require industrial investments totalling 1.7 billion ECU by 2005 (Statistics Finland, 1995, p. 8).

Process-integrated investments are becoming more important since environmentally aware companies have begun to scrutinize the whole product life cycle. In pulp plants recycling waste water also seems to be associated with increases in the pulp plant revenues (Hetemäki, 1996). Previously subsidized interest rates for environmental investments have been gradually abandoned, justified by the polluter pays principle and the adverse effects of subsidies, which may actually increase environmental emissions by decreasing the cost of capital and by increasing production as well as abatement.

Investments in **energy** saving are beneficial to growth, as it reduces imports and replaces investment in capital intensive energy production. However, it seems that the required return on energy saving investment has in general been relatively high both in industry and households.

Finnish policy towards **agriculture** has been adjusted to the common agricultural policy of the EU. The reform in the general support system from output support to hectarage and livestock unit support is expected to lead to extensification of production and hence to more environmentally sustainable production. Additional costs may result from investments in manure and urine storage facilities in order to meet environmental requirements. The total amount of agri-environmental support was 250 million ECU in 1995 or 13 per cent of total agricultural support. Although the costs of meeting environmental requirements vary from farm to farm, a majority, or 80–90 per cent, of all farms were participating in the five-year programme started in 1995. This would suggest that environmental commitment pays and that the support is covering the costs. However, farmers can leave the programme after three years without any sanctions. Another thing is that the economic conditions will be changing when the support for the transitional period ceases. The number of farms will decrease considerably as a result of the restructuring of Finnish agriculture, which in turn will also affect the environmental impacts of the sector.

According to preliminary calculations, organic production can offer an economically competitive alternative especially in the production of milk, beef and cereals. Moreover, consumers' environmental awareness is indicated by a willingness to buy food cultivated without fertilizers and other chemicals. The share of arable land area devoted to organic production is 2 per cent.

4.6   Environmental and Resources Issues in Public Opinion and Policy

Recently the major public debates on environmental issues in Finland have dealt with energy policy, nature conservation and the protection of old growth forests, and specifically with whether a fifth nuclear power plant should be built.

The previous parliament voted no to new nuclear power capacity, but active lobbying for and against a new reactor goes on. Given the high and increasing current consumption active measures to save energy will be needed. Reliance on biofuels, alternative energy sources or energy saving has not convinced industry at least as a final solution, and plans for large-scale investments in new capacity will continuously appear. However, as long as the public mentions problems connected with nuclear power plants as one of its principal environmental concerns, politicians are unlikely to take up the matter.

Finnish forest management and the principle of sustainable development have collided in both the domestic and foreign public arenas. The Finnish forest industry has been criticized for neglecting the importance of biodiversity by favouring commercial forest plantations and buying raw material from old growth forests. Greenpeace in particular has been actively campaigning for foreign pressure from German and British printing houses, for example, which would draw attention to the practices of the Finnish pulp and paper industry. As a result, the industry has become more careful in its environmental policy and, among other things, is yielding to the interests of the private forest owners, over half of whom consider wood production as the most important goal of forest ownership (Finnish Forest Industries Federation, 1993, p. 19). As far as the public opinion on forestry is concerned, Finns emphasize the vitality, aesthetic elements in nature and multiple use of forests – even at the expense of wood production and employment. A notable proportion of the Finns, about 40 per cent, have apparently contradictory views on the use of forests; they are doing a balancing act between opposing and agreeing with protection and the intensified commercial use of forests.

The latest phenomenon to get a great deal of publicity is attacks on fur farms by animal rights activists. Despite this new kind of 'fox-girl' pro-nature radicalism, the typical Finn still has only a relatively passive concern for the state of the environment, but lacks confidence in the politicians' and civil servants' ability and will to improve the environmental situation. For example, energy saving in households is not necessarily seen as a means to decrease the Finnish impact on global warming. Energy use in households has become a special concern of the Ministry of Trade and Industry, which is now financing programmes on consumer behaviour and energy saving.

According to some surveys, environmental degradation was considered as the most serious social problem in the boom years. During the recession, economic problems, particularly unemployment, were emphasized. Still, people recognized environmental problems as the second most important issue and were optimistic about the possibilities of combining economic growth and environmental protection (Wahlström et. al., 1996, p. 12). However, even though attitudes are ecologically sound, they do not necessarily imply environmentally responsible behaviour (Moisander, 1996). The Finnish Greens are among the strongest green parties in Western Europe (Hermanson and Joas, 1996; Joas, 1996).

Despite the contradiction between people's opinions and concrete actions on many environmental issues, the sorting of waste is perceived as something very concrete which households can do for the environment. The recycling ideology has been characterized as a kind of saving which goes well with the current economic situation and cautious consumption decisions in households. In general, waste management policy will, to a substantial extent, be based on the sorting and reuse of wastes. This is partly due to dwindling landfill capacity and public opposition to incineration plants in larger cities. However, especially in sparsely populated areas, this will entail higher costs for municipalities (Huhtala, 1995).

Research does not support the widespread perception of the division in environmental attitudes between educated urban people and those who are directly dependent upon exploitation of natural resources. It seems that the explanatory factors for positive attitudes towards the environment are sex and age rather than the place of residence; women and young people are more concerned about environmental issues.

REFERENCES

Finnish Forest Industries Federation (1993), *Forest Industry, Environment, Nature*, Helsinki: Finnish Forest Industries Federation.

Finnish Game and Fisheries Research Institute (1995), 'Fish and Game by Region', *Environment 1995* (12).

Hermanson, A.-S. and M. Joas (1996), 'Finland', in P.M. Christiansen (ed.), *Governing the Environment: Politics, Policy, and Organization in the Nordic Countries*, Research Nord (5), Copenhagen: Nordic Council of Ministers.

Hetemäki, L. (1996), 'Impact of Pollution Control on a Firm: A Distance Function Approach', *Research Papers* (609), Helsinki: Finnish Forest Research Institute.

Huhtala, A. (1995), 'Is Environmental Guilt a Driving Force? An Economic Study of Recycling', *Acta Universitas Lapponiensis* (6), Rovaniemi: University of Lapland.

Joas, M. (1996), 'Finland', in M.S. Andersen and D. Liefferink (eds.), *Environmental Policy in Europe: The Pioneers*, Manchester: Manchester University Press.

Koskela, E. and M. Ollikainen (1995), 'Optimal Forest Taxation with Multiple-use Characteristics of Forest Stands', *Discussion paper* (93), Helsinki: Government Institute for Economic Research.

Malaska, M., J. Luukkanen, J. Vehmas and J. Kaivo-oja (1996), *Environment-based Energy Taxation: Nordic Comparisons and Assessment of the Finnish Discussion*, Helsinki: Ministry of the Environment.

Ministry of the Environment (1995), *Finnish Action for Sustainable Development*, Helsinki: Finnish National Commission on Sustainable Development.

Ministry of Trade and Industry (1993), *Mobile. Energy and the Environment in Transportation*, Reviews, (B:136), Helsinki: Energy Department.

Moisander, J. (1996) 'Attitudes and Ecologically Responsible Consumption', *Research Reports*, (218), Helsinki: Statistics Finland.

Statistics Finland (1994), 'Environment Statistics', *Environment 1994*, (3), Helsinki: Statistics Finland.

Statistics Finland (1995), 'Finland's Natural Resources and the Environment 1995', *Environment 1995*, (10C), Helsinki: Statistics Finland.

Tahvonen, O., V. Kaitala and M. Pohjola (1993), 'A Finnish-Soviet Acid Rain Game; Non-co-operative Equilibria, Cost Efficiency, and Sulphur Agreements', *Journal of Environmental Economics and Management*, **24** (1), 87–100.

Wahlström, E., E.-L. Hallanaro and S. Manninen (1996), *The Future of the Finnish Environment*, Helsinki: Edita and the Finnish Environment Institute.

5. Norway: North Sea Oil, Resource Rents, and Long-Term Policies

Asbjørn Aaheim

5.1 Economic Growth after the Emergence of the Petroleum Sector

The Norwegian economy is characterized by a huge stock of natural resources and a small population, and the industrialization of the country in the late 19th century was completely founded on the utilization of natural resources. Even today, 65 per cent of Norwegian exports are based on these resources, in various degrees of manufacturing, including oil and gas, petrochemical products, wood products, fish and hydroelectric power.

The emergence of the **petroleum sector** has dominated the Norwegian economy since the late 1970s, about 10 years after the first oil discovery in the Norwegian part of the North Sea. Around 1980, the second oil-price hike and a major increase in the output from the petroleum sector caused a substantial increase in GDP, which increased by more than 5 per cent per year in real terms from 1975 to 1985. This was followed by a consumption growth which peaked at about 10 per cent from 1984 to 1985. These changes did not immediately provoke an economic policy response. Thus, the consumption pattern was still influenced by the old tax system which resulted in a negative real rate of interest for private loans. Resource based industries, such as aluminium and ship-building industries, were heavily subsidized which prevented restructuring, and the subsidies to agriculture and fisheries increased substantially during these years.

When the oil price collapsed in 1987, the annual oil rent dropped from more than 10 billion ECU, about 16 per cent of GDP, in 1986 to nearly zero in 1988. By then, the expected wealth of oil had been reduced by 300 billion ECU compared to expectations in 1981, or approximately 6000 ECU per capita. A reform of the private tax system brought about a collapse in residential prices around 1990, reduced domestic demand and increased unemployment, although this was counteracted for some time by high demand in export markets. Later, when the world economy slowed down, the problems in the

Norwegian economy grew rapidly, and eventually all the major Norwegian banks went bankrupt in 1992. Since then, the economy has recovered slowly, and unemployment has declined from 5.5 per cent in 1993 to 4.6 per cent in late 1995. In addition, 40 thousand people have been working in active labour market measures, making a total of about 6.5 per cent of the labour force outside the ordinary labour market. Although not acceptable, this rate of unemployment seems to be less problematic from a political point of view than it was only a few years ago.

Table 5.1   Long-term forecasts and targets for Norway, 1990–2030

	1990	2010	2030	*2030
GDP (1990=100)	100	150	200	-
Oil and gas	100	92	64	-
Electricity	100	170	216	-
Services	100	172	232	-
Wealth per capita (1000 ECU)	97	133	149	-
Financial	-3	18	14	-
Real	73	105	131	-
Petroleum	27	11	4	-
Electricity production (1000 TOE)	10 497	11 357	12 132	-
Energy intensive industry	2 581	2 633	2 633	-
Other domestic use	5 679	7 055	7 830	-
Net export	1 377	344	344	-
Emission targets and predictions				
NO_x (1000 t)	230	-	206	200
SO_2 (1000 t)	56	-	54	53
CO_2 (million t)	212	-	246	233

Note: Total wealth per capita declined from 138 in 1980 to 97 in 1990 due to a decline in oil wealth from 87 in 1980 to 27 in 1990. Pollution forecasts indicated as *2030 describe a scenario with a carbon tax, cf. below section 5.4.
Source: Ministry of Finance, 1993.

A **long-term programme** is presented by the government every forth year, most recently in 1993, covering the period 1994–1997 as well as prospects for the next decades for production and wealth and also for the environment (cf. Table 5.1). Future economic growth is critically dependent on the petroleum sector, where production is expected to decline slowly over the next 30 years so that its share of GDP will decline from 14.4 per cent in 1990 to 4.6 per cent in 2030. A moderate overall economic growth of 2.0 per cent until 2010 and 1.5 per cent thereafter is expected. Slower economic growth after 2010 is mainly due to lower labour supply, a slow-down in the petroleum sector and in resource based industries, and moderate productivity growth.

These prospects presuppose a slow depreciation of the Norwegian crown, and they are of course highly sensitive to the price of oil. Thus, the drop in oil prices in 1987 caused a 25 per cent depreciation. It is expected that Norwegian exports will continue to be resource based. Income from oil will decline in the future, which calls for active management of the petroleum wealth. In 1995, Norway's financial capital stock turned positive. This means that the wealth of petroleum is slowly being transformed into financial wealth and real capital, and most of today's oil wealth is expected to have been converted into real capital by around 2030 (cf. Table 5.1).

5.2   From Oil to Hydroelectric Power

The Norwegian energy market is characterized by a large share of electricity, which is completely based on hydropower. However, non-developed hydropower reserves are diminishing and expensive to develop. It is likely that further growth in electricity consumption will be based partly on natural gas.

Energy consumption per capita is 4.96 tons of oil equivalent, close to the OECD average, but high according to European standards, higher than Denmark and Sweden, but lower than Finland (cf. Table 1.2). This relatively high Norwegian consumption can be explained, partly by a generally high level of electricity consumption at rather low prices, and partly by a large energy intensive export industry. Total consumption has increased steadily since 1975, but halted between 1985 and 1990, mainly due to economic recession (cf. Table 5.2).

Table 5.2   Energy consumption in Norway by carrier, 1976–95

kTOE	1976	1980	1985	1990	1995
Electricity	5 760	6 429	7 863	8 341	8 986
Oil, transport oils	3 370	3 728	4 374	4 469	4 684
Oil, other oils	3 800	3 298	1 912	1 386	1 219
Coal and coke	1 123	1 147	1 362	1 195	1 315
Gas	24	980	1 243	1 243	1 243
Biomass	430	621	813	908	980
District heating	0	0	48	72	96
Total	14 507	16 203	17 615	17 614	18 523

Note: Energy consumption in the energy producing sectors themselves is excluded; 1 PJ = 23.9 kTOE (kilotons of oil equivalent).
Source: Statistics Norway, 1996.

A significant trend is the substitution from oil consumption for stationary purposes to electricity, especially from 1976 to 1985, despite the fact that the price of electricity has increased five times since 1975, while oil prices only trebled. The explanation is probably that the increase in crude oil prices in 1973 caused a shift towards electric equipment, based on the belief that oil prices would continue to increase. These expectations were confirmed around 1980. In the mid 1980s electric equipment had replaced most of the oil equipment, where possible. To switch back when oil became relatively inexpensive was, therefore, too expensive. Where possible, electricity is now used instead of oil. A further reduction of fossil fuels consumption therefore requires lower total energy consumption, as possibilities for substitution are nearly used up.

There is also a slight substitution from oil to biomass. All consumption of natural gas, which was introduced in the late 1970s, is for industrial purposes. In spite of huge reserves, natural gas is not being utilized as a source of heating in Norway, and there are no plans to develop a distribution net for gas. Oil consumption for transport purposes is expected to grow by approximately 0.9 per cent annually untill 2030, while oil consumption for heating purposes will grow by 0.6 per cent.

Norway plans to increase its export of **electricity** from an annual average of 2 TWh today to 10 TWh within a few years (cf. Table 5.1); the large figure for exports in 1990 is due to extreme weather conditions. The growth in exports may, however, be higher and depend on the extent of North Sea natural gas utilization. The expected 25 per cent growth in domestic electricity consumption from 1990 to 2030 will occur outside the energy intensive industries. The forecast production of 140 TWh in 2030 equals the total hydropower potential in Norway. In addition, there are protected rivers and waterfalls which constitutes an energy production potential of about 35 TWh.

A reform of the electricity market took place in 1992. In short, the reform aimed at deregulation, by separating the ownership of production, transmission and distribution. Common access to the transmission system was also introduced. Competition between producers contributed to the levelling out of regional differences in electricity prices, and to the reduction of prices in general. In some cases, the electricity bill was reduced by 30 to 40 per cent. In spite of these improvements, monopolies are still present on the supply side. This is particularly problematic for households, because they consist of small units with little bargaining power. There have been reported many cases where the local suppliers obstruct the possibility for single units to buy electricity from other suppliers. Moreover, supply of electricity to energy intensive manufacturing industries is excluded from the regular electricity market. These industries still draw advantage from highly subsidized electricity, and they are expected to sustain their level of energy use in the future.

The general reduction in prices and more emphasis on economic investment criteria caused huge economic losses for many hydropower plants developed recently. This caused a halt in further development of hydropower plants. The economic problems were strengthened by extraordinarily warm years with a high rate of precipitation. One of the most controversial on-going developments, Svartisen, were stopped half way. Most of these problems were, however, of a transitional character, and the economy of hydropower companies has improved significantly in later years.

Energy conservation policy is a rather vague item in Norway. The capital equipment in Norway is comparably modern and energy effective, in the sense that reducing energy consumption is considered to be quite expensive compared with expected costs in many other countries. However, the profitability of the energy intensive industries is partly based on low electricity prices, as these sectors are excepted from the deregulation. To the extent that these prices are indirect subsidies, a shut-down of some of these industries would be economically beneficial, although politically highly controversial.

Most active conservation policy has been directed towards households, in the form of information campaigns and cheap loans. The effects of this policy are disputed. Some surveys of energy consumption in households indicate that measures to reduce energy consumption result in higher comfort rather than lower energy consumption. Similar effects have been experienced in industrial sectors, and there are indications that subsidized technology would have been introduced regardless of the conservation policy.

5.3   Exploitation of Domestic Natural Resources

Exploitation of natural resources is very important in the Norwegian economy, notably exploitation of oil and gas, hydropower, forests and fisheries. There is also some extraction of minerals, but the activities have been reduced drastically during the last two decades, partly because of a collapse in metal prices and partly because of increasing extraction costs. Today, most of the metal extraction has been shut down, but extraction of industry minerals is profitable, although on a small scale. Agriculture is politically important, mainly because of heavy subsidies.

Resource based activities create substantial private income, but they are also a major source of **government revenue**, particularly from the petroleum sector. It is, however, difficult to separate resource revenues since the tax system does not charge resource rent, except for petroleum. The governmental revenues from the petroleum sector are highly sensitive to fluctuations in the oil price. The revenues amounted to about 7 billion ECU in 1995 and 1996. A resource rent tax for hydropower was considered in connection with the new energy law, but was not launched

There are also large governmental expenditures to resource based sectors, namely subsidies, first of all to agriculture. Although agricultural subsidies have been declining slowly since 1990, they are still twice as high as the average EU subsidies. In 1995 they amounted to more than 1.5 billion ECU, thereby exceeding the total agricultural contribution to GDP. Fisheries received 40 million ECU in 1995, which is only 20 per cent of the amount that was transferred to the fisheries five years earlier.

Table 5.3   Resource stocks, extraction, and rents in Norway, 1995

	Stock	Extraction	Rent
Oil and Gas	-	-	4750
Oil	1374	141	-
Gas	810	19	-
Hydropower	15	10	350
Metals	-	-	-66
Minerals	-	-	-3
Forests	625	-	238
Fisheries	-	-	13
Cod	2000	-	-
Capelin	190	-	-
Herring	3910	-	-

Notes: Resource rents are expressed in million ECU, 1991; stocks and extraction in 1995 are measured in million TOE (tons of oil equivalent) for energy, in 1000 m^3 forests, and in 1000 tons for fisheries.
Source: Lurås, 1994; Statistics Norway, 1996.

Extraction of oil and gas started in 1972, and has increased to 160 million tons in 1995, most of which is exported. Also hydroelectricity is a major product in the Norwegian economy, and contributes about 2.5 per cent of GDP. The direct contributions to GDP from forests and fisheries are small, but related activities are important. The value of the natural resource exploitation can be estimated by the resource rent, that is sector revenues in excess of a normal remuneration on capital, which is set at 7 per cent (cf. Table 5.3). The petroleum rent dominates the total resource rent, but rents from hydropower production and forestry are also significant. For other natural resources, the rent is small. Extraction of metals exhibits a negative resource rent. The main explanation for the differences of the resource rents among industries is the scale of the activities and costs of extraction, but government policies also influence the size of the rents.

The petroleum sector has developed during the latest 25 years, with active participation from the Norwegian authorities. The petroleum reserves have been considered as a national wealth of common property, not the property of the companies which operate the fields. Consequently, the authorities seek to make the rent from the sector as large as possible. The government collects its revenues from taxation of extraction (between 75 and 85 per cent) and to some extent as owner's income from the oil companies. The governmental revenues from the extraction correspond approximately to the rent.

Norway established the fully state-owned oil company Statoil in the mid 1970s to take care of the state-interests on the Norwegian continental shelf, and Statoil soon became the main actor in oil extraction in Norway. Ideally, Statoil is the state's representative in the Norwegian oil sector, and all of its revenues are in principle regarded as income to the state. To what extent the company should manage its own revenues is subject to political debate. In later years an increasing share of the revenues has been utilized by the company itself to invest in activities related to the extraction, such as petro-chemical industries, and in activities abroad.

Other national and international oil companies are also engaged in the petroleum sector. The main motivation for this is that the competence held by international companies is vital for a sound management of the oil fields. The companies are given concessions rights to explore and later produce oil and gas. Usually, several companies are given the concession on the same block as shareholders, but one company is given the main responsibility for opera-tion. Most concessions include a so-called gliding-scale, which allows the government to increase Statoil's share after a couple of years. The gliding-scale has been activated for the biggest oil and gas fields.

Practically speaking, direct political control over the activity is limited to the timing of the allocation of concessions to companies to explore blocks. To avoid too rapid growth in the activity, the government has mixed bright and less bright prospects in each concession round. The companies also need permission from the Storting to start extraction, but this opportunity for delaying the development of a field has in practice never been used.

In their management of oil and gas resources, the Norwegian authorities put greater emphasis on the economic outcome than on the management of **minerals**. One major explanation for this is historical conditions, such as ownership. The laws under which the ownership of natural resources is regulated trace back to 1539, when the Danish King Christian III stated that minerals belonged to the King. The substance of this law is still valid for mineral resources. It is custom now, as it was in the 16th century, to leave the operation of the resources to private agents.

However, private companies need some incentives to start business, and today these are established in terms of a reasonable tax regime from the operator's point of view. There are further rules for particularly valuable minerals, including minerals with an own weight higher than 5, that is iron ore, copper, pyrite, zinc and lead. The exploration is regulated, and discover-ies are regarded as state properties from the outset. In many cases, however, the property-owner also gets the rights to the metal.

The concession laws have had an important impact on the economic structure of the mining sector. Metal mines have been run by firms wholly or partly owned by the state, while other mineral mines are usually privately owned. During the 1970s, the prices of metals fell. The losses were considered transitional, and the mines received substantial support from the government. Today only a few mines are still operating, which in sum lose money.

For other minerals, which can be divided into sand and gravel, monumental stone and industry minerals, the problems have not been that visible. This is partly due to the fact that the prices are not subject to changes in the world market in the same way as metals are. Another important factor may be that the reserves are not as sensitive to changes in prices. Over the last couple of years, the mineral mining sector has earned a solid resource rent when compared to the size of the sector.

The Norwegian concession law is closely related to the development of the **hydropower** system. As for minerals, rivers and waterfalls above a certain power potential are regarded as state property. However, when this law was enacted in 1908, a large share of the hydropower resources were situated on private ground. The law therefore states that private owners may get a concession to develop and operate hydropower plants, but the plants will have to be given free of charge to the state after 60 years. Within the next 15 years, most of the privately owned plants will be transferred to the state.

The idea behind these concession laws was to prevent foreign companies from buying Norwegian waterfalls. Instead, this potential should be exploited with the aim of helping Norway develop into an industrialized nation. To keep electricity prices low has been a major issue in the resources policy ever after and still explains why energy intensive industries are protected by price subsidies. Previously, investments were dictated by the expressed 'needs' of industry, which resulted in substantial over-investment. Since 1970, the environmentalists have argued against further development. A protection plan for water resources has been established, and investment policies have become more economically oriented.

The resource rent of hydropower must be considered against this background. The figure in Table 5.3 does not take effects of price differentiation into account. Thus, the rent obtained by the electricity used in energy intensive industries is hidden in the accounts of these industries. This constitutes nearly one-third of the total use of electricity,

The stock of **forests** amounts to about 625 000 m^3 of wood. Most of this consists of spruce and pine trees. The stock grows by approximately 10 000 m^3 per year which is about twice as much as in the mid 1930s. The reason for the growth is mainly difficult accessibility and high extraction costs, although large parts of the forests are profitable (cf. Table 5.3).

The forests consist partly of a few big privately or state-owned properties, and partly of many small properties, often owned by farmers. It is hard to detect a governmental forest policy. However, Norske Skog, a big pulp and paper company and the major consumer of forest products, is owned by the forest owners. Prices are negotiated with a complicated interest structure, and there are rigorous rules about deliveries from the forest extracting sector.

The most complicated area of resource policy is, no doubt, the **fisheries**. One may say the policy consists of keeping interests apart and quiet. This is a successful policy as long as there is fish in the sea. In the past decades, however, there have been dramatic fluctuations in the fish stock, which are no doubt due to over-fishing, although natural cycles may explain part of it. The stock of herring was depleted during some prosperous years in the 1960s. Then, one started to fish capelin, which practically speaking disappeared towards the end of 1980s; the stock fluctuated dramatically from 7100 thousand tons in 1991 to 190 thousand tons in 1995. At the same time the stock of cod declined rapidly as well. In recent years the stock of cod has doubled from 1000 thousand tons in the 1980s, and the stock of herring has recovered from about 500 thousand tons in the early 1980s (cf. Table 5.3). The prospects for fishing have therefore been bright.

Fish policy is now focused on the international distribution of quotas, where Norway have been in conflict with Iceland and the EU for different reasons. The first regulations of participation in the fisheries were given in 1930. After 1972, permits have been required for all ships more than 27.5 meters of length. In 1989, when the stock of fish declined rapidly, quotas were introduced for all ships. The regulations have been maintained, but the official reason is no longer the risk of over-fishing, but rather excess capacity. During the gloomy years, the subsidies to the fisheries grew considerably. The authorities now see the opportunity to remove these subsidies by sustaining the quota policy, and thereby improving the profitability of the fishing fleet.

5.4 Environmental Effects

National inventories over **emissions to air** were established in the 1970s. Later came emission targets and international agreements on national emissions to air and water. Norway have today signed international agreements to restrict emissions of NO_x, VOC and SO_2. The Sofia protocol on NO_x requires the emissions to be cut back to the 1987 level by 1994. The emissions were 6.5 per cent lower in Norway in 1994 than in 1987. The reduction was due to reduced flaring of gas in the North Sea, introduction of catalysts in new cars from 1991 and a general decline in economic activity. The Norwegian government also had a national goal to reduce the emissions of NO_x by 30 per cent in 1998. This policy has been partly abandoned.

The Oslo protocol on reduction of emissions of SO_2 by 76 per cent from

1980 by 2000 is regarded as a realistic goal for Norway, and emissions have already been reduced by 70 per cent, partly because of an elimination of heavy fuel oils by law, partly because of the shut-down of a sulphate mine in northern Norway.

The Geneva protocol requires a 30 per cent reduction in VOC from 1989 to 1999. Northern Norway and off-shore activities are excepted from the agreement. The emissions from the oil sector constitutes nearly one-third of total national emissions. This total has increased by 10 per cent from 1989 to 1995. In addition, the Montreal protocol on stratospheric ozone, which restricts the use of ozone-depleting gases, and the Climate Convention have been signed. Norway is also bound by the North Sea agreement on the discharge of nitrogen and phosphate to the sea.

The energy sector contributes the greatest emissions of VOC and CO_2. This is in both cases due to emissions from oil and gas extraction, which account for about 80 per cent and more than 90 per cent, respectively, of the sector's total emissions. Manufacturing industries are the source of one-third of the total emissions of SO_2. Most of these are emitted in chemical and ferrous industries, which also make the biggest contribution to NO_x emissions from industry.

With a few exceptions, the emissions from other sectors are related to transport activities and heating. However, fertilization in agriculture causes emission of nitrates to air and drainage to soil. In 1993, 22.7 thousand tons of ammonia were emitted to the air from agriculture. The drainage partly flows into the North Sea with phosphorous and nitrates. In 1990 these amounted to 1.9 and 58 thousand tons respectively, about 4 per cent of the total inflow of these compounds to the North Sea from European countries. Most of the Norwegian plants for drainage cleaning are less than 30 years old. Today, the capacity of these plants are higher than needed, but there are still households in disparately populated areas, not linked to such a plant.

The development of emissions is closely related to economic activities. During the years with slow growth, the emissions tended to halt, but they have increased again in later years. The exceptions are SO_2 and lead, which have decreased rapidly. After unleaded fuel was introduced, emissions of lead are no longer regarded as a problem. Norway was one of the first countries to link economic forecasts and **forecasts of emissions** to air (cf. Table 5.1). The long-term forecasts are subject to assumptions about economic growth in Norway as well as in its main trade-partners, and to economic policy. Two forecasts are shown, one reference scenario and one scenario where a carbon tax is introduced in all countries and grows steadily to 30 ECU per ton of carbon in 2030.

The emissions of SO_2 and NO_x are expected to decrease in both scenarios, NO_x by about 10 per cent and SO_2 by approximately 5 per cent. The carbon tax will make this reduction slightly higher. This is sufficient to reach the official emission targets for SO_2, which actually allows for an increase, but is far from being enough to attain the target for NO_x, which requires a 30 per cent reduction from the 1990 level. The emissions of CO_2 will increase. The carbon tax will only reduce the growth in CO_2 emissions. The Norwegian government has given up its previous target for emissions of CO_2.

Norway was one of the first countries to realize problems of **transboundary pollution** by acidification, which is a significant problem in the lakes in the southern part of the country. The acidification was a result of sulphur originating mainly from Great Britain and Central Europe. These are still the main contributors, but imports of pollutants from Russia in the north-east corner of Norway cause huge local damage. In 1994, precipitation over Norway contained 43.3 thousand tons of reduced nitrogen, 63.9 thousand tons of oxidized nitrogen and 100.1 thousand tons of oxidized sulphur. The contributions from Norwegian sources were approximately 40, 10 and 3 per cent respectively, while between 30 and 40 per cent of each of the pollutants came from Great Britain and Germany. The content of oxidized sulphur has been reduced by nearly 45 per cent since 1980, while the reduction of reduced and oxidized nitrogen in this period is between 10 and 15 per cent.

Environmental **policy measures** are in principle chosen in accordance with the polluter pays principle. There are, however, different views with respect to how the principle should be implemented, partly due to conflicts of interests. The official environmental authorities, for instance represented by the State Pollution Authority, have a long tradition in assessing direct control measures and environmental standards and in monitoring activities subject to these rules. For a long time, this policy constituted the major activity by environmental authorities. However, attempts at implementing environmental concerns in other sectors of policy by the Ministry of Environment, and establishing an overall national environmental policy, were not very successful.

At the start of the 1980s, the Norwegian government started negotiations with other European countries in order to reduce long-transported pollution. They were eager to reduce the emissions of SO_2, notably in Great Britain and in Central Europe, which were considered to be the main sources of acid rain over Norway. The Norwegians clearly looked upon themselves as victims in this matter, and pushed forward to make the reductions as large as possible. After the agreement was signed, the first linkages between macro-economic forecasts as presented by the government and emissions were published. It became clear that economic forecasts were highly incompatible with the agreements made on emissions. Suddenly, the Ministry of Finance became concerned about environmental policy. This engagement has increased along with the number of international agreements on emissions, and has spread to other sectors of policy-making. As a consequence, the political control of emissions is now regarded a national policy issue, with links to all sectors of policy.

When the economic authorities became interested in the environment, they also claimed insight into what kind of instruments would be appropriate to control the emissions to air. The use of economic instruments has achieved widespread support, even to some extent among environmentalists. However, these measures are with few exceptions, such as taxation of fossil fuels, at a stage of assessment for the time being. A public report was made in 1992 to assess the potential of economic instruments in environmental policy. The report strongly recommended the extension of the use of economic instruments. A number of institutions and interest groups reacted against this view and claimed that competence within natural sciences was totally absent in the board. Another report was then made, which totally neglected use of economic instruments and made economists complain about the absence of economic competence. This is where the debate stands, and direct control remains the most widespread environmental policy measure today.

Charges on pollutants have been introduced to some extent, first to reduce emissions of lead from gasoline, later to reduce the emissions of SO_2, and Norway is one of the few countries that has introduced a CO_2 charge on fossil fuels. However, due to a rather flexible system of exceptions from this and other fuel charges, the average carbon charge in Norway is lower than in many other European countries. A governmental board has recently assessed the consequences of reducing the burdens of the present tax system at the expense of environmental taxation.

Toll zones on roads around the largest cities were introduced a few years ago, but not as an environmental policy measure. The tolls were to finance expansion of the road systems in the cities, and they were to be removed after a couple of years. Now, when the promised date of removal is approaching, environmental concern is becoming an argument to keep them in place.

One of the most successful measures of direct control is the protection plan for water-ways, which is an overall plan for protection of all non-developed water-ways in Norway and sets out priorities for future development. This plan emerged from the need to look at protection of single areas in relation to other areas. The plan therefore put strong emphasis on sustaining a reasonable geographical distribution of protected areas and on keeping the variety of the Norwegian rivers intact.

5.5 Constraints upon Economic Growth.

Norway is disparately populated, and therefore environmental costs are not serious constraints on economic growth. Material damage from pollution is estimated at 40 million ECU in 1995, and the reduction in short-time absence from work in Oslo, resulting from reducing the concentrations of pollutants by 50 per cent, is estimated at between 5 and 10 per cent.

The damage costs of global environmental and climatic change are difficult to assess. Another possible environmental constraint on economic growth is international agreements to reduce greenhouse gas emissions. How such agreements would affect the Norwegian economy depends on the distribution of commitments among participating countries, which is still an open question; the Norwegian government has firmly resisted agreements involving equal reductions of emissions for all countries. Instead, they argue that the distribution of reductions should reflect the costs of marginal reductions in each country. This is in better accordance with the polluter pays principle, as it is considered more expensive to reduce the emissions in Norway by a given per cent than in most other industrialized countries. Thus, electricity from hydropower has already replaced fossil fuels in most applications where possible. Moreover, coal is hardly used. The possibilities of substitution in energy consumption and production towards fuels with fewer emissions are limited. The only opportunity is to reduce total energy consumption.

From a Norwegian point of view, equal reductions in greenhouse gas emissions among countries have a direct and an indirect effect on the distribution of commitments. First, it becomes more expensive for Norwegians than for other people to satisfy the commitments given in the agreement. Second, Norway loses competitiveness. Because of the major dependency on energy in the Norwegian exports, the latter effect becomes substantial.

Welfare losses from a 20 per cent reduction in the emissions of CO_2 in the OECD countries have been estimated at less than 1 per cent of GDP (Torvanger et al., 1996). It is assumed that all countries use a carbon tax as the means to achieve the reductions. However, if the new carbon tax replaces other revenue motivated taxes, this so-called recycling may improve the efficiency of the tax system. The calculations do not take into account that abatement costs vary due to differences in the opportunities of reducing emissions. But abatement costs may differ as a consequence of different levels of carbon taxes prior to the new carbon tax. Thus, the loss is subject to terms of trade effects and to the properties of the existing tax system. The losses are estimated both before and after the revenues have been recycled.

For many countries, the positive effect of recycling more than counterbalances the negative effect of the emission target, thereby yielding a benefit of the climate policy. The loss prior to recycling is highest for the Scandinavian countries, Italy, Switzerland, Canada and Australia. However, the effect of recycling is large for Denmark, Switzerland, Canada and Australia. Norway is the only country which exhibits a loss greater than 0.5 per cent of GDP after recycling, mainly because of Norway's dependency on fossil fuel exports, but a high level of fossil fuel taxes prior to the new policy contributes to limit the effect of recycling.

Norway's dependency of natural resources causes problems which are partly exogenous to the economy and partly of a political nature. The main exogenous problem is the uncertainty of resource prices. The drop in national wealth caused by the collapse of the oil price in the 1980s lead to a substantial shift in the expectations in the economy. Observers, who prior to the drop had suggested that the government should encourage private consumption, suddenly became critical of the liberal policy. The period prior to the oil-price collapse has since been analysed in order to find out what the politicians did wrong – and a lot of different answers have been given. However, one tends to forget that at that time the oil wealth was expected to be substantially higher than it turned out to be. No wonder one had to make some rather inconvenient changes when this wealth disappeared. Thus, even if some policies in the early 1980s can be criticized, it is perhaps more important to ask what the best policy is, given the uncertainty that the Norwegian economy is subject to. Unfortunately, it seems that this lesson remains to be learned.

The standard view on how to deal with uncertainty is that one should spread the risk on several assets. In political terms, this has been interpreted as keeping the level of activity outside the oil sector as high as possible. This policy has been carried out with a very conservative view on the prospects for alternative activities. In particular, those industries that were supported by governmental policy when the oil revenues boosted were mainly the traditional industries, many of them resource based such as the energy intensive industries and the pulp and paper industries. Substantial support was also given to the ship-building industry. As a consequence, the oil sector has partly been subsidizing these old sectors, including agriculture and fisheries. This policy ended up with dramatic costs by the end of the 1980s. One may therefore say that the success of the oil sector made it possible to continue activities that should have been shut down, which partially became an obstacle to restructuring and growth.

5.6 The Role of Environmental and Resources Policy in Public Opinion

Norwegians indeed look upon themselves as environmentally concerned, but their environmental concern is closely related to outdoor life and conservation of nature. The environmental movement in Norway was motivated mainly by the struggle against further development of hydropower, and the major environmental non-governmental organization, Norges Naturvernforbund, was originally an organization with protection of nature as its main target. There have been conflicts within the organization on which issue, environment or nature, to emphasize. In this respect, the engagement against hydropower development has been important because it appeals to both sides: directly to natural conservationists, while those more concerned about environmental problems look upon this as a means to force through energy conservation.

Politically, environmental arguments are used frequently to defend certain policies. This indicates that the environment has a role to play in public opinion. An on-going debate about the development of power plants fuelled by natural gas clearly illustrates this. Gas-fired power plants will increase the Norwegian emissions of CO_2, and may explain why the Norwegian government, contrary to most other European governments, has left the goal of stabilizing these emissions. This is indeed problematic for a government than claims to take responsibility for the global environment. The government has therefore spent considerable effort in trying to convince the public that new gas-fired power plants may lead to global CO_2 reductions by substituting gas-fired for coal-fired electricity plants in other countries. The enthusiasm of the government in this debate can only be explained by a belief that acceptance from the Storting will depend solely on whether it can be convinced that the global emissions of CO_2 will be reduced. The environmental argument, as such, is highly speculative.

Unfortunately, the content of this environmental concern is illustrated by the very same example, because the economic return of the project has recently been questioned. Development was conditioned first on delivery of gas at prices below market prices, and second on exemption of the gas from the CO_2 charge. Enthusiasm has now turned to scepticism, neither because of the speculative environmental argument, nor because of the abolishment of the CO_2 charge and the emission target, but rather because of uncertainty about economic profitability.

REFERENCES

Lurås, H. (1994), 'Ground Rent and Wealth Value of Norwegian Natural Resources' (in Norwegian), *Økonomiske Analyser* (8), Oslo: Statistics Norway.

Ministry of Finance (1993), 'The Long-Term Programme 1994–1997' (in Norwegian), *Stortingsmelding* (4), Oslo: The Ministry of Finance.

Statistics Norway (1996), *Natural Resources and the Environment 1996*, Oslo: Statistics Norway.

Torvanger, A., T. Berntsen, J.S. Fuglestvedt, B. Holtsmark, L. Ringius and A. Aaheim (1996), 'Exploring the Distribution of Commitments – A Follow-up to the Berlin Mandate', *CICERO Report* (3), Oslo: Centre for International Climate and Environmental Research.

6. Sweden: Nuclear Phasing Out, Acidification, and Green Taxes

Eva Samakovlis

6.1 Recent Environmental Policy and Prospects for Economic Growth

The environmental policy pursued in Sweden can be characterized by its focus on limiting the emissions from point sources and for using administrative regulations, mainly permits. In general it is the northern European model with individual permits and best available technology that is applied. In later years the character of the environmental problems have changed, from being national, well defined industrial problems to being international and less concentrated, coming from non-point sources, like the emissions of carbon dioxide and CFC. This calls for more economic regulations. Recent policy initiatives in Sweden include an environmental classification of diesel and petrol, a tax on carbon dioxide and a charge on nitrogen oxide.

Since 1989 the Swedish economy has gone through the most serious crisis since the 1930s. In the early 1990s GDP decreased in three consecutive years, the national debt nearly doubled, the unemployment rate tripled and the budget deficit more than quadrupled. Since then economic policy has been successful in reversing this development and gaining confidence again. Sweden followed a strict budgetary policy, and in 1995 interest rates and inflation decreased, and the growth rate increased to 3.6 per cent. During 1996 Sweden was affected by the European economic development which brought down the growth rate to 1.1 per cent. In 1997 a new upward economic trend began, led by increasing exports and strong private consumption. The prospects for economic growth will depend on how economic policy manages to reduce unemployment, facilitate growth and strengthen public finances. The unemployment rate is expected to decrease, and the surplus of the current account is expected to end up at about 70 billion SEK in 1998, more than 4 per cent of GDP. The prognosis for the growth rate is 2.3 per cent in 1997 and 3.1 per cent in 1998.

The contribution of foreign trade to growth will continue to be strong, at least during 1997. Sweden is richly endowed with assets of forests, iron ore and water power. These natural resources dominated the country's comparative advantages and characterized the pattern of trade at the time of industrialization. Exports consisted of capital intensive refinement of natural resources and labour intensive natural resource based industry, like sawmills. Domestic industry was mainly labour intensive. The specialization of Swedish industry is still directed towards the natural resource assets, especially forests and water power, towards real capital and elecitricity intensive industry, mainly forest products, and away from labour intensive production (Hansson and Lundberg, 1995). The supply of natural resources is, however, limited, and the effect upon the environment usually exceeds what is sustainable in the long run. Sweden became a member of the EU in 1995. The future pattern of specialization will be affected by the creation of a European electricity market and general environmental policies of the EU.

6.2 Energy: Consumption, Efficiency and Policy

Since 1970 the relative importance of various **energy sources** has changed. The proportion of the country's energy supplied by oil has fallen from 76 per cent in 1970 to 44 per cent in 1994 (cf. Table 6.1). The electricity production from nuclear power and hydropower has more than doubled. Oil was the main source of energy for Sweden from the beginning of the 1950s to the end of the 1980s. Until the beginning of the 1970s the use of oil and energy increased dramatically.

Table 6.1   Energy supply in Sweden, 1970–2020

TWh	1970	1990	1991	1992	1993	1994	2020
Crude oil and oil products	350	187	181	188	186	204	259
Natural gas	–	7	7	8	9	9	112
Coal and coke	18	31	28	27	27	28	31
Biofuels, peat	43	65	70	71	76	79	99
Heat pumps for district heating	–	8	8	8	8	8	–
Water power, gross	41	73	64	75	75	59	121
Nuclear power, gross	–	68	78	63	61	73	0
Electricity import minus export	4	3	1	2	1	0	–
Total	457	437	434	439	442	461	662

Notes: Figures for 2020 show one of several scenarios, namely a high growth scenario with slow phasing out of nuclear power, cf. SOU 1995:139; 1 TWh = 86 kTOE.
Sources: SOU 1995:139; NUTEK, 1995.

The oil crises at the beginning of the 1970s led to high prices and an interest in discovering alternative sources of energy. The use of oil decreased; it was mainly fuel oil that was replaced by electricity for heating purposes. During the most recent years changed taxation in the industry sector and increased industry production has increased oil consumption. Most of the country's crude oil is imported from the North Sea.

The use of electric energy has increased dramatically since 1970, amounting to 138 TWh in 1994, mostly produced from hydro and nuclear power. Sweden has 12 nuclear reactors which were built between 1972 and 1985. The production potential of these reactors is around 72 TWh of electricity.

Coal was a major energy source during the first half of the century, but was then replaced by oil. Coal had a minor boom when the oil market was troubled by crises in the 1970s. Now, strict environmental standards keep consumption low. Coal is mainly used in large district heating plants. Sweden imported 1.7 million tons of coal for energy purposes in 1994, mostly from Poland and the USA (SOU 1995:139).

Natural gas is a relatively new source of energy in Sweden. In 1980 an agreement was made between Sweden and Denmark, concerning the import of natural gas to Sweden. Use has increased at the speed of the trunk pipeline extension. Natural gas is mainly used to replace oil in industry, and in combined heat and power plants. Sweden imported 9 TWh of gas in 1994.

Biofuels and peat are mainly used in forest product industry for heat and electricity production, in district heating plants, and in the single-family house sector. The use of biofuels in district heating plants has increased substantially since the 1980s, probably due to the increased taxation of fossil fuels.

The relatively high **energy consumption** in Sweden can to a large extent be explained by the cold climate, the energy intensive industry and the long transport distances. Industry and the residential and service sectors use approximately 40 per cent each of total consumption. The energy use in the transport sector has increased steadily. Total consumption of energy in 1994 was practically the same as in 1970, even though real GNP has increased by 44 per cent during the same period.

It is mainly a small number of sectors, with the pulp and paper industry in the forefront, that account for most of industry's energy use. The changes in this sector's use of energy are primarily due to variations in production volume, structural change and energy efficiency improvements. Structural change from energy intensive industries like mining and steel, towards less energy intensive industries like the manufacturing industry, will reduce the use of energy. All industries have decreased their use of oil in production. The use of electricity per unit of production value has been stable for most sectors. The total amount of energy used by industry was 141 TWh in 1994.

Energy use in the residential and commercial service sectors was approximately 156 TWh in 1994 for heating and domestic hot water production. It has decreased since 1970. There has been a change from oil to other energy sources, especially electricity. Increased use of district heating has reduced energy use, because of the reduction of conversion losses. To conserve energy, measures like retrofitting of additional insulation, and replacement of windows in older buildings have been made. Some attempts have also been made to improve efficiency of electricity use.

Energy amounting to 86 TWh in 1994 is used for transportation, mostly in the form of oil products, and it is increasing. Higher taxation on petrol and diesel fuels, the Kuwait crises and the economic recession made use quite turbulent during the 1990s. Transport by car is expected to increase. Local and regional collective traffic is going to increase in larger cities, and so will the number of flights and trains on the inter-regional market. To counteract environmental effects, energy savings are important, and the potential for higher energy efficiency is large for road traffic. Technological developments have resulted in a reduction of fuel consumption in new vehicles, but this development has stagnated recently. Using alternative fuels and improving the infrastructure would help create a better transport system.

It was not until the beginning of the 1970s that **energy policy** really became an issue in Sweden. The oil crisis in 1973 together with the fact that 70 per cent of the country's total energy needs was covered by oil, led to policies to lower energy consumption and oil dependency. The energy tax, which had been unchanged for a long time, increased substantially during the 1980s. Between the years 1970–94, energy consumption stayed on an unchanged level, and the share of oil in energy supply decreased. It is likely that the taxation contributed to this development together with the high oil prices. The Chernobyl accident in 1986 changed the direction of the energy policy, and the phasing out of nuclear power became an issue.

Policy instruments in Sweden are mainly administrative measures, such as concession applications and statutory standards, supplemented by some economic measures, including energy taxation. Even though the primary motive for energy taxation was not environmental but fiscal, energy policy considerations had an early influence on the design of energy taxation. Mostly, energy policy goals are in line with environmental goals, namely decreased oil dependency, electrification, nuclear power phasing out, increased use of domestic renewable energy sources, limited hydropower extension, limited increase in energy use, and decreased emissions of carbon dioxide. Exempt from energy taxation are biofuels, methane and ethanol. The importance of this exemption is expected to increase with the phasing out of nuclear power. Energy is from 1990 also subject to value added taxation. The energy tax is levied on delivered fuel and produced or distributed electricity. The tax burden is with some exceptions uniform, that is it is related to the fuel's energy content. A new energy tax system that was introduced in January 1993 distinguishes between taxes on industry and taxes on other users in order to preserve the international competitiveness of industry. Industry is exempt from the general energy tax and the tax on electricity and pays only 25 per cent of the carbon dioxide tax rate as compared to other users (cf. Table 6.4).

The general energy tax was introduced in 1957, for financial reasons. The sulphur tax was introduced in 1991, with the purpose of reducing emissions by 80 per cent in the year 2000 as compared to emissions in 1980, which is in fact already fulfilled. A limitation of the sulphur tax is that it is only levied upon sulphur from energy production (Eriksson, 1995).

After a referendum on nuclear power in 1980 it was decided to phase out nuclear power by 2010. A commission report with a plan for how the phasing out could proceed was presented at the end of 1995. The consequences of phasing out nuclear power were analysed, and it was concluded that one of the twelve reactors could be shut down during the 1990s without weakening the power balance considerably. Concerning the future role of nuclear power the commission concluded that a reorganization of the energy system should take place over a sufficiently long period of time, but no date for the completion of the phasing out was given. It is important for the adjustment process that the phasing out starts at an early stage. The speed of phasing out will be determined by the improvements in energy efficiency, the supply of renewable energy sources and the possibility of maintaining internationally competitive prices. The commission also pointed out a number of issues that need to be solved such as the effects of the phasing out on the climate, on employment, and on welfare.

The majority was not willing to give a date for completion of the phasing out. The most important task during the next years is to solve the problem of energy provision after the phasing out of nuclear power, taking into account international agreements on carbon dioxide emissions. Energy taxes will play an essential role. But energy policy is not always consistent, and industry for example is excepted from taxation.

In general the rise in the **prices of energy** until the middle of the 1980s were mainly the result of increased oil prices, while those since then are primarily the result of higher taxation. During the beginning of the 1980s the oil price was relatively stable, but the Swedish taxation on oil increased gradually. Since 1986 the price in real terms has been falling, except during the time of the war in Kuwait, with the Swedish tax increases counteracting. Oil prices in Sweden increased between the years 1992 and 1993, although they decreased internationally, due to the depreciation of the Swedish crown (SOU, 1995:139).

The price of coal in Sweden has followed world market prices, which rose over the period 1980–82. Since then, the price of coal has fallen in real terms, except for a small increase in 1990. Taxes on coal were very low until 1983, and since then they have gradually been raised. The price of biofuel has decreased since the middle of the 1980s, and biofuel has been cheaper than coal since 1990. The price of district heating varies between regions. The real price of electricity fell between 1980 and 1988, but then increased slightly.

The Swedish Parliament, Riksdagen, has, in order to increase competition, decided on a restructuring programme for the Swedish electricity market. The programme involves an active monitoring of competition by the competition board, the opening of transmission systems, and an appropriate organization of the national grid (NUTEK, 1995).

6.3   Domestic Resources: Exploitation and Policies

Swedish industrialization was export oriented and built on the exploitation of natural resources: forest, ore and hydropower. Sweden still has a comparative advantage in forestry and forest industry. The importance of Sweden as an exporter of ore has decreased.

Forest land covers 56 per cent of the total land area in Sweden. Pine and spruce are the dominating species, which account for approximately 85 per cent of the growing stock. General characteristics of the forest land is a lack of medium-aged forest and a surplus of forest older than 100 years. Felling has not been larger than growth since the 1960s. The growth has varied; in 1990 it was substantially higher with 100 million standing volume, than it was in the 1960s.

During the twentieth century the forest has been used systematically, that is with a cultivation form including sowing, cultivating and harvesting. All Swedish forests are subject to the regulations of the Forestry Act, according to which all forestry owners should manage the forest so that it gives a sustainable, high and valuable wood yield. Nature conservation and other interests should be taken into account in cultivation. The forestry owner should thin and clear the forest in a determined way. After felling, the forest owner is obliged to see to it that new forest is grown (Statistics Sweden, 1993). The new Forestry Act of 1993 is more deregulated and aims at consistent production and environmental goals. Thinning and clearing is not regulated anymore which gives the forest owner more choices of forestry methods. Several regulations concerning the age and the size of the felling forest were abolished. Sweden's total productive forest land area consists of 23.4 million hectares, 2 per cent of which is completely protected through the Nature Conservation Act.

Water power from **rivers** provides 13 per cent of the country's total energy supply. The largest energy contributors are the rivers Luleälven, Indalsälven, Umeälven and Ångermanälven. These rivers produce 38 TWh during a normal year of the total of about 61 TWh (cf. Table 6.1). Water power is going to be extended to a production level of 66 TWh during a normal year. The remaining rivers of northern Sweden, that have not been exploited, are protected. The harnessing of water power has entailed extensive encroachment on nature, most of it permanent. Agricultural land and reindeer pasture have been flooded, and parts of the rivers have been dried out.

Hydropower supplied 90 per cent of the country's total electricity needs until the middle of the 1960s and today accounts for about 50 per cent. The technical potential for hydropower development is 130 TWh and the economic potential about 90 TWh, or 7740 kTOE (SOU 1994:59). To protect the Swedish rivers from further exploitation, the Natural Resource Act was designed to include protection of some of the rivers. Four national rivers, Torne-, Kalix-, Pite- and Vindelälven and further 40 river basins are protected from the development of hydropower (Statistics Sweden, 1995). Hydropower construction requires permission from an independent body, the so-called Water Court (Vattendomstolen) according to the Water Act. Permissions from the Water Court are based on judgements of weighing the interest of power, against the interest of conservation. To further protect rivers against exploitation they have to be incorporated into the Natural Resource Act.

Ore has been mined in Sweden for more than a thousand years. Historically, mining was concentrated in areas with high contents of metals. At the dressing, parts with low metal content were sorted out and put as waste rock by the mine. This waste effloresces sulphide ore, which is a serious problem since hydrogen ions and metal ions are liberated. With increasing demands and decreased metal content in the ground, dressing techniques have developed in which the ore is grounded. This procedure creates waste sand that includes metal sulphides which oxidize in the same way as in waste rocks (Statistics Sweden, 1993). The mining of iron ore has decreased since the middle of the 1970s, due to increased competition from new producers in Brazil and Australia (cf. Table 6.2).

Table 6.2   Mining in Sweden, 1950–90

1000 tons	1950	1960	1970	1980	1990
Iron ore	14 730	23 920	36 000	30 900	15 540
Iron pyrite	407	413	575	396	252
Copper ore	61	73	114	181	296
Zinc ore	63	131	167	306	199
Lead ore	29	76	108	102	199

Source: Statistics Sweden, 1993.

6.4 Environmental Effects and Policies

Sweden has been able to reduce emissions of **carbon dioxide** by 40 per cent from 1970 to 1993, with the largest reductions being made in the industry and energy sectors by the transition from oil to nuclear power. Nearly all electricity production is now based on energy sources that do not emit any carbon dioxide. The phasing out of nuclear power will have a great impact on carbon dioxide emissions. Despite that, Riksdagen has set the objectives that by 2000 emission levels shall not exceed those of 1990, and after that they shall be reduced.

The ozone layer has during the past decade decreased by 3–5 per cent on the latitudes that cover Sweden, and is expected to decrease by the same amount during the next 20 years (Kriström and Wibe, 1992).

Acidification was one of the earliest environmental problems that were noticed in Sweden, and it has been given much attention since then. Scandinavia was the first area that suffered from acidification, since the ground's ability to neutralize acidification is small in this area. Even if the fall-out is smaller in Sweden than in Central Europe, the impact could still be significant. Fourteen thousand of the country's 85 000 lakes suffer acidification damage and 6000 of them have been treated with lime to counter acidification. The south-west of Sweden is the most exposed area; it is also there that damage to the forests has been observed. It is mainly sulphur and nitrogen compound that increases acidification. Major sources for emitting sulphur are industrial processes and the combustion of oil and gas in Sweden and in the rest of the world, and the major source for emitting nitrogen is road traffic.

Table 6.3   Air and water pollution in Sweden, 1980–94

1000 tons	1980	1984	1990	1991	1992	1993	1994
Emissions:							
Carbon dioxide (CO_2)	82 010	–	59 350	58 700	58 900	58 930	54 100
Sulphur oxide (SO_2)	508	–	134	110	104	101	–
Nitrogen oxide (NO_x)	424	–	400	394	402	398	–
Pollution load on marine waters:							
Phosphorus (tons)	–	4 700	4 600	–	4 200	–	–
Nitrogen (1000 tons)	–	131	123	–	133	–	–
Pesticides use (tons)	–	–	8 875	8 007	8 693	8 915	10 254

Source: Statistics Sweden, 1993, 1996.

As emissions of sulphur in western countries have declined sharply, an increasing share of the precipitation of sulphur in Sweden today comes from eastern Europe, but most of the precipitation of nitrogen comes from Germany and the UK (NUTEK, 1995). International agreements have led to large improvements in the emissions of sulphur. Nitrogen emissions are instead becoming a more serious problem, although there is very little Sweden can do domestically since approximately 90 per cent of the emissions come from abroad.

Nitrogen oxides together with organic substances, like solvent, contribute to the creation of ozone and other photochemical oxidants close to the surface of the earth. Ozone is created locally, and Sweden also receives an important amount from the continent during summer time. The so-called ozone episodes with short time high ozone content will decrease due to decreased emissions (Kriström and Wibe, 1992). These episodes occur primarily in the south of Sweden, and the effect is direct damage to plants. The background content of oxidants has increased in Sweden during the later decades and will probably continue to increase.

The main environmental problem in the densely populated areas is the traffic, which has been expanding and has brought with it increased air pollution and higher noise levels. In an international comparison, air quality in Swedish cities is good, but still people are troubled by air pollution and noise. The environmental quality will improve in the cities during the 1990s. Sweden can observe a decrease in the rates of sulphur dioxide and soot, although the country is still troubled by high rates of nitrogen oxides, ozone and some hydrocarbons (Molander, 1995).

Leakage of phosphorous and nitrogen through traffic, incineration and ammonia lead to eutrophication of **water** (cf. Table 6.3). The sources are both domestic and foreign. Increased rates of nitrogen are especially high in the south of Sweden. This stimulates the algae production which in the long term could lead to lack of oxygen and termination of some species. So far the effect on forest land has been increased growth, but in the long run increased rates of nitrogen could damage the forest and the quality of the ground water. Even though Sweden together with neighbouring countries have agreed to reduce the emissions, eutrophication will continue to be a problem probably until the beginning of the next century.

Organic substances are harmful for the whole environment, especially the long-lasting ones, since even if the emissions are small they accumulate and can damage in the long term. The most common are DDT, PCB and dioxins, although DDT and PCB have now been forbidden. Such substances emanate from pesticides in agriculture, chemical leakage, incineration processes and industrial processes. The increased use of pesticides in agriculture has led to an increased leakage of nitrogen. Since the ban on DDT and PCB, the rates of nitrogen and phosphorus emissions have decreased.

Other substances that are harmful for the environment, include the chlorinated organic pollutants from the bleaching activities in the pulp and paper industry. Those emissions have affected the Baltic Sea, and a lot of effort has been made to decrease those emissions. New technology for bleaching has been introduced. Air emissions from waste incineration plants and petrol have been improved through the cleaning of smoke from the incineration plants and through introducing unleaded petrol. The recommendation is still for fertile women not to eat too much fat fish from the Baltic sea.

Domestic emissions of mercury have been greatly reduced, and now most of the emissions in Sweden come from abroad. But the rate of mercury in fish is still high. Lead emissions have been reduced in Sweden, but the rate is still too high in forest lands. Cadmium affects agricultural land, and it emanates mainly from products like batteries, fertilizers and from incineration. The use of cadmium had decreased due to a ban that was introduced in 1982.

6.5 Environmental policy

Since the end of the 1960s environmental policy has used administrative regulations like limits, prohibitions and other legal restrictions to effectively limit pollution from point sources. Health and ecological effects from industry emissions are today probably very small. In the 1970s large subsidies were given to firms for environmental protection measures; at present such instruments only play a minor role. The change from point to non-point sources makes economic regulations more appropriate and they are becoming more important. The economic regulations used today are primarily taxes and charges (cf. Table 6.4).

The carbon dioxide tax was introduced in 1991, payable at the rate of 0.25 SEK per kg of carbon dioxide emissions (1 ECU = 8.25 SEK). Since then, the tax has gradually been raised and amounted to 0.37 SEK per kg as of January 1996. The purpose of the tax was to keep the emissions unchanged during the 1990s. The tax is levied on the input of the fossil fuels. Biofuels are excepted from the tax. Since the energy tax reform in 1993, the tax burden on industry is reduced to only 25 per cent of what other users pay in order to preserve competitiveness. It is difficult to evaluate the specific effects of this tax, since fuels also are subject to a general energy tax. What is obvious is that district heating has substituted biofuels for fossil fuels. Whether this is due to the energy tax or to the carbon dioxide tax is hard to judge (Kriström, 1995).

Simulation experiments with a 100 per cent increase of the tax show that carbon dioxide emissions would be reduced by 0.5 million tons in Sweden. Whether this would also lead to a reduction globally remains unanswered since it is possible that production would move abroad (Brännlund, 1996).

The charge on nitrogen oxide was introduced in 1989 for domestic air traffic, and in 1992 for large combustion plants. The purpose of the charge is to reduce the emissions by 30 per cent as compared to 1985 emissions. In contrast to the carbon dioxide tax, this tax is levied on the output of the emissions. Domestic air traffic pays 12 SEK per kg of nitrogen oxide emitted and large combustion plants pay 40 SEK per kg. The levy applies to plants with an annual energy production of 25 GWh or more. The charge levied on combustion plants has an interesting feature, as it is neutral relative to the national budget. Repayments are made to operators of plants with the lowest emissions. In this way plants producing low emissions relative to their energy production will be favoured, and investments in equipment to reduce nitrogen oxide emissions will be encouraged. Emissions from combustion plants have decreased by 35 per cent since 1992 (Kriström, 1995).

Table 6.4   Main environmental taxes in Sweden, 1995

Type of tax	Tax Revenue billion SEK	Tax rate SEK/unit
Electricity tax	-	Industry: 0
		Other: 0.09/kwh
Energy tax on fossil fuels		Industry: 0
	18.35	Petrol: 3.30/litre
		Oil for heating: 0.59/litre
Energy taxes, except petrol	11.50	–
Carbon dioxide tax	0.00	Industry: 0.09/kg
	12.26	Other: 0.37/kg (petrol: 0.86/litre)
Sulphur tax	0.16	30 SEK/kg
Producer tax on electricity	1.70	Hydro: 0.04/kwh, nuclear: 0.012/kwh
Tax on nitrogen fertilizers	0.09	1.80/kg
Tax on pesticides	0.20	20/kg
Tax on domestic air traffic	0.18	CO_2: 1/litre, Hydrocarbons: 12/kg, and Nitrogen Oxides: 12/kg
Charge on nitrogen oxides	-	40/kg (large scale combustion)
Battery charge	0.03	Lead: 40 per battery, Alkali: 23/kg, and Nicad: 25/kg
'Junk' car charge	0.20	1300/car
Revenue, per cent of GDP	3	–
Revenue, per cent of total revenues	6	–

Notes: Tax rates are quoted in Swedish crowns; 1 ECU = 8.25 SEK; the 25 per cent VAT on energy introduced in 1990 is not included. Tax revenues and tax rates in the table are reported using slightly differing criteria and are therefore not completely consistent.
Source: Treasury of Sweden; Brännlund, 1996; NUTEK, 1995.

Diesel and petrol have been differentiated to favour the production of cleaner fuels. Diesel has been differentiated with regard to the emissions of sulphur and hydrocarbons, together with other parameters. The difference in the tax between the environmental classes was from the beginning based on the marginal cost from producing the different qualities. This principle has partly been abandoned for an incentive creating principle. The differentiation has been an environmental success, and fuel has become cleaner (Brännlund, 1996). In 1985 the requirements on exhaust purification became more stringent. Since this required unleaded petrol the government used administrative regulations to force forward a supply, together with tax differentiation to encourage the use of this petrol. The market share of unleaded petrol has increased at a high rate. Exhaust purification through catalysts must be given some of the credit for this change, but most of the transition from leaded to unleaded petrol is due to tax differentiation (Eriksson, 1995).

The tax on domestic air traffic introduced in 1989 made the domestic airline company change the combustion chamber of some of its aeroplanes, which reduced hydrocarbon emissions by 90 per cent. The taxes on fertilizers and pesticides were introduced to finance environmental measures within the agricultural sector. The use of nitrogen in fertilizers has decreased by 20 per cent, and the use of phosphorous has decreased with 50 per cent since the middle of the 1980s (cf. Table 6.3). The experience from the charge on batteries and from the differentiated car excise have been less favourable (Eriksson, 1995). Sweden has not used tradeable emission permits yet.

In the spring of 1995 the Swedish Green Tax Commission was launched with the purpose of analysing a possible 'double dividend' in the form of improved environmental quality and reduced unemployment, by taxing pollution more and labour less.

A recent government white book discusses principles for environmental policy (SOU 1994:133). Some of them are broad and are regarded as general guidelines, like the principle concerning sustainable development and the precautionary principle which is strong in Swedish environmental policy. The purpose of other principles is to declare the responsibility of the polluter, like the polluter pays principle and the principle of best available technology. The cyclical principle and the critical load principle are both principles that help to develop sustainable development in an operative way. Critical loads have been helpful when it comes to cut-downs of acidifying material in polluted regions. In 1993, the Swedish government made the 'cyclical proposition', in which guidelines for a cyclically adjusted development for society are given. The last in the row of principles is the substitution principle, which states that one should never use unnecessarily risky material or methods.

6.6 Resources and Environmental Costs as Constraints on Growth

Environmental policy has increased direct investment and operation costs for the industry, amounting to 4.3 per cent of total investment costs in 1985. In mining the share was 11 per cent, and because of its size the pulp and paper industry accounted for almost 40 per cent of the total environmental investments made by industry. More indirectly, environmental investments also have effects on productivity and growth. Intuitively, a more strictly regulated production process would affect growth negatively, but there is growing research in beneficial processes where regulations lead to innovations, which lower the cost of production and improve the environment (Porter and van der Linde, 1995). Most of the studies regarding the relationship between environmental regulations and economic growth have been done for the USA (Christiansen and Haveman, 1981).

The main general conclusion is that the negative effect on productivity has been small. In Sweden, only a small part of the productivity growth stagnation during the 1970s could be explained by the environmental regulations, and this is probably due to adjustment costs which will diminish over time. The dominating cause was the overall stagnation of growth. At the business level the textile and manufacturing industries had higher productivity growth rates compared to other industries and also relatively small environmental investments, which is possibly part of the explanation. In the forest industry environmental regulations had little or no effect on productivity. Environmental costs have not been higher for smaller companies, possibly because industries with larger companies like the forest industry and the steel industry have been subject to stricter regulations than other industries. It is reasonable to approximate the degree of environmental regulation by the share of environmental investment in total investment; generally, environmental regulations could have had a negative effect upon productivity growth, but the effect is small (Wibe, 1986 and 1991)

A case study of the pulp and paper industry showed that the impact of environmental regulations on firm profits varies substantially among mills, and that large firms suffered more than small firms (Brännlund et. al., 1995).

Swedish producers have argued in favour of international harmonization of environmental law in order to make competition more fair, and in order to prevent translocation of production to countries with less strict regulations (Molander, 1992).

6.7   The Role of Environmental and Resources Policy

For **public opinion** environmental policy presents large problems of information. First, environmental policy is not only based on the views of experts but also on those of elected politicians eager to satisfy voters' opinions as to which problems are serious. Second, the scientists are not clear on the relationship between cause and effect, particularly if the effect is irreversible or if it occurs far into the future. Environmental research and policy tends to be directed towards problems that society finds important rather than towards what scientists find important.

The importance of environmental issues among the voters according to election data largely follows the space these issues have been given in media. The environment was not an important issue in the election of 1964. In 1967 the problem of mercury was given a lot of attention, pictures of poisoned fish were publicized by the media, and environmental opinion started to take form. An increase in interest can be seen in year 1973. In 1976 the debate changed because of the oil crises, and the important issues in this election became energy use, oil dependency and nuclear power. In 1979 the dominating issue was the phasing out of nuclear power, and in 1980 the referendum on nuclear power took place. In the election of 1982 other issues like the wage-earners' investment funds took all attention in the debate. The 'victory of the environment' came in 1988, when almost half of the voters considered environment as one of the most important questions. After the peak in 1988 the interest declined (Bennulf, 1994).

In Sweden, public reactions towards policies to support the environment have in general been positive. Concrete proposals during the last decade, like restrictions to lower traffic and to prohibit chemical pesticides, have been supported by a majority of the people. The only exception to this positive attitude is the proposal to lower the speed limit on the roads and to raise the tax on petrol (Bennulf, 1994). Opinion on nuclear phasing out has oscillated, depending on nuclear accidents and information from the political parties. Generally, the Swedes are positive towards environmental policy. One thing to bear in mind here is that Sweden has a long tradition of being a strictly regulated society.

Environmental issues have consequences for **economic policy**. The government gives grants for different forms of environmental protection. The share of government grants to environmental protection was large in the 1970s, when major subsidies were given to firms and local government to improve environmental protection measures, particularly to develop and extend municipal sewage treatment works. Total government grants are about 3.2 billion SEK annually, much less than revenues from environmental taxes, which include 30 billion SEK energy taxes and 12 billion SEK carbon dioxide taxes. The total amount is 50 billion SEK, that is 3 per cent of GDP and 6 per cent of total tax revenue (cf. Table 6.4).

The role of environmental and resources policy in economic policy will depend on how international undertakings regarding the climate are designed, and on the timing of nuclear power phasing out. Because of the already low emission levels, a freezing or a percentage reduction in relation to earlier levels would be more expensive in Sweden in relative terms as compared to a per capita based undertaking. Other environmental problems appear to be less costly. The costs of measures against acidification have been estimated at about 0.5 per cent of GDP, and the level of costs concerning over-fertilization is similar. These costs are offset by some gains like better health. Problems regarding both biodiversity and waste are difficult to appraise. Nonetheless, the total restrictions from environmental problems have been estimated to cost about 5 per cent of GDP, plus or minus 2 per cent. These estimates are based on the strong assumption that policies are stable and effective (Molander, 1995).

REFERENCES

Bennulf, M. (1994), *Environmental Opinion in Sweden* (in Swedish), Lund: Dialogos.
Brännlund, R. (1996), *Where have Eco-taxes worked?*, Stockholm: Ministry of Finance.
Brännlund, R., R. Färe and S. Grosskopf (1995), 'Environmental Regulation and Profitability. An Application to Swedish Pulp and Paper Mills', *Environmental and Resource Economics*, **6** (1), 23–36.
Christiansen, G. and R. Haveman (1981), 'Environmental Regulations and Productivity Growth', *Natural Resources Journal*, **21** (3), 489–504.
Eriksson, A. (1995), 'Swedish Legal Report: Environmental Taxes' (in Swedish), pp. 247–61 in Nordiska Skattevetenskapliga Forskningsrådet (ed.), *Miljöskatter*, skriftserie Nr. 32, Uppsala: Justus.
Hansson, P. and L. Lundberg (1995), *From Basic Industry to Hightech* (in Swedish), Stockholm: SNS Förlag.
Kriström, B. (1995), 'Swedish Economic Report: Environmental Taxes' (in Swedish), pp. 247–61 in Nordiska Skattevetenskapliga Forskningsrådet (ed.), *Miljöskatter*, skriftserie Nr. 32, Uppsala: Justus.
Kriström, B. and S. Wibe (1992), *An Efficient Environmental Policy* (in Swedish), Långtidsutredningen (1992), Bilaga 6, Stockholm: Finandepartementet.
Molander, P. (1992), *Free Trade – A Menace to the Environment or not?* (in Swedish), Rapport till expertgruppen för studier i offentlig ekonomi, Stockholm: Almänna Förlaget.
Molander, P. (1995), *The Environment as a Long-Term Restriction* (in Swedish), Långtidsutredningen (1995), Bilaga 2, Stockholm: Finandepartementet.
National Board of Forestry (1995), *Statistical Yearbook of Forestry*. Stockholm: National Board of Forestry.
NUTEK (1995), *Energy in Sweden, Facts and Figures*, Stockholm: NUTEK (Swedish National Board for Industrial and Technical Development).
Porter, M. E. and C. van der Linde (1995), 'Towards a New Conception of the Environment-Competitiveness Relationship', *Journal of Economic Perspectives*, **9** (4), 97–118.
SOU 1994:59, *Which Waters Should Be Protected?* (in Swedish), Stockholm: Miljö- och Naturresursdepartementet.
SOU 1994:133, *The Principles of Environmental Policy* (in Swedish), Stockholm:

Miljö- och Naturresursdepartementet.

SOU 1995:139, *Restructuring of the Energy System* (in Swedish), Stockholm: Näringsdepartementet.

SOU 1996:73, *Swedish Nuclear Regulatory Activities* (in Swedish), Stockholm: Energidepartementet.

Statistics Sweden (1993), *Environmental Figures* (in Swedish), 4th ed., Stockholm: Statistics Sweden.

Statistics Sweden (1995), 'Protected Nature', *SM*, **9501** (Na 41), Stockholm: Statistics Sweden.

Statistics Sweden (1996), *Statistical Yearbook of Sweden*, Stockholm: Statistics Sweden.

Wibe, S. (1986), *Regulations and Technological Progress* (in Swedish), Rapport till ESO, Serie Ds Fi 1986:15, Stockholm: Liber.

Wibe, S. (1991), 'Regulation and Productivity' (in Swedish), in *Konkurrens, regleringar och produktivitet*, Expertrapport Nr. 7, Produktivitetsdelegationen, Stockholm: Almänna Förlaget.

7. Denmark: Energy Efficiency, Water Purification, and Policy Instruments

Anders Christian Hansen

7.1 Economic Growth and Growth Policies

The Danish economy has developed at very different GDP growth rates during three periods since 1982: a period of strong growth from 1982 to 1986 (average annual growth rate 3.7 per cent), a period of low growth from 1987 to 1993 (1.0 per cent), and a period of high growth, starting in 1994 (3.0 per cent 1994–96). The size of the population remained at 5.1 million in the 80s and is now slightly increasing. The years 1982 and 1993 were turning points in Danish politics as they were in economic trends. From 1982 to 1992 Denmark was ruled by a conservative government with centrist participation. In January 1993 a social democratic and centrist government took over.

Shifts in economic policy have had considerable impacts on economic growth. The low growth period from 1987 onwards was not entirely but primarily caused by a tightening of fiscal policies in 1987 and then – in the first years of the 90s – prolonged by weak export market growth. The policy of the new government was to use the comfortable position of the Danish economy and the rise in the export market growth rates as background for a fiscal expansion in 1994. This was done, and the government succeeded to 'break the unemployment curve' as its slogan put it.

Denmark will not join the European Monetary Union, but the Danish economy fulfils most of its convergence criteria. With respect to inflation, current account balance, and interest rates the performance of the Danish economy has improved considerably in recent years. However, the structural problems in the economy persist. The surplus on the current account and the lower inflation rate was achieved at the expense of a rise in unemployment to a high of 12.3 per cent in 1993. Conversely, the improved employment situation since then, with unemployment at about 8.0 per cent in 1997, entailed a gradual elimination of the comfortable current account surplus which is anticipated eventually to vanish in 1998. Energy production in the

North Sea profoundly influences economic performance; declining energy imports correspond to about one third of the improvement of the current account since 1985, and growing energy production and exports account for about 0.5 per cent GDP growth during 1995–97 (Economic Council, Autumn 1996, pp. 45, 79).

The government presents the choice of growth strategy as a choice between a leisure oriented and a service oriented strategy resulting in annual per capita GDP growth rates of 0.85 per cent and a 1.75 per cent, respectively (Ministry of Finance, 1996). In the low growth alternative, structural unemployment is stabilized at 9.5 per cent, while it is reduced by half in the high growth alternative. According to the Ministry of Finance, the latter can be achieved by reducing the opportunities for paid leave and early retirement and increasing the share of the younger generations that complete their education. The high growth alternative will provide the public sector with comfortable room for reducing taxes or improving public services. The low growth alternative will allow for more leisure, and a large group of the population will receive public transfers on a more or less permanent basis.

The government unambiguously prefers the high growth strategy. The simultaneous commitment to improvements in the environment, however, gives rise to a dilemma. A primitive calculation shows that if everything, including the environmental pressure from economic activity, grows at 1.9 per cent per year, there will be almost twice as much of all variables in 2030. But the leisure strategy would not produce a qualitatively different outcome. It would result in a 42 per cent increase in 2030. In both cases it is a challenging task to achieve economic growth and a better environment at the same time. The government's answer to this dilemma was first of all to use green taxes in order to direct increasing consumption in a less polluting direction and to subsidize consumption of the less polluting household services. The latter is, however, only indirectly related to environmental concerns. Other, minor green issues include environmental assessment of all government proposals and the introduction of green national accounts.

The energy and environmental policies in many respects continue policies initiated under the former government because a broad parliamentary consensus is not unusual in Danish environmental policy. At least on the rhetorical level there is a broad consensus about the polluter pays principle and the principle of sustainable development. The price of the broad consensus is, however, that the meaning of the two principles is somewhat ambiguous and the concepts are open to different interpretations.

7.2   Energy Consumption, Efficiency, and Policy

Denmark belongs to the part of the world with high levels of **energy con-**

sumption. Danish per capita consumption of energy is above the average level in Western Europe, which again was about twice the world average, but it is lower than the overall OECD level which is pushed upwards by the high levels of energy consumption in the USA (cf. Table 1.2).

Energy consumption per unit GDP decreased by 36 per cent from 1970 to 1988. This was a larger decrease than in any other OECD economy, and it placed Denmark as the third most energy efficient OECD economy in 1988 (OECD, 1991).

Table 7.1   Energy consumption and production in Denmark, 1970–94

	1970	1980	1990	1992	1994
Energy consumption (1000 TOE)	17 800	18 600	17 000	17 300	17 900
of which (per cent):					
Coal	6	29	40	39	35
Oil	92	67	43	42	44
Natural Gas	0	0	11	11	14
Renewable sources	2	3	7	7	7
Fossil fuel extraction (1000 TOE)					
Oil	100	250	6 000	7 800	9 200
Natural gas	0	100	4 800	5 800	5 900
Energy intensity (index, 1980=100)					
Households	117	100	69	70	-
Industries	110	100	92	80	-
Total	124	100	73	74	-
Energy price (index, 1980=100)					
Households	51	100	98	97	-
Industries	46	100	70	63	-
Total	50	100	81	78	-

Notes: Energy intensity for households is defined as the ratio of energy consumption to household consumption expenditure in constant prices; for industry it is similarly defined as the ratio of industrial energy use to the industrial use of intermediate goods in constant prices; 1 PJ = 23.900 TOE (tons of oil equivalent).
Sources: Statistics Denmark, 1994; Danish Energy Agency.

The general intensity of energy consumption was reduced by roughly a fifth during the 70s and a fourth during the 80s. Due to this improved energy efficiency in 1994 a GDP, which was more than 70 per cent larger than in 1970, could be produced and consumed with roughly the same energy consumption as in 1970. In the first half of the 90s, this positive development does, however, seem to be drawing to a close.

The improvements in energy efficiency have taken place in both sectors but primarily in the household sector. Households as well as industries reacted to the price increases in 1973 and 1980 with a remarkable reduction in their intensity of energy consumption. The drop in oil prices in the second half of the 80s only affected industries since household prices were kept constant by levying a tax on household consumption of energy.

Several potential savings in industrial energy consumption remain unexploited partly due to insufficient price incentives, but also partly due to a surprising inability of industries to undertake profitable energy saving investments. For many well known energy saving measures in a long range of industries the net costs are negative. Savings of energy exceed the investment costs. Even with a 30 per cent rate of interest, 10 per cent of industrial energy consumption could be saved without any net costs (Economic Council, 1995; Ministry of the Environment, 1990).

Danish **energy policy** emerged in the wake of the first oil price shock, and the first coherent energy policy programme was presented by the Danish government in 1976 based on a broad parliamentary consensus like subsequent energy policy programmes in 1981, 1990, and 1996. In the early 70s Danish energy supply was extremely dependent on oil which provided 92 per cent of primary energy requirements (cf. Table 7.1). The major response to this vulnerability of supply security after the first oil crisis was to convert the fuel basis of power generation from oil to coal and generally to use a greater variety of energy sources. In 1994 the share of oil had dropped to 44 per cent, and the share of coal had increased to 35 per cent. Denmark has no hydropower resources, but the intention of the present government is to increase the share of energy supply from renewable sources to 13 per cent in 2005. The strategy is to substitute coal by natural gas and renewables in electricity generation before 2030 (Ministry of Environment and Energy, 1996).

The second objective besides supply security was to reduce overall energy costs by improving energy efficiency. The problem of the current account impact of energy imports was relieved during the 80s as Denmark's oil and gas production increased, international oil prices dropped, and the current account became positive. Improvements in energy efficiency have primarily been promoted in the household sector by subsidizing energy saving investments since 1976. In the year 2005 energy intensity should be reduced to 80 per cent of the 1994 level and in the year 2030 to 45 per cent. These targets may seem very ambitious, but they simply imply an annual decline of energy intensity by 2.2 per cent as from 1970 to 1994 (cf. Table 7.1).

Nuclear power was removed in the programme's 1986 revision, after being turned down in a referendum. Instead, electricity generation was to be based on coal, and more efforts were devoted to the development of renewable energy sources, particularly wind power and natural gas. Contrary to the 1976 programme, which was mostly concerned with local and regional pollution due to energy use, recent plans focus on the CO_2 reduction target.

Energy consumption in **transportation** has increased despite improved energy efficiency. Person transportation, measured in passenger-kilometres, increased by 80 per cent from 1970 to 1994, that is an annual rate of 2.5 per cent, and another 30 per cent increase is expected by 2005. Freight transportation only increased by an annual 1.5 per cent, but in the coming years the growth rate is expected to be as high as 1.75 per cent. In both transport categories, the largest and most expanding transportation type is road transport. The share of public transportation in total passenger transportation decreased from 20 per cent to 15 per cent in the period 1984–94, while the prices of public transportation relative to private transportation increased by 75 per cent during the same period (Ministry of Transportation, 1993; Economic Council, 1996).

Transportation causes environmental problems locally (particles, lead, HC, CO, NO_x, and SO_2), regionally (NO_x and SO_2), and globally (CO_2). According to a recent study, the average costs of air pollution, accidents, noise, and road maintenance by motor car driving are DKK 0.40 per passenger-kilometre. The gasoline tax would have to be DKK 11.00 (1 ECU = 7.25 DKK) instead of the current DKK 4.10, in order to cover the social costs of car driving. The before-tax gasoline price is DKK 2.50 (Economic Council, 1996).

7.3 Domestic Resources

In the 60s Danish **energy resources** were expected to be insignificant, and in 1962–63 the concession for the North Sea and the entire Danish underground was given away for literally nothing to one Danish corporation, Maersk, which shared the concession with oil companies in DUC (Dansk Undergrunds Consortium). Following the discoveries of some reserves the concession was renegotiated in 1979–81 leading, first, to more competition in exploration and extraction activities and, second, to the signing of a contract in 1981 about gas supplies from 1984 onwards. This contract has an important role in Danish energy policy concerning security of energy supplies and in relation to the CO_2 reduction strategy since carbon dioxide emissions from natural gas are only 60 per cent as compared to coal.

The presently known oil reserves amount to 216 million TOE corresponding to 24 years of exploitation at the 1995 level (Danish Energy Agency, 1996) (cf. Table 7.1). The contribution of oil and gas extraction to the economy has been considerable, and it is part of the explanation of the rapid improvement of the Danish economy. Self sufficiency in oil and gas consumption was attained in 1991, and self sufficiency in total primary energy requirement including wind power is anticipated in 1998. This is, however, also when the maximum oil production is reached.

The government aims at expanding the share of renewable energy to 13 per cent in 2005 and 35 per cent in 2030. Approximately half of the expansion is expected to be biomass based energy production while the other half should originate from climatic energy sources such as wind, sun, and geothermal energy. Coal fired power and heating should be completely phased out before the year 2030 (Ministry of Environment and Energy, 1996).

The costs of wind power are still declining. At good locations, the new generation of large windmills, which are only running experimentally today, will be competitive with coal based power plants. They do, however, require a flexible power system, which can accumulate power when the wind is blowing and back up when it is not. Difficulties with finding appropriate locations and with getting the electricity suppliers interested in wind power have delayed the programme, but potential locations seem to have been found by now, including open sea locations, and the arrangement of taxes and subsidies provides sufficient incentives.

Renewable resources in Denmark include **fish stocks** among which cod is the economically most important. In recent years cod fishing in the Baltic Sea has been severely restricted in order to relieve the pressure upon the stock from intensive fishing efforts and deteriorating natural conditions for the growth of cod larvae. The fisheries are regulated under the EU fisheries policy, which determines the maximum sustainable catch, distributes quotas among the member states, and financially supports the reduction of surplus capacity of the fishing fleet.

Forests cover 10 per cent of Denmark's area, almost twice as much as a century ago. At the end of the 18th century, the forests that once covered the country completely had been reduced to 2–3 per cent. The present 10 per cent is the result of long-term planning starting back in the 19th century. It is the intention of the government to double the forest area to 20 per cent in less than a 100 years. Multipurpose forestry with products other than the traditional (timber, firewood, and paper) is gaining in importance. For the benefit of biodiversity 2 per cent of the present forests are kept as unmanaged reserves.

Today, **agriculture** is only employing 85,000 persons, but it occupies about two thirds of Denmark's total area. The recent completion of the Uruguay Round in GATT implies that EU has to reduce its agricultural output by letting up to 15 per cent of the cultivated area lie fallow. As a consequence the agricultural subsidies are being redirected from production subsidies to cultivated area subsidies. According to the Danish government, there are environmental benefits to be harvested from this policy (Ministry of Environment and Energy, 1995). The pressure from very intensive cultivation can be relieved, and some of the fallow areas could be used for buffer zones along water courses, for forestry, and for production of biomass for power and heat production. Agriculture is also subject to regulation by a number of government programmes concerning fertilizers, pesticides, ground water protection, use of genetically manipulated crops, use of sludge and other waste products as nutrients, and – for some farmers – conversion to organic agriculture.

7.4   Environmental Policies

Danish environmental legislation concerns four separate fields of regulation: area planning, nature protection, environmental protection, and natural resource use (Basse, 1994). The Ministry of the Environment was established in 1972 and was merged with the Ministry of Energy in 1995. Together with the municipalities and counties it administers the environmental policy.

The characteristics of the **environmental regulation** in Denmark are an ambient quality approach, a decentralized administration, and a consultation and consensus relation between the authority and the regulated firm (Andersen and Hansen, 1991). The ambient quality approach implies that emission limits are differentiated according to the dilution and absorption capacity of the actual recipient. With this approach it is more likely to find optimal balances between economic and environmental concerns than if all emission sources are subject to the same emission limits. The decentralized administration means that decisions are made by municipality and county officials and politicians and that control is conducted by local authorities. The consultation and consensus relation is more a matter of practice than of statutory provision.

How sympathic these principles may appear, their interplay has led to highly undesirable outcomes. Many local politicians interpreted the principle of balancing environmental gains against economic costs as giving economic costs in terms of local jobs and tax base a much higher priority than intended by parliament. Moreover, in the absence of a more general responsibility for the environment, municipalities could pursue the traditional dilution strategy, building stacks still higher and waste water pipes still longer. In the 70s, the municipalities invested rather large sums in the construction of waste water treatment   plants but were reluctant to invest in the necessary technical equipment.

Although the polluter pays principle was praised in the political rhetoric it has been neglected at several occations. For instance, the fee for industrial waste water was usually the same as for household waste water disregarding its much higher pollution contents. Another example was the increasing ochre-pollution problems due to draining in agriculture, the costs of which eventually were paid by the tax payers (Andersen and Hansen, 1991).

Recent revisions of the Environmental Protection Act have added two new principles to the environmental policy consensus. First, the introduction of clean and cleaner technologies are seen as a much more appropriate answers to pollution problems than dilution or end-of-pipe solutions. Second, environmental efforts with a given cost can have much larger effects in developing and transition economies than in Denmark (cf. Chapter 15).

Table 7.2   Pollution of air and water in Denmark, 1972–94

1000 tonnes		1972	1980	1985	1990	1994	target
Global air	ODS	-	-	-	4.2	0.6	0.0
pollutants	CO_2	-	-	61 000	61 000	59 000	49 000
Acidification	SO_2	721	450	-	180	157	90
	NO_x	237	274	-	269	-	203
	N_2O	10	10	10	10	-	-
Tropospheric	VOC	-	154	-	165	-	122
ozone	CO	622	673	-	770	-	647
	CH_4	10	12	-	14	-	0
Agri-	N	-	-	379	326	339	247
culture	pesticides	7	-	8	6	4	3
	N	-	-	20	17	10	7
Waste water	P	-	-	6	4	2	1
	BOD	-	-	60	29	10	12

Notes: ODS designates ozone depletion substances; CO_2 emissions are net of electricity exports and emissions due to climatic variations; tropospheric ozone is caused by laughter gas (N_2O) with volatile organic compounds (VOC), carbon monoxide (CO), and methane (CH_4); BOD is an abbreviation for Biological Oxygen Demand which is an indicator of the concentration of organic matter in water as measured by the oxygen consumption in the decomposition process; target levels are related to the year 2000 except for ODS (2002), CO_2 (2005), waste water and pesticides (1995–96).
Sources: Data from Statistics Denmark; cf. also Ministry of Environment and Energy, 1995; Fenhann and Kilde, 1994.

Some forms of **emissions to the air** have been considerably reduced (cf. Table 7.2). The emission of ozone depleting substances (ODS) has been phased out almost totally since the introduction of government regulation in this field in 1986, from 6800 t in 1986 to 600 t in 1994. They will be totally phased out before 2002. Four regulation instruments have been used in order to achieve these results. First, technical standards eliminating the use of ODSs has been used, and the date from which the use of particular ODSs is banned has been announced in advance to give the producers time to develop alternatives. Second, taxes have been used; all ODSs including the less harmful but still ozone depleting transitionary substitutes, HCFC and HFC, have been taxed according to their ODS. Third, voluntary agreements with industries on recycling have been established. Fourth, a technological development programme has been launched in order to support the development of ozone layer neutral substitutes. The revenue from the taxes has been used to finance recycling and research and development projects.

Denmark is the 16th most carbon dioxide releasing country in the world (cf. Table 1.2). Although the other Nordic countries also have emissions above the world average, except for Norway which has large gas flaring emissions, they have lower emission rates than Denmark. Increases in CO_2 emissions during the 70s and 80s were due not least to the conversion of the Danish power generation sector from oil to coal. While other OECD countries have committed themselves to stabilizing CO_2 emissions at the 1990 level from 2000, Denmark has obliged itself to cut emissions to 80 per cent of the 1988 level in 2005. Emissions have been slightly declining during the period from 1990 to 1995, but only one sixth of the reduction target was reached.

Denmark is a net exporter of sulphur dioxides and nitrogen oxides (cf. Table 15.1). Power generation has been responsible for most of the sulphur dioxide emissions and regulation has primarily been applied to power plants. The government and the power industry have agreed upon an emission reduction schedule. It is left to the power producers to decide just how to satisfy a given power demand taking into consideration the complex interplay of prices and sulphur content of the various fuels as well as the fuel efficiency and emission abatement capacity of each power plant. In this sense the regulation can be classified as economic, and recently a tax upon sulphur dioxide emissions has been introduced. If this looks like a command-and-control regulation, it is primarily because of the quasi-public character of the power production sector. Sulphur dioxide emissions have been reduced at a rate which makes it realistic to achieve the target in the year 2000. In contrast to this, NO_x emissions have been steadily increasing, and it is obvious that the trend points for future emissions are substantially above the targets, as is emission of substances causing tropospheric ozone increase, not least related to transportation. The critical levels for tropospheric ozone concentrations recommended by WHO are frequently exceeded in Denmark. The problem is not only related to urban air quality. An estimate of 10 per cent reduction of crop yield due to ozone pollution is regarded as reliable (DMU, 1993).

Emissions to the aquatic environment and particularly eutrophication of Danish lakes and streams have been a central issue of environmental concern since the 70s, and the environmental policy in this field was mainly directed towards waste water treatment, since waste water was perceived as the major threat to the aquatic environment. In the mid 80s, however, the public became aware that eutrophication was also a severe problem to coastal marine areas.

The targets have been maintained without major changes throughout three programmes. The total loading of nitrogen should be reduced by 50 per cent of the 1984 level or 145 000 tonnes of which 127 000 tonnes should be saved in agriculture. Phosphorous should be reduced by 80 per cent of the 1984 level or 12 000 tonnes of which 4 000 tonnes in agriculture and 8 000 tonnes in urban activities. Nutrient limits in waste water were set at 8 mg N/l, 1.5 mg P/l, and 15 mg BOD/l. The target levels were originally planned to be reached before 1993, but the target year was postponed to year 2000 in the 1991 plan for sustainable agriculture.

While the waste water targets seem to be approached as scheduled, there is only very modest progress regarding the agricultural nitrogen leaching (cf. Table 7.2). The outcome of efforts to reduce the regularly reoccurring oxygen deficit in marine areas is poor. A modest increase in the oxygen concentration was observed in the early 90s, but this was followed by a severe deterioration in 1994 (DMU, 1995). Throughout all of the programmes aimed at reducing the agricultural contribution to eutrophication, the preferred approach has been command-and-control instruments combined with government subsidies including investment subsidies for manure storage capacity, technological and economic advice about fertilizer management to farmers, production standards regarding crop composition and rotation, methods of fertilizing, and compulsory accounting of fertilizer and manure use. A common characteristic of these instruments is also that instead of addressing the actual use of fertilizer itself they address the conditions for fertilizer use.

Another major agricultural pollution problem is the use of pesticides. Pesticides have been found in 12 per cent of the ground water sources, although only in a very few cases in concentrations above the maximum admissible level. They seem to be present almost everywhere they are looked for, including food. When they spread to nature, particularly to lakes and streams, they can do considerable harm to wild flora and fauna. In 1986 an action plan was launched for the reduction of pesticide consumption as well as the average frequency of treatment by 25 per cent before 1990 and by 50 per cent before 1997. Since 1990 there has been a steady decline in both variables but the Ministry of the Environment and Energy (1995) concludes that the 1997 target for frequency can hardly be reached in due time. The 1997 target for consumption can probably be reached because the Danish parliament, Folketinget, in 1995 passed a law which increases the pesticide tax considerably. The pesticide tax is differentiated according to the harmfulness of the various pesticides. The government revenue is returned by lowering real estate taxes for agriculture.

In Denmark practically all drinking water comes from the abundant ground water resources; 1.8 billion m^3 can be used per year, and only 1 billion m^3 of this is utilized. Water shortage is, however, a regional problem in the Copenhagen region due to large consumption and limited regeneration of ground water (Ministry of Environment and Energy, 1995). In recent years, several pollution sources have been detected in ground water reservoirs. One of the major elements in the 1996 ground water protection plan is to point out a number of ground water reservoirs of vital importance where activities including pesticides use on the soil above must be restricted.

Soil pollution is the result of point source pollution as well as diffuse pollution. The most recent figures for point source polluted land plots includes 25 000 properties on 14 000 locations. Diffusely polluted land comprise 420 km². Eight hundred km² urban land which have been urban since 1940 and earlier are also considered polluted in the same category although the pollution is not documented. Public expenditure on cleaning polluted plots has increased from about 15 million ECU in 1990 to 200 million in 1994 and future annual expenses have been estimated at about 50 million ECU. According to these estimates, 30–50 years would be required to clean up all known pollution plots with this level of activity.

Solid waste has traditionally been taken care of by deposition in landfills and by incineration. In Denmark as in other countries the space requirements and the soil and air pollution related to this approach have proved to be enormous. Thus, the Danish policy is to reduce the solid waste flow through promoting clean technologies and recycling. The municipalities are responsible for handling the solid waste and many of them are engaged in the development of expedient systems for sorting solid waste at source in order to ease recycling.

Recent government plans (Basse, 1994) intend to reach a recycling rate of 54 per cent in the year 2000; 25 per cent should be incinerated and at most 21 per cent deposited in landfills. The shares in 1993 were 50 per cent, 23 per cent, and 26 per cent respectively; 1 per cent is hazardous waste which is treated in a special plant for incineration of chemical substances. In order to reach these targets, the tipping fees were raised and differentiated in 1997. The highest fee is DKK 285 per ton landfill deposition. For incineration a lower fee of DKK 210 per ton has to be paid, but if the incineration is used for power production the fee is only DKK 160 per ton (Ministry of Environment and Energy, 1995).

7.5 Resources and Environmental Costs as Growth Constraints

Generally, the Danish economy is not as dependent on its natural resource base as on its real and human capital. The primary industries only contribute 5 per cent of GDP while manufacturing and service industries provide 95 per cent. But the decline of the primary sectors is not always and not in all regions off-set by increases in the secondary and tertiary sectors. On the small island of Bornholm, for instance, the crisis in cod-fishing entailed severe economic difficulties in the local economy.

Economic sustainability requires that depleted natural resources are replaced by increased man-made capital. For most of the period from 1966 to 1994 it seems that increases in man-made capital exceeded the extraction of oil and gas. In 1980–81, however, the capital stock decreased due to consumption of total man-made plus natural capital, in excess of gross accumulation of man-made capital. The reason for this unsustainable development was not increased extraction of natural resources, but rather a reluctant macroeconomic adaptation to changes in terms of trade and other circumstances requiring reduced aggregate consumption at that time (Hansen, 1995, 1996).

In some cases environmental policies have been successful in the sense that means have led to ends with only modest complications and have followed the desired time schedule. It is tempting to try to extract a universal recipe for successful environmental policy from these cases, but it would probably soon turn out not to be universal but on the contrary very specific. Some broader conclusions can, however, be drawn about why different means are used for different ends in Danish environmental policies.

The phasing out of ODSs and the abatement of SO_2 emissions are success stories. In both cases strictly binding emission standards were combined with economic instruments that gave the agents involved the opportunity of reducing emissions in the least costly ways. It was also the case with phasing out of leaded gasoline and partially with the reduction of volumes of pesticides used. In these cases, the desired result was obtained simply by making it sufficiently attractive to the polluters not to pollute. The restoration of the waste water treatment system was also relatively successful. In this case, the instruments were more of the command-and-control type, and obviously economic incentives cannot play the same role within the public sector as in relations between the public and the private sector.

In other instances, the instruments that were used seem highly inappropriate, and the targets are not likely to be met. This is first of all the case with industrial CO_2 emissions and leaching of nitrogen from agriculture. Industrial CO_2 emissions, that is industrial energy use, have been left untaxed while taxing of household energy consumption related to its CO_2 emissions gives a tax rate of approximately DKK 600 per ton of CO_2. This difference in taxation results in marginal costs of CO_2 emission reduction in households of DKK 600 per ton CO_2 while emission reductions that could be made for far less in industry are left unattended. Obviously, this policy is not only ineffective, it is also inefficient (Economic Council, 1995).

The 'energy package' passed by Folketinget in 1995 partly solved the problem. The industrial consumption of energy for heating is taxed at a rate gradually increasing to the level of household energy taxation. Energy used for industrial processes is, however, only lightly taxed and practically untaxed for the firms that comply with an energy savings programme that has been approved by the authorities.

While effective regulation does not necessarily imply efficient regulation, it is certain that ineffective regulation, if it costs anything, is inefficient. The regulation of agricultural nitrogen leaching belongs to this category. Investment costs alone were in 1993 estimated at DKK 400 per capita with no reduction in nitrogen leaching. During 1991–95 the total costs amounted to 1.5 billion ECU (Economic Council, 1993, p. 94).

Table 7.3   Fiscal aspects of environmental policy in Denmark, 1970–94

	1984	1990	1992	1994	1995
Government environment related accounts (billion DKK)					
Expenditures	-	7.4	8.8	10.1	10.8
Revenues	-	5.5	8.3	9.5	10.1
Net expenditures	-	1.9	0.5	0.6	0.7
Energy and emission taxes (per cent of GDP)					
Energy	1.6	2.0	2.0	2.0	2.1
Emissions	0.0	0.2	0.4	0.6	0.6
Total	1.6	2.2	2.3	2.6	2.8
Energy taxation					
Average energy tax (DKK/TOE)	462	840	840	880	-
Fossil fuel tax (per cent of total)	97	93	93	92	91
Implicit CO_2 tax (DKK/tonne)	137	245	261	271	-

Notes: 1 ECU = 7.25 DKK.
Sources: Statistics Denmark.

Energy and emission taxes have been increased to 2.8 per cent of GDP in 1995. Most are energy taxes and they are primarily related to the use of fossil fuel (cf. Table 7.3). Contrary to the widespread belief that economic instruments are always more efficient than command and control instruments, the Danish experience shows that they can be designed in ways that make them hopelessly inefficient. The taxes used for regulating fossil fuel combustion and related emissions are primarily addressing household consumption while less costly energy savings and emission reductions can be found in industrial energy use. The ultimate defence for using these insufficient means for so ambitious ends is that if tougher economic means are used, the industries in question will lose competitiveness and thus market shares to foreign competitors. This can be very costly to industries concerned and also to society. If the foreign competitors really have a cost advantage due to more lax environmental regulation, it will also be disadvantageous from an environmental point of view. At best the pollution source will just move outside the country and at worst the total of domestic and foreign pollution will increase. For this reason economic instruments are not used to control industrial CO_2 emissions and agricultural nitrogen leaching.

Although it is hard to find any major examples of countries that have gained market shares by means of lenient environmental regulation, there are reasons for taking the argument seriously. If trade barriers continue to be torn down in the coming decades leading to equalization of other costs, then costs of environmental regulation could end up being important. The solution to the competitiveness problem is not necessarily no taxes. It can also be considered as 'smart taxes' or 'smart instruments', which only hit the primary target without hurting the surroundings.

In the Danish debate a number of suggestions of this kind have been presented in recent years. Recognizing that the approval of energy savings schedules in larger firms and in industrial branches is likely to develop into a regular quota system, it has been suggested that the quotas should be tradeable (Economic Council, 1996). The CO_2 emission tax could be progressively increasing with the emission level, or each firm could be granted a tax free emission quota. This would put a high tax on the marginal emission and a low tax on the other emissions. Thus it would affect emissions more and competitiveness less (Jespersen, 1995; Clemmensen, 1995).

The problem of the competitiveness effects that would result from a fertilizer tax can be solved or at least drastically diminished if the total nitrogen loss on the farm rather than the fertilizer use is taxed, for example by a deposit-refund system where the farmer pays a deposit for all nitrogen that enters the farm in agricultural inputs such as fertilizer and feed, and receives a refund for all nitrogen that leaves the farm in its sold output such as corn, meat, vegetables, etc. In this way only the nitrogen that actually escapes into the environment will be taxed (Hansen, 1991).

7.6   Environmental Policy Principles and Public Opinion

The increasingly more ambitious environmental policy since the mid-80s reflects an increasingly environmental concern among the voters. The decisive shift in environmental concern occurred in the years 1982–84 and culminated temporarily in 1987, maybe because of tighter fiscal policy and increasing unemployment in the following years (Andersen, 1988).

A recent survey analysis provided some figures as to how much the population would be prepared to pay for an improvement in the environment. The willingness to pay for improved protection of air and ground water amounted to approximately 4000 DKK in 1994 per respondent with about half the amount being devoted to each problem. The willingness to pay for reduction of noise pollution, which was also included in the two sets of questionnaires was close to nothing (Jensen, 1995). This study has, however, not been used as an argument for changing the general course of the environmental policy. The authors confined themselves to the conclusion that taking account of the estimated costs of environmental protection it was not unrealistic to assume that the population would be willing to pay for this.

REFERENCES

Andersen, J.G. (1988), 'Environmental Policy Attidudes in Denmark' (in Danish), *Politica*, **20** (3), 393–413.

Andersen, M.S. and M.W. Hansen (1991), *The Marine Environment Plan. From Negotiation to Symbol* (in Danish), Aarhus: Niche.

Basse, E.M. (1994), 'Introduction to Danish Environmental Law', *CeSam Working Paper* (1), Aarhus University.

Clemmensen, F. (ed.) (1995), *Green Growth* (in Danish), Copenhagen: Arbejderbevægelsens Erhvervsråd.

Danish Energy Agency (1996), *Oil and Gas Extraction 1995* (in Danish), Copenhagen: Danish Energy Agency.

DMU, Danmarks Miljøundersøgelser (1995), 'Monitoring the Marine Environment Programme' (in Danish), *Faglig rapport fra DMU* (141, 142).

Economic Council, *Denmark's Economy* (in Danish), various issues, Copenhagen: The Economic Council.

Fenhann, J. and N.A. Kilde (1994), *Inventory of Emissions to the Air from Danish Sources 1972–92*, Systems Analysis Department, Risø National Laboratory.

Hansen, A.C. (1995), 'Sustainable Savings in Denmark' (in Danish), in P. Lübcke (ed.), *Miljøet, Markedet og Velfærdsstaten*, Copenhagen: Fremad.

Hansen, A.C. (1996), 'Energy Consumption and Economic Growth in Denmark', *Research Papers*, Roskilde University, Department of Social Sciences.

Hansen, L.G. (1991), *Regulation of Nitrogen Losses in Agriculture* (in Danish), Copenhagen: Amternes og Kommunernes Forskningsinstitut.

Jensen, P.R. (ed.) (1995), *A Welfare Indicator for Denmark 1970–90* (in Danish), Copenhagen: Rockwoolfondens Forskningsenhed.

Jespersen, J. (1995), 'Green Taxes in Theory and Practice' (in Danish), in P. Lübcke (ed.), *Miljøet, Markedet og Velfærdsstaten*, Copenhagen: Fremad.

Ministry of the Environment (1990), *Energi 2000* (in Danish), Copenhagen: Ministry of the Environment.

Ministry of Environment and Energy (1995), *Report on Denmark's Nature and Environmental Policy 1995* (in Danish), Copenhagen: Ministry of Environment and Energy.

Ministry of Environment and Energy (1996), *Energi 21* (in Danish), Copenhagen: Ministry of Environment and Energy.

Ministry of Transportation (1993), *Traffic 2005* (in Danish), Copenhagen: Ministry of Transportation.

Ministry of Finance (1996), *The Budget 1996* (in Danish), Copenhagen: Ministry of Finance.

OECD (1991), *The State of the Environment*, Paris: OECD.

OECD (1995), *Environmental Data Compendium*, Paris: OECD.

Statistics Denmark (1994), *Data on Nature and Environment* (in Danish), Copenhagen: Statistics Denmark.

PART THREE

Baltic Countries

8. Estonia: Oil-Shale, Environment, and Growth Scenarios

Erik Terk

8.1 Domestic Resources

Estonia is sparsely populated with 34 inhabitants per km². The total population is 1.5 million, and the total area is 45 215 km² of which 9.2 per cent is made up of more than 1 500 islands and islets. After significant decreases in the 1950s and again in the early 1990s the share of agricultural land is 33 per cent. Forests cover 44 per cent of the country with a total standing volume of 285 million solid cubic metres, increasing by 5 per cent since 1991. The peat land area is 22 per cent of the territory including parts of the forests.

There is a long tradition of nature conservation in Estonia, and landscapes, flora and fauna are remarkably well preserved and rich in variety. Although 69 animal species and 167 higher plants are threatened to some degree, there has also been a net increase in several mammal species, including species protected under the Berne Convention like wolf, elk, beaver, boar, lynx and brown bear. Forestry laws were introduced in the 18th century, when Estonia was under Swedish rule, and later, from the 1760s under Imperial Russian rule, protected forests were established along the coast. The beaches are predominantly in their natural state. In north-eastern Estonia one of Europe's most unique primeval forests is located, and in its immediate vicinity is found an important and highly polluted industrial area (Kaasik, 1995).

As is apparent from Table 8.1, Estonia is quite rich in various resources. The most important mineral resources are oil-shale, phosphorite, dictyonema (alum) shale and carbonate rocks, which are all located in the northern and north-eastern parts of Estonia. Peat and sand-gravel resources are distributed relatively evenly over the whole country. Estonia's natural reserves of building materials include active deposits of limestone – the country's national stone – and dolomite, clay and sand. Curative mud has been used since the beginning of the 19th century. There are a few deposits of sea mud which can be used and some deposits of lake mud in Värska in the south-east of Estonia.

111

Table 8.1   Exploitation of mineral resources in Estonia, 1991–96

	1991	1992	1993	1994	Deposits 1996
Oil-shale (million tons)	19.6	18.8	14.9	14.5	3 988
Peat (million tons)	1.8	1.4	0.6	1.1	1 512
Phosphorite (million tons)	0	0	0	0	500
Limestone and dolomite (million m³)	3.1	1.4	0.9	0.9	471
Clay (thousand m³)	300	170	80	90	43 000
Sand and gravel (million m³)	6.9	2.2	0.4	0.9	383
Curative sea muds (thousand tons)	5.0	1.3	2.2	0.7	2 100

Notes: Phosphorite has not been mined since 1991.
Source: Statistical Office of Estonia, 1996.

The world's largest exploited deposits of oil-shale are located in the north-east of Estonia. Furthermore, the phosphorite (P_2O_5) deposits in the northern part of Estonia are the largest in Europe. Phosphorite used to be mined to produce a phosphoric fertilizer, but because of concerns over its environmental and health effects, production was discontinued in 1991. Uranium was produced in north-eastern Estonia in Sillamäe in the 1950s.

Other economically significant natural resources for the Estonian economy include the forests, the soil, fish resources in the coastal sea and the large lakes, Peipsi and Võrtsjärv.

8.2   Economic Growth, Environment, and Resources until 1990

Although Estonia cannot be considered rich in natural resources, its economy has been relatively resource intensive. At the turn of the century Estonia was one of the areas of rapid economic and industrial growth for the quickly developing and militarizing Imperial Russia. But most Russian enterprises, like large textile mills and naval shipbuilding plants, were based on imported raw materials, and only a smaller proportion used local raw materials including cement factories and logging and timber factories. The first attempts to exploit oil-shale resources also took place during the Imperial Russian period, in 1916.

After the establishment of the independent Republic of Estonia industrial employment was drastically reduced. Economic policy was focused on agriculture which turned out to be an effective export industry. Particularly in the 1930s, a tendency to use local land and natural resources was strengthening. Oil-shale, peat and cellulose industries were built up with state support, and hydropower plants were constructed. This economic policy was related to the introduction of ideas of self-sufficiency and some elements of planning, which became internationally popular in the 1930s.

After Estonia's incorporation into the USSR the economic structure was reoriented, and large programmes of industrialization and industrialized agriculture were centrally decided. Oil-shale production was expanded in the 1960s, large power stations based on oil-shale fuel were built, cement-production capacity in Kunda was significantly increased, phosphate production in Maardu expanded, and at the same time a number of enterprises were built, which used imported raw materials from the east and exported their production, also to the east. Growth rates were high in the 1950s and 1960s, close to 10 per cent annually, significant immigration from Russia took place, and the problems of technological backwardness, like high depreciation of technological equipment and environmental pollution, were not yet evident.

In the 1970s the growth rate slowed down according to official statistics, from 5.6 per cent annually in the first half of the 1970s, to 4.2 per cent in the second half of the 1970s and 3.0 per cent in the first half of the 1980s (Estonian Economy, 1988, cf. Table 1.1). At the same time ecological problems emerged in connection with production increases in production complexes established earlier, often ignoring ecological criteria.

The most important 'all-union' roles of the Estonian SSR in the Soviet Union were supplying the north-western part of the Soviet Union with energy, that is electricity produced from oil-shale, and the production of dairy and meat products. The all-union ministries competed and tried to maintain their positions; many decisions were irrational, and environmental effects in particular were neglected. For example, the biggest consumer of water in Tallinn was the cellulose plant with its outdated technology which was located quite near the city centre without any sanitary zone surrounding it. Against the background of the cellulose production of the Soviet Union, its production volume was quite low. Though the city was short of water in draught years and the plant polluted the city, the all-union ministry never agreed to close it down. Instead, a water pipe-line from Lake Peipsi to Tallinn was planned. The cost of the pipe-line was greater than the value of the plant's production in ten years while the dominant motivation for its existence was the maintaining of cellulose production in Tallinn's city centre.

Agriculture became highly concentrated. Estonian agriculture was more productive than elsewhere in the USSR because of cheap fuel and imported, cheap combined fodder, but it caused environmental problems concerning, for example, the disposal of pig manure, soil structure effects from the use of heavyweight farming equipment, water pollution, and side-effects from large-scale soil improvement investments.

A sceptical and hostile attitude developed in Estonia towards the large all-union projects, mainly because of the fear of further labour immigration, but also because of ecological concerns. The ecological awareness of Estonian society was quite well developed at that time, and comparative sociological studies reveal that the Estonians of the late 1980s were ecologically better informed than several Western European populations (Lauristin et. al., 1985). Several large projects were prevented including the exploitation of the Estonian phosphate deposits near Rakvere, planned to be realised in 1987, which posed an immense threat to ecology, especially the ground water. The use of the deposit was prevented by an unprecedented popular movement. Other projects were, however, realised, and among the largest was the Muuga Port, then named The Tallinn New Port or 'Novotallinskij Port', whose first stage was opened in the middle of the 1980s. The port was designed as a base for the Soviet import of grain and tropical fruits, but is now one of the key elements of Estonia's transit business.

The most-polluted areas are located in north-eastern Estonia in a narrow west-east belt between Kiviõli and Narva. The power stations, oil-shale processing and chemical plants located here cast large amounts of various waste products into the air. The greatest polluters were and still are the Narva power stations which emit flying oil-shale ash, SO_2, and NO_2. A large part of the area has been covered with open-cast mines, of which only some have been recultivated, as well as waste products, ash piles and plateaux of ash. Spontaneous combustion was a frequent phenomenon in the waste piles. The territories over the underground oil-shale mines have their own problems with the frequent sinking of ground. The Sillamäe chemical plant with its radioactive waste dump poses a separate problem.

In particular, emissions of sulphur, SO_2, were high by international standards; per capita emissions were three times higher than in the other Baltic states and Finland and even higher as compared with other Scandinavian countries (Tables 8.2, 1.2 and 15.1). Water pollution was also becoming critical. The biggest polluter of Estonian waterways was the insufficiently treated or untreated waste water. Only a quarter of the sewage water was treated biologically.

8.3 Economic Structure and Economic Growth During the Transition

The restoration of Estonia's independence in the early 1990s and the transition to a market economy were accompanied by a sharp decline in GDP, by 37 per cent from 1989 to the lowest level in 1994, by a geographical reorientation of the economy from Russia towards Northern European countries, and by radical changes in the economic structure including decreasing volumes of industry and agriculture and the emergence of a service sector. The use of mineral resources has decreased and the pressure on the environment has also been reduced at least initially, thanks to the drop in volume of agriculture and industry. The increased export of timber and peat to the west, regrettably as raw material rather than processed goods, has also become a characteristic feature of transition economy.

The Estonian economic reform is notable for its remarkable lack of centralized industrial policy. No branch of production received official favours, the enterprises' ability to adjust themselves to the economic conditions, especially the ability to reorient to the western market, has been practically the only decisive factor in the development of the new structure.

The economic growth has been significantly influenced by predominantly western investments, which have enabled the enterprises to update their technologies, to introduce organizational know-how, and to reach foreign markets. Foreign investments have been made primarily in joint ventures and in new enterprises; investments in enterprises privatized by official privatization channels, particularly the Estonian Privatization Agency, to foreign owners have been less significant, although investments in these enterprises have been considerably larger than in those sold to domestic owners.

The results of privatization have become apparent primarily in trade and services, as well as in transport, where the process was conducted during the so-called small-scale privatization. The privatization of large and medium-sized enterprises began more massively in 1993. The process was largely complete by the end of 1995, with the exception of mainly large infrastructure enterprises and some firms with rather complex production and economic relations, including the rare metals processing plant Silmet, where the usual methods of privatization could not be used. Some of these enterprises have strategic importance for the Estonian state.

The most direct consequence of the changed economic environment has been the sudden drop of productivity in all branches of economy. Although macro-stabilization policies are accompanied by zero growth or a certain reduction even in market economies, the effects are rarely as dramatic as in Estonia where large price and foreign trade shocks occurred simultaneoulsy. As a result GDP fell 36.6 per cent in 1990–94. Value added in agriculture decreased 31.5 per cent in the period 1990–94. It can, however, be presumed that real economic decline was somewhat less extreme than described by official statistics.

Economic growth began from 1995. A key determinant is investment, which has been increasing from 21 per cent of GDP in 1992 to 24 per cent in 1993, 27 per cent in 1994 and 28 per cent in 1995. Considering the progress of the property reform and the accelerating integration of Estonia into the international economy, quite high economic growth can be expected at this rate of accumulation. The preceding steep downfall also enables the achievement of high growth rates since the base levels were consequently low.

Significant structural changes have taken place. The share of trade in GDP has increased from 8 per cent in 1991 to 16 per cent in 1995, and the share of real estate, leasing and business services increased form 2 per cent in 1991 to 9 per cent in 1995. The declining sectors were first of all manufacturing, declining from a share of 36 per cent in 1991 to 15 per cent in 1995, and agriculture including hunting and forestry, the share of which declined from 17 per cent to 7 per cent.

The most important reasons for the decline in **agriculture** have been the disappearance of the eastern market, the continuing property reform, the absence of a consistent agricultural policy, and the technical backwardness of the food processing industry, for example the lack of slaughterhouses meeting European Union requirements, which results in uncompetitive domestic products. Collective and state farms were liquidated from April 1993 as part of the land reform, and they have been replaced by joint-stock companies and co-operatives but only a few new privately owned farms.

The fuel industry and **energy** production are mainly based on oil-shale mining which has dropped from 22.5 million tons in 1989 to 14.5 million tons in 1994 (cf. Tables 8.1 and 8.3). Most of the oil-shale, 88 per cent, was used for primary energy production in 1994. Production of electricity remained at the 1993 level in 1994, 9152 gigawatt-hours, whereas the production of thermal energy in 1994 decreased by 5 per cent as compared to 1993. The role of exports has decreased as compared to previous years. The wear and tear of existing production capacity is a problem both in oil-shale mining and in power stations. The modernization of these branches requires extensive investments and is linked to a comprehensive analysis of economic efficiency of energy production from oil-shale. The existing production capacity can be used for the next 10 years, but will also need maintainance investments in that period.

Some **manufacturing** enterprises have been aided by foreign partners with investment and technology. But the price has often been a restructuring from the manufacture of end products to production of components and semi-manufactured products for western enterprises.

The production of **food products** provided the main part of total production of the manufacturing industry in 1996. The production of that branch has decreased less than that of the others, since a large portion of the goods is being consumed by the domestic market. Estonian food was also significantly cheaper than imported food, especially in the months immediately following the monetary reform in June 1992 which undervalued the Estonian Kroon and pegged it to the Deutschmark. But this branch is now facing serious problems connected with price rises. Since one of the components of the Estonian economic reforms has been the refusal to use custom barriers to protect the domestic market of agricultural products and foods, further growth can only be based on the inflow of foreign capital and the renovation of technologies.

Before 1990 the light **industry** as well as engineering industries were oriented towards eastern raw material supplies and eastern markets for their products. Thus the textile industry was particularly hard hit in the second half of 1992 after the monetary reform. The largest textile industry enterprise – the Kreenholmi Manufaktuur in Narva, which employed nearly 7000 workers in the 1980s – maintained only a few per cent of its production volume in 1993. The sewing industry fared somewhat better as it managed to reorient more efficiently to the western markets.

The **forestry**, timber and paper industry has suffered badly during the economic reform. The production of cellulose has stopped, paper production has been relaunched. The volume of final felling dropped by more than 40 per cent after 1991 but is now recovering. The most important products of wood working industry are timber, plywood, fibreboard and chipboard, and products like skis. The furniture industry is a profitable sub-branch which has also found a market for its products. While the forests used to be predominantly state-owned, land reform will transfer 40–50 per cent of them into private ownership, mainly as relatively small farm forests. The Ministry of the Environment prefers that the forests that are particularly important for environmental protection should remain under state control.

The export of timber became an important source of revenue in the first half of the 1990s. The situation is not critical here, according to the Ministry of the Environment, since the logging was supposed to have amounted to only 40 per cent of the natural increase in the forests. The volume of logging may even rise to more than half of the annual increase.

Several features of the processes of the transition and the restoration of national independence have an impact on the state of the **environment**. The changes in agriculture and the disintegration of the large-scale production significantly change the structure of the landscape. Agricultural reform has also left many sources of pollution ownerless, for example, warehouses of pesticides and toxic chemicals. The metal trade, which has spread in Estonia since the beginning of the 1990s, has in several cases resulted in the circulation of radioactive metal. The structure and ownership forms of industry are changing; unfortunately, environmental protection requirements or criteria have only extremely rarely been applied in the privatization of enterprises. According to the estimates of the Ministry of the Environment, the privatized enterprises – partly because they frequently suffer from lack of capital – have not displayed significant technological improvements for the reduction of pollution. The Kunda Cement Plant, presently Nordic Cement, which was privatized by foreign capital, is a positive exception.

Serious problems have emerged in recent years primarily in the privatization of chemical plants, for example the Silmet and Kiviter enterprises, in connection with the transfer of the environmental rehabilitation and waste dumps liquidation obligations to the new owners.

Military-related pollution is a problem of its own in Estonia; its full extent became apparent only after the completion of the Russian troops withdrawal from Estonia some years ago.

Table 8.2   *Air pollution in Ida-Virumaa County in north-eastern Estonia, 1990–94*

1000 tons	1990	1991	1992	1993	1994
Particles	193	154	142	108	91
Sulphur oxide (SO_2)	218	198	150	116	114
Nitrogen oxide (NO_2)	18	16	14	11	11
Carbon oxide (CO)	15	12	10	10	14
Others	16	15	9	5	4
Total	459	394	327	249	234

Source: Liblik and Kundel, 1995.

Fears have been expressed that the Central and Eastern European countries may become dumping grounds for Western European hazardous waste or waste products, whose recycling would be too difficult. Some cases of that type became known in Estonia in 1992–93, for example, the stockpiling of old tyres in the Muuga Port for incineration. Some legislative moves to eliminate such threats have been taken.

As a whole, it can be concluded, however, that the state of Estonia's natural environment has improved significantly during the transition period, not due to technological improvement, a rise in environmental awareness or rapid construction of treatment plants, but due to the sharp decline of production in industry and agriculture, which significantly reduced the burden on the environment. As for agriculture, the reduced use of fertilizers due to their high price and the farmers' financial hardships should be mentioned. The use of natural resources has declined as well. Besides the drop in oil-shale mining, the use of peat has also been reduced. The use of mineral building materials has declined by more than 90 per cent.

While approximately 480 000 tons of waste products were emitted into the atmosphere in 1992, the amount was 100 000 tons less in 1993 (cf. Table 8.2). One of the main reasons for this was the reductions in energy production. While a steady increase of nitrate and phosphorus compounds in rivers took place in the 1970s and 1980s, this has significantly declined since the end of the 1980s especially regarding nitrate compounds, particularly because of the reduced use of fertilizers. The content of organic waste in the rivers has decreased by 25–50 per cent as compared to the indices of the 1970s. The reasons are both the installation of biological water treatment plants, often with Scandinavian financial assistance, and the decreasing levels of production. The declining ground water surfaces of the Tallinn, Tartu and Kohtla-Järve water supply areas, caused by excessive use, have begun to recover.

There are still problems concerning the quality of the air in the north-eastern Estonian industrial towns, which has improved rather slowly despite reduced production. Part of the explanation is that a certain improvement of the state of the environment together with other difficulties connected with the economic transition have driven environmental problems into the backgound in social awareness. Yet it is clear that production volumes, at least in industry, will increase again in the near future, and the environmental situation may deteriorate again unless a radical modernization of production according to ecological requirements is undertaken.

8.4   Prospects for Economic Growth: Alternative Scenarios

In order to analyse various aspects of the future development of economic growth in Estonia a number of economic scenarios have recently been worked out by working groups headed by Dr Alari Purju and Garri Raagmaa of the Estonian Institute for Futures Studies.

The construction of the scenarios proceed from the idea that further economic development of Estonia as a country with a highly open economy will depend entirely upon the degree to which it succeeds in integrating large-scale international flows of trade, transit and international co-operation and continued large foreign investments. It is presumed that this potential economic activity will be directed predominantly between the east and the west, that is the Western and Northern European countries, Russia and the CIS area, and particularly Estonia's closest neighbours Sweden and Finland, but also larger actors in the world economy like Germany and the USA.

While the scenarios worked out by the Estonian Institute for Futures Studies is mainly used for the analysis of Estonia's success in exploiting its geo-political and geo-economic potential, they also have applications as the bases for a prognosis of Estonia's energy demand and for determining the developing pressure on Estonia's natural environment in the future, its type, strength and geographic dispersal within Estonia.

According to the type of geo-economic integration, two main types of scenarios are:

-   The 'West-East' scenario, where Estonia, while continuing its integration in the western political and economic structures, primarily the European Union, combines this with quite close economic ties with Russia and CIS. Besides the development of a transit-related economic cluster, the Estonian agriculture and food industry will probably find a profitable market in Russia; some not too modern branches of industry like engineering and chemical industry may also receive a new lease of life.

– The 'West-West' scenario, where Estonia will continue its successful integration into the European Union, but where the economic ties with Russia and CIS will weaken as compared to the present. The reasons may be Russia's increasing isolationism, deteriorating relations between Russia and Estonia or uncontrolled processes in Russia.

According to the calculations of the Institute for Futures Studies the possible rates of economic growth in Estonia will be quite different in the two scenarios, with an annual average of 6–7 per cent in the 'West-East' case and 3–4 per cent in the 'West-West' case. The structure of economic growth will also vary between the scenarios, and the relative growth of industry and transport will be larger in the 'West-East' scenario.

Within the framework of these two general scenarios, several sub-scenarios have been established. One version of the 'West-West' scenario, called 'Periphery of Finland', essentially means that an additional hypothesis is used that Estonia will develop into a hinterland for the Nordic countries and will specialize in functions requiring cheap labour. Estonia will be drawn into the common infrastructure system of the Baltic Sea basin. The integration of Tallinn and Helsinki will strengthen, regional differences within Estonia will increase. The north-eastern Estonian industrial and south-eastern Estonian rural regions will face great difficulties. The growth of GDP will not exceed 3–4 per cent per year, and rather high unemployment will persist.

Another sub-scenario, called the 'Ferryman' scenario, is a version of the 'West-East' scenario, where economic relations with Russia will be improved and a transit branches cluster will develop predominantly as a combination of sea and rail transport, but without progress concerning export of high-technology products and services. Economic growth will be relatively rapid, approximately 5–6 per cent annually until the year 2005, and some traditional branches of economy, which faced difficulties in 1992–96, will recover, like agriculture and branches of industry based on Russian raw materials. A relatively low qualified employment will prevail, and the share of industry and agriculture will be relatively high as compared to the other scenarios. A crisis and depression can be foreseen after some initial growth, because a number of industries based on low labour costs will move to cheaper countries like Belarus and Ukraine.

The 'Grand Slam' sub-scenario combines the positive aspects of the 'Ferryman' scenario with an enlargement of intellectual employment which presupposes that serious efforts towards this purpose are made in the 1990s. In that case there would be no depression and economic development could continue after 2005 at a rate of 6 per cent per year or even accelerate.

The environmental pressures would differ between the scenarios. In the 'Finland Periphery' scenario environmental pressures would be the smallest among all the scenarios. A large part of the polluting enterprises would be closed down for economic reasons, or the pollution would be relatively limited due to continued low production volumes. The strict Nordic regulations and standards would apply. Some problems could be caused by the increasing tourism in scenic places like western Estonia and the islands, but these would not be too serious thanks to the well-disciplined tourists.

Environmental problems could become serious in the case of the 'Ferryman' scenario. Industrial production volumes would increase, including in the chemical industry, combined with high traffic pollution in the cities. The dispersed pollution by agriculture may also start growing. Transit trade has been concentrated in certain lanes, border crossing checkpoints and ports. There may be conflicts in connection with the building of new transit lanes. Risk will increase in the arrival at and departure from the highly burdened Port of Muuga and others. Positive aspects are that the infrastructure facilities built by western owners will probably be highly modern and consequently not particularly harmful to environment. High economic growth may also strengthen public interest in environmental improvements and willingness to pay for them.

The environmental problems of the 'Grand Slam' scenario will be similar to those of the 'Ferryman' in the initial period. But the situation will gradually improve, because the new technologies being introduced will favour energy savings and efficient use of raw materials and low-waste production. Pressure on the environment will be reduced by the development of information-intensive production and export services.

8.5 Energy Consumption and Efficiency

Oil-shale is the main fuel for energy production in Estonia, and almost all electricity is produced at two huge oil-shale based power plants constructed in the 1960s, the Estonian and the Baltic Power Stations, with capacities of 1610 MW and 1435 MW, respectively. Electricity production is totally monopolized in Estonia, all electricity is produced by the State enterprise 'Eesti Energia' (Estonian Energy). Practically all electricity production is based on oil-shale. Heated debates on the method of privatization of the enterprise are going on at present.

Oil-shale will probably also dominate Estonian energy production in the near future and its share of the primary energy supply will remain at least one third. But the situation may change quite significantly in the coming decades where natural gas can be expected to become more important particularly in the high growth, 'West-East' scenario (cf. Table 8.3).

Coal and nuclear fuel are not expected to become significant sources of energy before the year 2025. The use of hydropower and wind energy and the burning of peat will probably increase, but their significance will remain rather marginal. In case a new cellulose plant should be built in Estonia, it will probably cover its energy requirements by burning wood. The growth rate of energy demand will lag behind the growth rate of economy and more so in the high growth 'West-East' scenario. But in absolute terms, the energy demand of the 'West-East' scenario will of course be higher than that of the 'West-West' scenario.

Table 8.3   Sources of primary energy in Estonia, 1995–2020

per cent	1995	2000	2005	2010	2015	2020
Renewable resources	0	0	1	1	1	1
Timber products	5	6	6	6	4	7
Peat	2	2	2	2	2	2
Coal	1	1	1	1	1	1
Natural gas	10	15	29	35	41	36
Oil products	21	21	24	25	27	26
Oil-shale	61	55	37	30	24	27
Total (per cent)	100	100	100	100	100	100
Total (1000 TOE)	5488	5619	5744	5929	6119	6786

Notes: Projections of energy consumption and distribution according to primary sources are calculated from the assumptions of the 'West-East' scenario as described in the text; 1000 TOE (tons of oil equivalent) equal .042 PJ.
Source: Liik, 1997.

Natural gas is presently supplied by the Russian firm Gazprom and delivered by the pipe-line coming from the south of Estonia. The amount of gas was not metered at the border to Russia until 31 August 1994, when the gas metering station was put into operation in Värska. The project was financed by 1.4 million USD from the EBRD (European Bank for Reconstruction and Development). Gas consumption has decreased since 1991. Temporary increase in consumption took place at the end of 1994, when Russia cut fuel oil exports. Estonia is interested in the long run in overcoming the one-sided dependence on Russian natural gas and hopes to gain access also to the gas pipe-lines' circle around the Baltic Sea based on gas produced in the Norwegian Sea (Baltic Gas Supply, 1996). The share of gas, however, is increasing in the Estonian fuel market where gas competes with fuel oil.

The environmental impacts of the energy sector is largely related to the Estonian oil-shale industry. In the 1980s the output of oil-shale reached its maximum when about 32 million tons were extracted per year. In 1995 the mining had decreased to 14 million tons. Half of the oil-shale is mined in open-cast pits, half underground. Open mining causes damage to the natural landscape and entails waste of other resources. About 2000 ha of land in north-eastern Estonia have been used in every five year period for oil-shale mining. In current practice most other natural resources are destroyed while the mining industry is not interested in their protection. A total of 11 240 ha of land were spoiled by open mining, of which 8730 ha had been technically recultivated by January 1993. Underground mining in turn causes serious ground water problems and subsidence of the land surface. The area over the underground mines totals about 22 000 ha. Land under the waste heaps from oil-shale separation facilities should be added here.

Air pollution originating from power plants is to a large extent deposited outside Estonia (cf. Tables 15.1 and 15.2). Sulphur is the main problem. The oil-shale power plants were constructed in the 1960s and no sulphur purification technology was used in the whole former Soviet Union nor in Estonia at that time. Solid particles, that is fly ash, cleaning equipment only was used. Therefore, annual emissions of sulphur compounds were huge in the 1980s, when oil-shale output and electricity production, respectively, were at their height. As a result annual sulphur emissions exceeded 200 thousand tons. Due to significant decreases in economic activity starting from 1991, the emissions of all pollutants into the air have declined (cf. Tables 8.2 and 1.3).

Millions of tons of alkaline ash, containing a variety of micro-elements plus heavy metals, are disposed of in ash fields, covering territories of more than 2000 ha; until 1990 about 6 million tons of ash had been ejected annually into ash dumps. Over 200 million tons of ash have been disposed of in this way until now. The length of protection dikes amounts to 25 km and their maximum height is 30 m. Nevertheless, there is a permanent threat to neighbouring water courses of pollution by strongly alkaline water (pH =12–13) in the event of extraordinary weather conditions.

There exists, however, a use for oil-shale ash. Since the 1970s some dry ash from the hoppers of the cyclones and electric precipitators has been delivered by air-screw pumps via air ash pipes to storage and ash loading plants. About 40 per cent, or 4 million tons, of the ash is delivered to agriculture as fertilizer for acid soils and to the building materials industry.

8.6 Resources and Environmental Cost as Constraints upon Growth

Since a very sharp turn towards service production has occurred in the Estonian economy in the 1990s and the present Estonian export industry is only partly based on local natural resources, neither the local resources nor the threat of their exhaustion can be considered a significant constraining factor upon economic growth. This will probably hold true in the longer term as well. According to the 'periphery of Finland' sub-scenario, the growth constraint will be the low level of economies of scale and the failure to use the potential of the country's geographical location, while service branches dominate the economic structure together with industrial subcontracts to the Northern European countries. In the case of the 'West-East' scenarios the volume of economic branches based on local resources will be only slightly greater.

The decrease of agricultural raw materials production in Estonia can have a constraining effect on the development of the food industry, but in that case, the reason would not be the exhaustion of natural resources, but the decline of agriculture, caused by a combination of several factors, as well as difficulties with access to foreign markets for agricultural products. The production of timber and furniture is a significant branch of the Estonian export industries, as the forest resources of the country are significantly larger than the needs of the timber and furniture industries. The problem of the sufficiency of the forest resources may arise in connection with the project currently under discussion to build a large modern cellulose factory in the Baltic region. But in that case the timber supply area of the plant should be wider anyway than the territory of a single Baltic country. The building materials industry, where Finnish and Swedish capital have made significant investments in the last 10 years, has been built in order to exploit local raw material resources, so that limited resources should not pose a problem.

The constraint on energy production from oil-shale will probably not be the exhaustion of oil-shale deposits, but the introduction of pollution taxes, which could make the oil-shale industry incapable of competing with other fuels and turn the major reconstruction projects of the oil-shale power stations economically shaky.

Phosphates have been exhausted in the Maardu deposit near Tallinn, but the immensely larger Rakvere deposit is unused. The time of its opening depends primarily on the emergence of a sufficiently environment-friendly mining technology, since the deposit is located in a highly vulnerable area. Disregard for ecological criteria could cause irreversible harm to Estonia's ground water.

Neither is the lack of water a significant constraint on economic growth in Estonia as a whole. It poses local problems in some regions, notably northeastern Estonia, but the problem can be solved by eliminating the present large losses of water.

The problem of environmental restrictions and taxes may become more important than that of natural resources. Estonia has signed quite strict agreements on the limitation of pollution. The limits can be met at present, because output volumes have significantly dropped during the transition. The restrictions concerning air pollution may become the most critical. In the event of a hypothetical increase of the power stations' production to the 1990 level, the pollution limits would probably not be met in an economically acceptable way. The water pollution restrictions could become a somewhat less important constraint, because waste water treatment plants have been constructed during the 1990s, often with Scandinavian financial assistance. Although the waste water treatment plants of some regions are even oversized, their absence in other areas presents serious problems. The situation is critical in that respect in Kohtla-Järve, the centre of the north-eastern Estonian industrial region, where the capacity of water treatment plants has been exhausted.

Several large enterprises, vital for the Estonian economy, are in a situation where they do not directly pollute the air or the water, but are stockpiling large quantities of waste products. Unless these enterprises make a move towards low-waste technologies, the attitude towards stockpiling waste products may become stricter in the future.

In the 'West-West' scenario the limiting effect of environmental constraints on economic growth will be somewhat less strict than in the 'West-East' scenario. But the latter scenario has higher growth rates which allow the allocation of more finance for environmental improvement.

REFERENCES

Baltic Gas Supply (1996), Material presented at the conference *Future Integration of the Baltic Sea States' Gas Supply*, mimeo, Tallinn: Estonian Institute of Future Studies.

Estonian Economy (1988), *Problems of the Development of the Estonian Economy* (in Estonian), Tallinn: Valgus.

Kaasik, T. (1995), 'The Natural Environment', in *Estonia in the European Union*, Tallinn: Estonian Institute of Future Studies.

Lauristin, M., P. Vihalemm and R. Timak (1985), *Environmental Conscientiousness of the Population and Attitudes towards Natural Environment*, Tartu: Tartu University.

Liblik, V. and H. Kundel (1995), 'The Quality of Atmospheric Air in Ida-Virumaa' (in Estonian), *mimeo*, Tallinn: Stockholm Environment Institute.

Liik, O. (1997), 'On the Planning of Estonian Energy Industry', Paper presented at the conference *Does Estonia know, where it goes*, mimeo, Tallinn: Estonian Institute of Future Studies.

Lugus, O. and P. Vartia (eds.) (1993), *Estonia-Finland. A Retrospective Socio-economic Comparison*, Helsinki: ETLA (The Research Institute of the Finnish Economy), TAMI (Institute of Economics at the Estonian Academy of Sciences), VATT (The Government Institute for Economic Research, Finland).

Statistical Office of Estonia (1996), *Statistical Yearbook of Estonia 1996*, Tallinn: Statistical Office of Estonia.

9. Estonia: Energy Prices, Environmental Taxes, and Policy Implementation

Tiit Kallaste

9.1 Institutions and Legislation for Environmental Protection

Estonia passed its first law on nature conservation in 1935. Among the Soviet republics Estonia enjoyed a good reputation concerning environmental protection, and Estonia was the first of the union republics to pass a law on nature conservation, in 1957. After regaining independence in 1991 much Soviet legislation remained temporarily in force provided it did not conflict with Estonian laws, but it is being adapted to the transition of the economic system, particularly the introduction of private property rights, and since 1991 environmental legislation has undergone profound changes.

Estonian environmental legislation is based on two main framework laws, the Law on the Protection of Nature in Estonia (1990) and the Law on Sustainable Development (1995). The Law on Sustainable Development gives a legal basis for implementation of the decisions of UNCED in Rio de Janeiro in 1992. Another framework for environmental legislation is the Association Agreement with the European Union from 1995, and harmonization with EU legislation is actively pursued and progressing. This also implies the ratification of several international conventions. Recently Estonia has ratified the 1992 Helsinki Convention on the Protection of the Baltic Sea (Hjorth, 1992; UN ECE, 1996), the 1973 International Convention for the Prevention of Pollution from Ships, the 1985 Vienna Convention for the Protection of the Ozone Layer, and the 1992 UN Framework Convention on Climate Change. But so far Estonia has not ratified the 1979 Geneva Convention on Long-Range Transboundary Air Pollution or the 1991 Espoo Convention on Environmental Assessment in a Transboundary Context.

The Law on the Protection of Nature in Estonia provides the main principles for environmental protection policy, including the polluter pays principle as the basic type of regulation and the precautionary principle. Although economic incentives have been introduced, including environmental taxation, it is generally a major problem that there is a lack of follow-up regulations and of government capacity to monitor compliance at the national, regional and district level. The framework laws are rarely supported by relevant regulations governing their implementation. In general terms Estonian environmental policy is in accordance with that of the European Union.

9.2 Energy Policies

Energy sector development is a strategic element in the government policy of transition towards a market economy. The main goal of Estonia's energy policy is to encourage energy efficiency in the production, distribution and transmission processes and also in the final use. Increased energy efficiency will also contribute to the improvement of the environmental situation in the oil-shale region in the north-east of Estonia. High energy prices alone are not sufficient for progress in the energy sector, and market forces cannot guarantee efficiency or solve the related environmental problems. Therefore government energy policy is extremely important. The main problems are an inadequate legislative and institutional framework, low technical standards, low efficiency of heating systems, inefficient household subsidies, dependence on imported fuels, serious pollution problems, and lack of financial resources for investment.

Electricity production technology with outworn and obsolete cleaning equipment for fly gases and also lacking sulphur cleaning technologies cause severe pollution in north-eastern Estonia (cf. Table 8.2). This in turn causes significant health problems among the local population, where there are also serious social, demographic and employment difficulties. Various indicators of health and welfare problems such as occurrence of the cardio-vascular, respiratory and allergic diseases, and of pregnancy and childbirth anomalies are substantially above average in this region (Kallaste, 1991).

Estonian industry has been quite energy intensive for decades. The economic recession is the main reason for the significant decline in energy consumption since 1991 (cf. Table 1.3). Due to the ongoing privatization and restructuring an improvement in energy efficiency by the companies themselves is expected. However, taking into account the scarcity of investment capital, the government is supporting energy efficiency measures in industry by providing soft loans and by assisting in carrying out energy audits. Household consumption of energy is now increasing, but big fluctuations have taken place.

Energy prices have been increasing continuously since 1990, and energy costs form a significant share of the expenses of households, industry and the public sector. They are a major burden for the structural adjustments of trade and of the economy in general. Prices of natural gas, coal and petroleum products have moved towards world market levels, and prices of oil-shale, electricity, oil-shale, and district heating are increasingly covering the costs of production. The resulting price structure with wide differences between various types of energy has significantly influenced consumption patterns (cf. Table 9.1).

Table 9.1   Comparative energy prices in Estonia, 1995

Type of fuel	Price in EEK per MWh	Price in USD per MWh
Electric energy	390	33.1
Natural gas	185	15.7
Heavy fuel oil	81 – 144	6.9 – 12.2
Coal	62 – 111	5.3 – 12.2
Peat briquettes	60 – 99	5.3 – 9.4
Wood waste products	38 – 89	5.1 – 8.4
Peat	37 – 62	3.2 – 7.5
Firewood	36 – 79	3.1 – 5.3
Oil-shale	34	2.9

Note: The rate of exchange was 1 US dollar for 13 Estonian Kroons in 1994, and 11.5 Kroons in 1995. For a comparison with Latvian energy prices cf. Table 11.1.
Source: Ministry of Economic Affairs, 1996.

Considering the most probable energy policy option, Estonia will have to continue to rely on local fossil fuel, that is oil-shale, in the future. Therefore, it is vital to develop new oil-shale boilers, based on modern technologies of combustion and flue gases purification. Boilers currently in operation at the Baltic and Estonian Power Stations do not apply recent discoveries on fouling and corrosion processes in boilers. Studies on new combustion technologies like 'fluidized bed' and others are conducted by various firms in Sweden and Finland, including Åhlström, Vatenfall and Imatran Voima. There is some interest from enterprises in Great Britain, Germany and particularly in the USA (Kallaste, 1996).

To improve the scope for utilization of oil-shale ash in agriculture and in the building materials industry the application of pulverized combustion is essential. To reduce atmospheric pollution it is expedient to introduce a three-stage flue gas cleaning system using cyclones to remove coarse particles, electric precipitators to capture fine fly ash particles and a third stage to capture sulphur dioxide and aerosol particles.

This requires huge investments in energy production in the near future. It is expected that privatization of the presently fully state owned energy sector will call forth investments. Significant participation of foreign investments is needed as well. In 1996 preliminary negotiations with the US electrical company NRG Energy on the possible investment of 259 million USD in Estonian electricity generation by selling half of the enterprise shares have started. Until now the negotiations have reached the phase, where a principal decision about partial selling of the state-owned enterprise 'Estonian Energy' has been taken.

The large investment costs for updating purification systems for solid and gaseous emissions in energy production in Estonia and elsewhere in Eastern Europe can become a major obstacle for the realization of the widely publicized idea of a so-called 'Baltic Ring', that is the development of cheap energy production in a number of countries in economic transition, like Poland, Estonia and Lithuania. The costs of producing clean energy from coal or oil-shale in the former socialist countries could be relatively high as until now very little has been invested in the cleaning of flue gases.

Other domestic resources are being exploited as well in order to improve the diversity of energy supplies. The share of local fuels, biofuels in heat generation in the municipal sector, particularly in smaller towns and villages, and also renewable energy could be enlarged. This allows the dependence on imported fuels to decrease and reduces local unemployment. It is of high importance particularly in rural areas and on islands. Policies include subsidizing the use of local fuels by giving favourable loans either for fuel production or for consumption, for example by reconstructing boiler houses.

Simultaneously with the development of domestic energy supplies, the government actively attempts to replace imports of natural gas and heavy fuel oil from Russia with more reliable supplies. However, there is still a political interest in further intensive development of the Estonian oil terminals for transit of liquid fuels in order to make Estonia the main mediator for Russian oil exports to western countries. Availability of alternative gas supplies would facilitate the use of gas turbines for electricity generation at peak hours and reduce the need for construction or rehabilitation of the very polluting coal, oil-shale or heavy oil fired boilers.

Despite the relative closeness to natural gas deposits in the North Sea and Norwegian Sea, the share of natural gas in the energy balance of the Baltic Sea countries is mostly small and remains below the average for Western Europe, which was about 21 per cent in 1994. The present gas supply to Finland, the Baltic States and Poland, in contrast to the Western European countries, is entirely dependent on one source of gas supply, namely Russia. A north–south, trans-Baltic gas pipeline project has been suggested, which would start in the North Sea or the Norwegian Sea, pass through Sweden and Finland, proceed through the Baltic States and finally be connected via Poland to the gas network of Central and Western Europe. The realization of the project would make it possible to meet the gas demand of these countries, as well as to create a strategically important European gas transmission ring system which would provide stable gas supplies regardless of possible complications or economic blackmail, technical malfunctions, or other circumstances in Russia. This gas transmission ring system would incorporate the unique natural underground gas depositories in Latvia, providing the possibility of storing up to about $20*10^9$ m^3 of gas within the network. In the first stage of the project the existing gas pipeline network in the Baltic States may also be used, in particular the high pressure pipeline from the Latvian gas depository constructed in the 1980s to Tallinn, but presently unused. The north-south pipeline may be connected to the gas pipelines from Russia. Later on the pipeline could also be used for transporting gas from the Stockman deposit in the Barents Sea to Europe.

9.3   Policies Concerning Domestic Resources

Large areas with unspoiled nature such as forests, mires, bogs and peat-lands are among Estonia's resources, and there is a long tradition for **nature conservation**. At present 7.8 per cent of the territory is to some degree protected, while 1 per cent is under a strict protection regime. Protected areas include nature reserves, areas of specific protection and areas of limited management. Estonia has four national parks, Lahemaa, Karula, Soomaa and Vilsandi. The West Estonian Archipelago Biosphere Reserve is also protected, and in total there are 311 protected areas, 155 of which are larger than 50 hectares. In addition, there are some five hundred parks currently under protection (Estonian Environmental Information Centre, 1995; Statistical Office of Estonia, 1996, p. 255).

Significant changes in nature conservation took place recently with the passing of the new Act on Protected Natural Objects in 1994. This act lays down procedures for the protection of areas and natural monuments as well as plant, animal and fungi species and fossils. It determines the rights and obligations of land owners, land users, and other persons in regard to protected natural objects. The act establishes a list of all possible restrictions and obligations. It states, for example, that economic damage or loss arising from the protection regime shall be compensated. Spatial planning of protected areas and establishment of the protection regime is performed according to protection zones. The territory of a protected area may be divided into four different zones: strict nature reserve, special management zone, limited management zone and general zone of a programme area.

Policies concerning the use of domestic resources have been changed profoundly starting in 1991, when **resource pricing** was introduced in Estonia. Large-scale use of local natural resources, particularly oil-shale and phosphate resources, during the period of central planning has significantly damaged the natural environment in Estonia, most significantly in northern and north-eastern Estonia. There has been serious deterioration affecting all components of the environment as a result of pollution which also has negatively affected human health. In the former Soviet economy natural resources did not have a price; they were assigned to the concerned ministry free of charge. At the eve of the transition period in Estonia the basis for change towards pricing of resources and taxation of environment was worked out in a government regulation in November 1990, which laid down two main principles for the use of natural resources, namely firstly resource payments for the use of land, water, mineral and organic resources like mineral building materials, oil-shale and peat, and secondly compensation charges for changing the type of land use in urban areas, in rural areas and in wooded areas.

Now resource pricing is a vital part of environmental taxation policy which aims at improving the efficiency of resource use. At first, these kinds of payment were designed for more efficient and sustainable use of oil-shale, water, mineral building materials and peat resources. They are based on the total volume of resources used, not the actual production outcome, in order to avoid the former large production losses. All the charges are index-linked. Resource payments or charges are also levied on the use of land. Differentiated compensation charges have been established for changing the kind of agricultural, forest and urban land use, which have been put in force stepwise starting from 1991.

However, resource payments still represent an extremely small proportion of the sales price of the resources, for example 1.8 per cent in the case of oil-shale and 0.5 per cent in the case of peat. In practical terms, the incentive mechanism has not yet achieved its objective. A principal shift should be undertaken in the near future (Estonian Environmental Information Centre, 1995).

Resource payments and charges on the use of natural resources are paid into the local and state budget. There are certain differences in resource pricing as regards the recipient of the revenues. Payments for the use of natural resources like oil-shale, peat, mineral building materials and water resources are paid both to the state, county and municipality budgets. For example, 80 per cent of the payments for oil-shale and water resources are paid to the state budget and the remaining 20 per cent to local budgets. As for peat and mineral building materials, only 30 per cent of payments are paid to the state budget and 70 per cent to local budgets. Considering the requests of local governments, from 1996 the shares to be paid to local and state budgets have been changed. Also, in 1996 the prices for the right to use mineral resources were increased by 2.5 per cent of their sales price, and the prices for mineral water and Cambrian-Vendian ground water were increased twice. The shares of payments received by local governments were increased, so that 50 per cent of the payment for the use of water and 80 per cent for the use of oil-shale resources are to be allocated to local and municipal budgets, excluding deposits of national importance, where the share of local budgets is to be 20 per cent (Estonian Environmental Information Centre, 1995).

The resource payments have been designed for the total use of a certain deposit of the resource, not only for the actual use of the resource. They reflect the principal difference as compared to the practice before 1991. Payments for the use of fixed amounts of natural resources are imposed by executive bodies of the local governments on the basis of specific entrepreneurship contracts.

The payments for the use of natural resources made up 23.9 million EEK in 1994. The share of local budgets was 5.3 and of the state budget 18.6 million EEK. Revenues from water consumption were 48.5 per cent of the total and the share of oil-shale 48.3 per cent. In 1995 the revenue from resource payments reached a value of 40.7 million EEK, including 13.1 million EEK for the use of oil-shale. However, resource payments contributed only 0.3 per cent of the total state budget revenue. Nevertheless, their shares in many local budgets were significant (Estonian Environmental Information Centre, 1995).

The range of **institutions** which share the responsibility for extracting and using natural resources for productive purposes is very wide. Different ministries and agencies share responsibilities for regulating the affairs of these sectors. The responsibility for the management of natural resources lies with the Ministry of the Environment. This provides the possibility for unified accounting, supervision and regulation of the use of natural resources and environmental protection. The Ministry of the Environment is also in charge of nature conservation and natural resources management via a number of boards like the Board of Forests, The Land Board and The Board of Fisheries. The Ministry and the subordinated boards work out draft laws, develop national policies, control nature conservation and resource management, and implement relevant conventions. The practical implementation of laws and obligations on nature protection and natural resources is ensured by the Nature Protection Inspectorate and the State Marine Inspectorate. Monitoring of the state of protected assets and updating of the Nature Conservation Register are the responsibility of the Minister of the Environment.

The regional environmental departments implement the laws at the county level. County officials have to validate the restrictions on land use in their area. The lack of a specific interpretation of the land reform legislation and of detailed guidelines is making this task difficult. The division of responsibilities between the state and county levels is not fully clarified yet. It is not established by law either. At present there is no overall strategy or any practical guidelines on nature conservation or rational use of natural resources for county and municipal authorities. The administrative structures are not yet working satisfactorily as the duties and the responsibilities of the different levels are not clearly defined by law and the activities of the bodies involved in nature conservation and use of natural resources are not specified.

9.4 Environmental Policies

Environmental policies are implemented by means of administrative methods as well as economic instruments. At present the Ministry for the Environment is the national environmental protection authority. The state functions at local levels are performed by the boards of environmental protection of the county governments and municipalities. In Tallinn and in Narva the state functions are carried out by the boards of environmental protection of the local governments. Obligations may be imposed upon local governments only in accordance with the law or with the agreement of the local government. For example, in the Waste Law and in the Water Act special articles are included regulating the competence of municipalities.

Among the administrative methods a system of **environmental impact assessment** (EIA) is required by the 1995 Act on Sustainable Development, and a law describing the procedures for EIA is currently being drafted. The system presently in use is partly carried over from the former Soviet Estonia's attempts to harmonize its environmental policies with Western European practices in the late 1980s. The draft law describes EIA as the mandatory assessment of the compliance of planned activities, such as development or construction projects, programmes and planning documents, with environmental protection requirements and principles of sustainable development with the aim of finding the optimum alternative. EIA is a mandatory part of the system of decision making so that not only economic feasibility, but also environmental impacts of human activities are taken into account. EIA is also required for issuing permits for the use of natural resources. The draft law is supplemented by methodological guidelines, and both regulations suggest the important role of the public in the EIA procedure. It is important to consider both the relevant European Union directives and international conventions. Thus Estonia is already participating in the process initiated by the UN ECE aiming at joining the Espoo 1991 Convention on Environmental Impact Assessment in a Transboundary Context.

According to the new draft law the state will only have the reinforcement function, and everything related to the organization of the EIA will be the responsibility of the object of the EIA and the licensed EIA experts. This adds to the responsibilities of objects of the EIA and also indicates that the national authorities trust the licensed EIA experts. Licences are issued by the Commission under the Ministry of the Environment. The reliability and quality of the work of the licensed experts will be regulated by normal market forces in this sphere. Recent EIAs were mostly concerned with fuel terminals and construction or enlargement of ports. One EIA was carried out in Latvia, concerning the planned new port in the transborder area Heinaste, where the transboundary environmental impact of the Latvian port was assessed.

Another policy instrument closely related to EIA is the **environmental audit** which assesses the compliance of environmental administration and activities of an operating enterprise with environmental protection requirements in regard to sound environmental practices and to principles of sustainable development. It has recently been introduced in Estonia according to methods used in Western European countries, where the use of environmental auditing has proved an effective tool of environmental management. The introduction of environmental auditing in Estonia has been supported by the EBRD and World Bank, and a draft government regulation has been worked out in co-operation with the Stockholm Environment Institute, Tallinn Centre. The aim of this policy instrument is to encourage entrepreneurs to learn about the benefits of auditing. When environmental impacts of business activities are assessed in advance, it might be possible to reduce risks in the loan policy of the banks and to avoid fines and penalties concerning pollution charges.

Besides administrative methods and direct regulations the new system of economic control of environmental protection uses **economic instruments** which take advantage of economic incentives to achieve the goals of environmental improvement. As in other countries they are used as a complement to other policy instruments like regulations and co-operative agreements with industrial enterprises (Bye et al., 1990). Economic instruments as a policy tool offer a number of inherent advantages over regulations, not to speak about moral suasion: greater cost-effectiveness, permanent incentives to decrease pollution and greater flexibility in application and modification, and they are in addition a source of revenue. Economic instruments typically involve either a financial transfer between polluters and the community or the actual creation of new market systems, for example for tradeable emission permits. Among the types of instruments listed by the OECD (1992) – charge systems, subsidies, deposit-refund systems, enforcement incentives and market creation – all of them, except market creation, have been implemented in Estonia.

One of the most promising policy instruments is undoubtedly the **taxation of environment**, which was introduced in Estonia in 1991, with a variety of aims, not only environmental protection and efficient use of resources, but also encouragement of a private environmental industry and the provision of earmarked funds for environmental purposes, which has been a very prominent purpose. The most important source of revenue is pollution charges, forming about 90 per cent of revenues. These have been implemented in air and water pollution control and in solid waste management. Pollution charges are channelled into the Estonian Environmental Fund, and the charge rates are based mainly on the empirical knowledge of experts without much use of classical economic theory and optimum calculations. Besides pollution charges, user charges, product charges, administrative charges and tax differentiation are used in Estonia, but their significance is much smaller.

Table 9.2   Tax rates on pollution and waste disposal in Estonia, 1993–95

Tax rates in US dollars per ton	1993	1994	1995
Air pollution			
Sulphur dioxide	.05	1.13	1.60
Carbon monoxide	.01	0.16	0.23
Non-toxic dust	.04	0.81	1.15
Oil-shale fly ash	.05	1.13	1.60
Soot	.08	1.62	2.30
Nitrogen oxides (accounted as NO_2)	.12	2.59	3.67
Water pollution			
BOD (>15.0 mg/l)	19.2	46.2	68.3
Solid Waste (>15.0 mg/l)	11.5	23.1	34.1
Oil products (>1.0 mg/l)	92.3	92.3	136.4
Phenols (>1.0 mg/l)	323.1	323.1	477.5
Phosphorus (>1.0 mg/l)	69.2	69.2	102.3
Nitrogen (>12.0 mg/l)	38.5	38.5	56.9
Fats	69.0	-	-
Waste disposal according to hazardousness class			
Inert wastes (non-toxic)	.008	.038	.056
Low toxic wastes (class IV)	.023	.115	.170
Moderately toxic (class III)	.230	.323	.477
Toxic (class II)	2.300	3.230	4.774
Very toxic (class I)	23.100	32.300	47.737

Notes: The tax rates apply for emissions and disposals within allowed limits. For waste disposals above the agreed limits or in the event of no permit for disposal, the tax rates are increased fivefold for class IV wastes, 50 fold for class III wastes, 100 for class II wastes, and 500 fold for class I wastes; BOD (biochemical oxygen demand) is a common measure for organic pollution.
Source: Estonian Environmental Information Centre, 1995.

Pollution charges are applied on various air and water pollutants and on waste disposal (cf. Table 9.2). For air and water there is a difference between discharges below a negotiated limit and above this limit. Charges per unit of discharge also vary according to type and location. Uniform rates are set nation-wide but may be adjusted within limits by local authorities, depending on local conditions, the economic situation of the enterprise and its willingness to install abatement equipment. All pollution charges are subject to indexation, so that their real values are no longer eroded because of inflation as they were during the first four years. The revenues from pollution charges are earmarked and paid into the Environmental Fund.

Pollution charges in general equal the predetermined tax rates on direct releases into air or water, or on waste disposal. As far as air pollution is concerned, direct charges have been established for six pollutants: SO_2, CO, non-toxic dust, oil-shale fly ash, soot and NO_x. For about 50 other types of pollutants, charges are calculated on the basis of health standards and maximum permissible concentrations (Kallaste, 1994a).

For air pollution control the charge system is based on permits which are issued by the local environmental boards, based on the requirement of the various environmental and health standards, that is maximum permissible concentrations for each of the pollutants. Emissions from all sources, including stationary sources where emission permits are not yet required, are added, and the total volume of emissions is used for calculations of diffusions for local areas. On this basis permitted emission quotas are issued, and predetermined taxes are computed. In the event of violation of emission quotas non-compliance fees are levied according to an exponential tax rate related to the toxicity of the waste. For air pollution four toxicity classes and for waste deposition five classes are used (Kallaste, 1994b).

As for water pollution emission, charges have been established for suspended solids, oil products, organic pollutants as measured by BOD (biochemical oxygen demand), total nitrogen, total phosphorus, phenols, sulphates and fats.

The solid waste disposal charges are paid by enterprises for wastes deposited in landfills, dumps and repositories. There is no levy on reused or recovered wastes. The charges are graduated according to the hazardousness of the waste. Depending upon the hazardousness class of the waste, but also upon the location and the sanitary conditions in which the waste is stored, the basic pollution charge rates may be increased by a factor of up to 500. The waste charges are paid to the Environmental Fund.

The **Estonian Environmental Fund** is organized as an extra-budgetary fund. It was founded in 1983 as an All-Union economic experiment as a mechanism for collecting revenues from violations in resource use and pollution of the environment. Up to 90 per cent of revenues remained in Estonia, the rest was transferred to the central government in Moscow. It was a real innovation in the former Soviet Union. The revenues totalled up to about 1 per cent of the total expenditure on environmental protection in Estonia at that time. In 1990, the Fund was reorganized into the extra-budgetary Estonian Environmental Fund. The Fund is divided into a centralized Republican Fund, 20 local (county or municipal) funds and various special earmarked funds. The Republican Fund is attached to the Estonian Ministry of the Environment, local Funds to the local county or municipality Environmental Protection Boards. The activities of the Fund are run by the Council of the Fund, the composition of which is determined by the government according to recommendations from the Ministry of the Environment. Its legal basis is the Environmental Fund Law of 1994 and the Statute of the Fund.

At present the major part of the Fund's revenues comes from pollution charges. The remaining revenues, which consist mostly of non-compliance fees, are to some extent unforeseeable, since they depend on the polluters' environmental strategy which they choose each year under the changing economic conditions. The strong emphasis on economic incentives implies that even legal regulations, sanctions and fines are considered mainly from an economic point of view rather than a legal or moral one.

Environmental expenditures and revenues from environmental taxation are still relatively small (cf. Table 9.3). The share of the Environmental Fund is negligibly small, only about 4 per cent of total environmental expenditures, but it is increasing.

Table 9.3   Pollution charges and expenditures in Estonia, 1991–95

Source of revenue, per cent	1991	1992	1993	1994	1995
Pollution charges					
Water emission charge	59	50	33	32	40
Air pollution charge	15	8	18	28	19
Waste disposal charge	23	15	35	31	41
Other sources	3	27	14	9	0
Total revenue (per cent)	100	100	100	100	100
Total revenue (million EEK)	57.9	7.5	22.9	22.7	35.3
Total revenue (per cent of GDP)	.40	.07	.10	.08	.09
Environmental expenditures					
State and regional budgets	-	7	13	-	-
Environmental funds	-	4	4	-	-
Enterprises	-	79	59	-	-
International loans and grants	-	10	24	-	-
Total expenditure (per cent)	-	100	100	-	-
Total expenditure (million EEK)	-	228.3	454.5	-	-
Total expenditure (per cent of GDP)	-	2.09	2.07	-	-

Notes: Environmental revenues are the revenues of the Estonian Environmental Fund. The total revenue in 1991 is indicated in million roubles.
Sources: Estonian Environmental Information Centre, 1995; COWI-Consult, 1995.

Pollution charges and non-compliance fees are partly paid to local funds established at the respective environmental boards. In its turn, the Fund's financial means are used partly by local and partly by state authorities. As for the centralized Republican Fund, its revenues are formed on the basis of the redistribution of local Funds' revenues between the Republican Fund, which gets 50 per cent of total revenue, and the 20 local funds. Local Funds have the right to decide how to use their revenues.

The Environmental Fund is earmarked and managed independently from the state budget. Despite its low share in total environmental expenditures in Estonia, still only about 4 per cent, it has great importance for institution building. The Council of the Fund examines the financial plans presented by the departments and submits summarized budgets and reports to the government.

International assistance is a significant source of finance for environmental expenditures. Estonia has received investment finance from Finland in relation to co-operation concerning air pollution (cf. Table 15.3). At present Estonia is not a party to the 1979 Geneva Convention on Long-Range Transboundary Air Pollution, but Estonia did conclude a bilateral treaty on air pollution abatement with Finland. Under this agreement Estonia is obliged to reduce its NO_x emissions to the 1987 level by 1994, to reduce its SO_2 emissions by 50 per cent of the 1980 level by 1997, and by 80 per cent of that level by 2005 at the latest. Estonia is currently meeting the requirements under the agreement, but this is primarily the result of the economic recession.

In connection with bilateral agreements on co-operation in combating marine pollution concluded in 1993, Finland and Sweden have contributed to the investment costs of oil-combating equipment. Finland also assisted Estonia to build up an oil-drift forecasting system for Tallinn to manage major oil spills.

The Baltic Sea Joint Comprehensive Action Programme, adopted in 1992, identified 132 pollution hot-spots, of which 13 are located in Estonia (cf. Table 14.1). Estimated investment costs are also 10 per cent of the total, 1.5 billion ECU (UN ECE, 1996). On the top of the list is the reconstruction of the oil-shale power plants in Narva with costs of about 70 per cent of the overall estimated investment costs, more than 1 billion ECU. Other hot-spots are related to Tallinn municipal and industrial water pollution, the Matsalu Bay management programme, Pärnu municipal and industrial water pollution problems and the Gulf of Riga management programme. In practice the Programme is being implemented through a number of ongoing projects. A desulphurisation pilot plant at one boiler in Narva has been the first experimental step. In Tallinn, the first stage of a biological waste water treatment facility was started in 1993, which has already cut the pollution load by two thirds. Also the Haapsalu waste water treatment plant has been started (UN ECE, 1996). The projects are jointly financed by foreign investments and local funds. Foreign funding usually comes through bilateral assistance and loans from international financial institutions. Also the private sector is increasingly involved in the implementation of the Baltic Sea Programme in Estonia, and this trend is encouraged politically.

9.5   The Role of Environmental and Resource Policy in Public Opinion

During the last five years environmental problems have lost the prominence in public opinion, which they enjoyed in the last Soviet years, and have been replaced by more urgent problems of economic recession, criminality, stress and so on (Kallaste, 1994a).

A questionnaire survey of decision makers, namely politicians and authorities, revealed practically no discrepancies as to the determination of environmental priorities. But for both groups, particularly the politicians, environmental protection stands as no real priority area. It seems that economic and political problems absorb most of the respondents' energy, so that ecological problems are pushed into the background. The general attitude seems to regard environmental problems as being important yet without real urgency.

According to another questionnaire in 1994, only 4 per cent of the general population regarded environmental problems as the most pressing. The environment obtained fifth place after criminality (14 per cent), cost of living increases (13 per cent), economic recession (6 per cent), and nationality problems (5 per cent).

The political interest in Estonia, and in other Eastern European transition countries, is focused on immediate economic issues, not long-term strategic environmental problems. This explains the increasingly positive attitude towards possible phosphorite mining in Virumaa, as well as the tolerance towards further expanding the Ignalina Power Plant in Lithuania and the establishment of a huge waterpower plant in Daugavpils in Latvia. Mass awareness of the environment seems much harder to obtain in Eastern Europe than in western countries because of the economic depression. On the other hand various types of wasteful habits – like non-reusable dishes and many types of goods for which advertising and packaging costs exceed their proper value – are less widespread in Eastern Europe. It is of utmost importance that ecological awareness in Estonia reaches a higher level in the near future (Kallaste, 1994a).

Politicians and administrators will have to reconcile the long-term demands of society as a whole with those of sectoral and competing short-term interests within society. Ensuring the practical compliance with rapidly changing legal requirements in the economy and in the environment is also one of the greatest challenges in Estonia's efforts to join the European Union. The adoption of EU environmental legislation in national environmental legislation is progressing well at present, but still much remains to be done. The adoption of the Act on Sustainable Development in 1995 at least gives a legal basis for future implementation of main directions adopted at UNCED in Rio de Janeiro in 1992.

REFERENCES

Bye, B., T. Bye and L. Lorentsen (1990), 'Taxation of Fossil Fuels. The Impacts on Economic Activity, Energy Markets and Pollution', in K. Halsnaes and G.A. Mackenzie (eds.), *Nordic Workshop on Integrated Energy and Environmental Modelling - Risø National Laboratory, 15-16 February 1990 (Nord 1990:74),* Copenhagen: Nordic Council of Ministers.

COWI-Consult (1995), *Case Study on Environmental Expenditure and Investment in Six Selected CEE Countries,* Paris: OECD.

Estonian Environmental Information Centre (1995), *Estonian Environment 1995* (in Estonian), Tallinn: Estonian Environmental Information Centre.

Finnish Ministry of the Environment (1995), *East Europe Project, Activity Report 1994,* Helsinki: Ministry of the Environment.

Hjorth, R. (1992), 'Building International Institutions for Environmental Protection. The Case of Baltic Sea Environmental Co-operation', *Linköping Studies in Arts and Science 81,* Motala: Department of Water and Environmental Sciences.

Kaasik, T., K. Peterson and H. Kaldaru (1996), *Man and Environment. Changes in Estonian Public Environmental Awareness 1983–94* (in Estonian), Tallinn: Stockholm Environment Institute.

Kallaste, T. (1991), 'The Environmental Problems in Estonia and Some Ways to Solve Them', *Research Institute of Nothern Finland Working Papers* (76), Oulu: University of Oulu.

Kallaste, T. (ed.) (1994a), *How to Upgrade Environmental Protection in Estonia,* Project Report by the Stockholm Environment Institute Tallinn Centre for the Finnish Ministry of the Environment, Tallinn: Exactica.

Kallaste, T. (1994b). 'Taxation and Environment in Estonia. Case Study on Estonia', in OECD (ed.), *Taxation and Environment in European Economies in Transition,* Paris: OECD.

Kallaste, T. (1996), 'Environmental Implications of EU Membership of Estonia, Latvia, Lithuania and Poland, Estonian Case Study', in B. Hägerhäll (ed.), *Environmental Implications of EU Membership of Estonia, Latvia, Lithuania and Poland,* Stockholm: Stockholm Environment Institute.

Kallaste, T. and A. Tarand (1996), *The First National Workshop on Climate Change,* Working paper, Tallinn: Stockholm Environment Institute - Tallinn Centre.

Ministry of Economic Affairs (1996), *The Present Situation in the Gas Sector in Estonia* (in Estonian), Working paper, Tallinn: Ministry of Economic Affairs.

OECD (1992), *Environment and Economics. A Survey of OECD Work,* Paris: OECD.

Peterson, K. (1995), 'How Many Environmental Conventions Are Feasible to Implement for Small Countries with Economies in Transition: Baltic Context', in *Proceedings of the Second Workshop on the Environmental Conventions and the Baltic States,* Pärnu, 27–8 April 1995, Tallinn: Stockholm Environment Institute.

Statistical Office of Estonia (1996), *Statistical Yearbook of Estonia 1996,* Tallinn: Statistical Office of Estonia.

UN ECE (1996), *Environmental Performance Review of Estonia,* Working paper, Geneva: UN ECE Economic and Social Council.

10. Latvia: Energy Imports, Eutrophication, and Forest Resources

Valdis Mežapuķe

10.1 Prospects for Economic Growth and Restructuring

The current environmental situation in Latvia is determined by the legacy of the Soviet era and by the present economic decline. The increased levels of pollution resulting from the industrialization drive under Soviet rule have been reduced since 1991 because of the sharp industrial decline. Consumption of primary energy resources is rather low, although energy intensity per unit GDP is high, and pollution levels are not very high, but there are several areas of the country where pollution is highly concentrated. Except for forests, which cover 44 per cent of the territory, and agricultural lands, Latvia's resource base is narrow, so most resources and raw materials must be imported. There is a dense network of rivers and streams in Latvia. The rivers discharge directly into the Baltic Sea or into the Gulf of Rīga and the Gulf of Finland.

The population of Latvia is 2.5 million, of which 69 per cent is urban and 31 per cent is rural. The average population density is 39 inhabitants per km^2. Nearly one third of the population is concentrated in the capital, Rīga.

During the period of Soviet occupation from 1940 until August 1991 Latvia experienced fast industrialization as well as implementation of the kolkhoz system in agriculture. There were high rates of economic growth, especially in the 1950s and 1960s, and like the other Baltic Soviet republics Latvia was among the most well-off areas in the Soviet Union with levels of production 10-20 per cent above the Soviet average (cf. Table 1.1). The industrialization brought about an influx of immigrant industrial workers from other parts of the Soviet Union, and the share of Latvians in the total population dropped from 83 per cent in 1945 to 52 per cent in 1989. The industrialization also entailed environmental problems. Investments in such infrastructural elements as sewage treatment and waste disposal systems were neglected. Significant damage to the environment was also caused by the Russian military forces, who took over approximately 100 000 hectares of Latvian land. A major source of ground pollution was the contamination of extensive territories with various chemicals, as well as motor and rocket fuel dumped by the Russian occupation forces (Environmental Protection Committee, 1992, p. 3).

Beginning in 1991, Latvia experienced a serious decline in GDP. In 1995 GDP had dropped to 51 per cent of its level in 1989 (cf. Table 1.3). The decline was caused by the systemic and structural changes which occurred as Latvia transferred from a Soviet-style command economy to a market economy based largely on the principle of private ownership, and the inevitable decline was most pronounced in industrial production. This has reduced pressures on the environment. Between 1990 and 1995 there were significant declines in non-household use of water and energy resources, in the amount of toxic waste, in the amount of non-household sewage, and in the use of pesticides and artificial fertilizers. However, there are three economic developments which are increasing the environmental pressure: wood cutting in the nation's forests has increased; this also applies to extraction of peat moss; and the number of vehicles in the country is growing.

It is generally expected that the economic decline in Latvia has now been halted and that gradual recovery and economic growth will resume in the future. Various estimates for GDP per capita exist; thus, according to the official exchange rate of the lats (LVL), in 1994 Latvia's per capita GDP was USD 1463 or some 5 per cent of GDP per capita in the USA (Central Statistical Bureau of Latvia, 1997a). Estimates using purchasing power parities yield higher figures (Guļāns, 1995, p. 17), and according to the figures in Tables 1.1 and 1.3 a reasonable estimate would be a current level of about 20 per cent of the US level taking the sharp GDP drop in recent years into account.

There are also different opinions concerning the time required to reach the production level of 1990. The forecasts which have been developed by the Ministry of Economic Affairs contain two developmental scenarios – the slow development scenario and the dynamic development scenario. The former scenario anticipates that GDP will begin to increase in 1996 and will maintain a growth rate of approximately 1 per cent per annum through the year 2000. The latter scenario, the implementation of which would require considerable local and foreign investment, anticipates an annual GDP growth rate of 3–5 per cent, beginning in 1997 (Ministry of Economic Affairs, 1996a, 107). A memorandum on Latvia's economic policies which was submitted to the International Monetary Fund suggests a feasible GDP increase of 2–3 per cent in 1996 (Ministry of Economic Affairs, 1996a), and it turned out to be 2.8 per cent. There are no official predictions concerning the structure of GDP by sector. It can be expected that the number of workers in agriculture will decline. The leading role in industry must be taken by those sectors which process and export local resources, which engage in production without requiring excessive energy consumption, and which make active use of Latvia's scientific potential.

Economic development in Latvia requires utilization of the developmental assets of the country. The human capital is at a fairly high level; a well-developed educational system was carried over from the Soviet period, but so also were attitudes concerning work and labour relations which necessitate psychological changes in order to meet the demands of a market economy where enterprises are based on private capital. The real capital base was also comparatively well-developed under Soviet rule, including infrastructure, three large freight harbours, major oil refineries and oil products pipelines, and a network of railways and highways. The natural capital consists mainly of forest resources, which could be more fully utilized by increasing cuttings to the point where they are equal to regrowth and by further developing the wood processing industry. It is of major importance to create legal and economic conditions for attracting foreign investment, and Latvia's top priority in foreign policy and foreign economic relations is to strengthen the ties with the European Union with full membership of the EU as the ultimate goal. A free trade agreement between Latvia and the EU took effect on 1 January 1995. On 27 October of the same year Latvia submitted an official application for membership. Along with economic and political considerations, Latvia hopes that joining the EU will help the country improve its environmental legislation and environmental protection plans on the basis of EU standards (Institute of Economics, 1995, p. 25).

10.2 Energy Consumption and Efficiency

Although there is some potential for discovering oil deposits in Latvia, there are currently no fossil fuel resources. Domestic energy resources consist of wood, peat and hydropower. Consumption of energy grew quickly in the 1970s and 1980s. Domestic power production has never met demand. In 1988 Latvia was able to supply 11.7 per cent of energy needs by domestic production, and in 1994 the share of local energy resources in total energy consumption reached 15.8 per cent. During the 1990s a significant decrease in the consumption of energy resources took place (Table 10.1) due to a general decline of living standards and industrial production and the rising prices of energy resources.

Primary energy consumption has declined by 47 per cent since 1990. Per capita consumption of primary energy in Latvia is about one third of the level in the Scandinavian countries, and in 1993 per capita consumption of electricity was approximately 15 per cent of Scandinavian consumption. Today Latvia has a one-sided fuel supply system. Natural gas and liquified gas, 80 per cent of oil products, including 100 per cent of heavy fuel oil, as well as most of the coal used is imported from CIS countries, mainly Russia. Often, this is fuel with low environmental standards and significant sulphur contents, in some cases up to 3 per cent. Diversification of fuel supply sources is considered to be one of the top priorities (Ministry of Economic Affairs, 1996b). In 1990s the relative shares of natural gas and heavy fuel oil have oscillated depending on variations of prices, but the general trend is that the relative share of natural gas has decreased from 28 per cent in 1990 to 22 per cent in 1995. The increasing use of the relatively less expensive heavy fuel oil is damaging to the environment. It is likely that the substitution of heavy fuel oil for natural gas, as well as increased use of peat and wood, will continue. This inevitably will lead to increasing emissions of sulphur, carcinogens and dust, unless power stations are equipped with the necessary anti-pollution equipment (Ministry of the Environment, 1995, p. 5). Household energy consumption consists largely of district heating and natural gas. The industrial sector uses heat, natural gas, oil and electricity. The agricultural and transportation networks mostly use petroleum products. Latvia uses little coal, only 9 per cent of total consumption, unlike most Eastern European countries, and as a result has relatively clean air. Oil products constitute 55 per cent and electricity 10 per cent of energy consumption.

Table 10.1   Energy consumption in Latvia, 1990–96

	1990	1991	1992	1993	1994	1995	1996
Energy use (kTOE)	9010	7650	6180	5206	4815	-	-
per capita (TOE)	3.37	2.87	2.33	2.00	1.88	-	-
per unit GDP	3.05	2.89	3.59	3.55	3.26	-	-
Electricity use (GWh)	9044	8708	6899	5250	4975	4963	4895
Industry	3883	3695	2853	2031	2020	2066	2146
Agriculture	1680	1548	1107	605	304	221	176
Transportation	390	350	294	222	231	235	178
Households	1297	1299	1184	863	950	1161	1093
Other uses	1794	1816	1461	1529	1470	1280	1302

Notes: Energy consumption per unit GDP is measured in KOE (kilograms of oil equivalent) per 1000 LVL; GDP was calculated in 1993 prices; at the end of 1993, the exchange rate for one USD was 0.548 LVL. 1 PJ = 23.9 kTOE (kilotons of oil equivalent); 1 GWh (1 million kWh) equals 86 TOE.
Sources: Ministry of Economic Affairs, 1996b, p. 9; Central Statistical Bureau of Latvia, 1997a, p. 229.

One of the main problems of Latvia's energy supply system is deficiencies in electricity generation capacity. In 1994 Latvia consumed 4975 GWh of electricity, which is 45 per cent less than in 1990 (cf. Table 10.1). Per capita electricity consumption in Latvia is lower than in any other Baltic or Scandinavian country. About 50 per cent of electric power demand is imported from Estonia, Lithuania and Russia. Development of the generating capacity so that the Latvian power system will be able to supply 85 per cent of demand by domestic production is formulated as another top priority. The Latvian generation system consists of three hydropower stations with a total capacity of 1500 MW on the Daugava river and two thermal power stations in Rīga with a capacity of 500 MW which are fuelled by heavy fuel oil or natural gas. There are a certain number of smaller stations scattered throughout Latvia. Electricity production by hydropower stations, which on average is 2730 GWh a year is naturally dependent on annual rainfall and therefore is not stable. Analysis of the consumption and production of electricity on a weekly basis shows that Latvia is able to satisfy its demand for a few weeks in spring only (Bataraga, 1994, p. 2).

According to the World Bank (1993, p. 111), per capita energy consumption in Latvia in 1990 was 3668 kilograms of oil equivalent, which is average by European standards but high in relation to GDP. Compared to 21 countries with climactic conditions similar to Latvia's the consumption of energy per capita in Latvia was about 35 per cent higher than expected on the basis of its GDP per capita. In the same World Bank (1993, p. 114) survey Latvia's energy consumption per unit GDP was calculated as 1.091 kilograms of oil equivalent per 1000 USD. Among the analysed countries, higher consumption was found in Bulgaria, Poland, the Czech Republic and Hungary, but consumption per unit GDP was lower in the Scandinavian countries. Estimates for energy consumption per unit GDP differ widely. According to another survey (Zēbergs et. al., 1992, p. 50), Latvia uses as much as four times more energy per unit GDP than the USA and six times more than Japan (cf. also the data offered in Tables 1.2 and 1.3). This is probably exaggerated, but energy efficiency is low in Latvia, and the major reasons for this are slow long-term technological progress, as well as an economy structured around high consumption of energy.

The current energy intensity in Latvia is higher than the levels in the Scandinavian countries according to the Ministry of Economic Affairs (1996b, p. 8). The slight increase in the country's energy intensity per unit GDP since 1991 (cf. Table 10.1) can largely be explained by the decline in GDP by nearly 50 per cent during this period. Certain kinds of energy consumption are not directly connected to production, notably energy consumption for heating, lighting and other common needs.

It is expected that due to structural changes in production and implementation of energy savings, the energy consumption level of 1990 will not be reached before the year 2010. According to the forecasts for energy consumption the energy intensity per unit GDP may decline by 18 per cent in 2010 as compared to the rate in 1994 (Ministry of Economic Affairs, 1996b, p. 36).

10.3 Exploitation of Domestic Resources

Latvia is not rich in natural resources. Most of the resources which are needed for the country's economy must be imported. An important domestic renewable resource is water for use in households and in production, and rivers play an important role in providing hydropower. Forest resources are also important, and timber and wood products are Latvia's leading export commodity. Other renewable resources include peat and fish. Latvia has exhaustible resources of minerals which are used directly or indirectly in construction. Areas of unspoilt nature could become an important resource for tourism. Of the total area of land, forests cover 44 per cent, bogs 10 per cent, and preserved territories 7 per cent or 441 thousand ha, including the Gauja Natural Park of 92 thousand ha and six nature reserves.

Table 10.2   Exploitation of natural resources in Latvia, 1990–96

	1990	1991	1992	1993	1994	1995	1996
Water consumption (million m³)	642	596	531	407	370	334	323
of which industrial use	226	193	158	103	167	161	158
Timber logging (thousand m³)	3800	4500	4000	4800	5730	6886	6764
of which state forests	2400	2500	3100	3800	4729	5298	4483
exports of round timber	-	-	-	1028	1950	-	-
exports of processed products	-	-	-	366	1200	-	-
Peat extraction (thousand tons)	-	-	-	400	647	522	552
used for fuel	-	-	-	312	435	300	356
agricultural use	-	-	-	78	202	198	163

Notes: In 1995 exports of round timber increased to 3240 thousand m³ and exports of processed forest products to 1537 thousand m³.
Sources: Central Statistical Bureau of Latvia, 1997a, pp. 184, 212, 220; Dienas Bizness, 15 March 1996, p. 18.

Latvia has had considerable experience with **hydropower**, which supplies nearly half of the country's electricity. The hydropower potential of the main river, the Daugava, is now fully exhausted. The total installed capacity of the Daugava Hydropower Plant cascade is about 1500 MW, and at present construction of new hydrotechnical buildings on the river is being considered by state programmes, also with a view to decreasing the threat of spring floods. The economically and environmentally profitable potential of the Latvian small rivers is estimated to be at most 8 MW, but the theoretical potential could be as much as 70 MW (Ministry of Economic Affairs, 1996b).

Currently 10 small hydropower plants with a total capacity of 2.5 MW are operating.

Some of the power stations, however, especially the Plavinas hydropower plant, were constructed with insufficient attention devoted to environmental issues. There was considerable damage to aquatic life and to the national historical heritage. Proposed hydroelectric projects at Daugavpils with a capacity of 300 MW and Jekabpils with a capacity of 160 MW were suspended, not only because of strong environmental opposition, but also because the limited amount of energy that would be produced did not justify the construction of the objects on economic grounds.

Still, given the major expenses which are involved in importing energy, new debates arose in 1996 concerning the possible construction of a power plant at Daugavpils with a lower raising of the Daugava river than was anticipated in the proposals for power plant construction developed in the 1980s. In 1996 a modernization and upgrading of the hydropower plants on the Daugava river was initiated. The benefits of the project will be an increased share of renewable energy and a reduced dependence on imported electricity.

The annual average run-off **water resources** of Latvian rivers amount to 35 milliard m^3, and the annually exploitable ground-water resources are estimated at 2.2 milliard m^3. The total water extraction is 1.7 per cent of the water resources. In 1994 477 million m^3 were extracted, a decrease from 712 million m^3 in 1990, and of this 216 million m^3 were extracted from ground water. Extraction declined further to 456 million m^3 in 1995 and 429 million m^3 in 1996, of which 195 and 181 million m^3 were extracted from ground water (Central Statistical Bureau of Latvia, 1997b, p. 54). Water consumption in 1994 amounted to 435 million m^3 (cf. Table 10.2). Of total water consumption 56 per cent was used in households, 16 per cent in industry, 7 per cent in energy production, 9 per cent in agriculture and 5 per cent in fishery. This pattern differs considerably from the European average where 53 per cent of water supply is used by industry, 25 per cent by agriculture and only 19 per cent by households (ECAT, 1996, p. 107). Household consumption of water is relatively high in Latvia, especially in the major cities, namely 550 litres per resident per day in Rīga, 334 litres in Daugavpils and 530 litres in Ventspils. Since 1991, as industrial production has decreased, industrial consumption of water has decreased correspondingly (cf. Table 10.2).

Approximately 95 per cent of the residents in Latvia's major cities, as well as 50 per cent of residents in smaller towns, use centralized drinking water systems which exploit both above-ground and subterranean water resources. Individual water supplies on farms and in small villages are usually obtained by means of shallow-bored wells. Until 1969, only underground sources were used for water supplies. Industrial development and the rapid increase in Latvia's urban population were the main reasons why lake and river water were eventually exploited as well. In the Rīga region, as well as in Liepaja, where the use of subterranean waters exceeds the natural renewability of the resource, depression funnels have occurred in the underground strata where water use is most intensive.

Latvia has adequate water resources to supply its population and its economic needs. The quality of Latvian drinking water, however, is inadequate, especially in centralized systems. Transboundary water pollution, eutrophication of water courses, degradation of water ecosystems, and low quality of drinking water are stated by the National Environment Policy Plan to be among the most important environmental problems in Latvia (Ministry of the Environment, 1995, p. 5).

Today **forests** cover 44 per cent of all Latvian land, a considerable increase over 1923, when forests covered only 25 per cent of the land. This increase took place mainly after 1945 concurrently with industrialization. Many family farms located in remote areas far from major roads were abandoned and not included in the kolkhoz system. The land was no longer meliorated and was left to turn into swamp and to become overgrown with brush and forest. This also happened to parts of the kolkhoz lands which were not cultivated with sufficient intensity (Boruks, 1995, pp. 349–50).

Coniferous trees make up 60 per cent of all trees, of which 40 per cent are pine and 20 per cent are spruce. Among deciduous trees, the most common is the birch which constitutes 28 per cent of the trees. Soft-leaf trees make up 39 per cent of all forest trees, while hard-leaf trees like oak and ash account for only 1 per cent of the trees (ECAT, 1996, p. 120). The total amount of potentially available wood in Latvia's forests is approximately 490 million m^3. The average annual growth in Latvia's forests is approximately 16.5 million m^3, and the permissible forest cutting rate for 1995 was 8.4 million m^3, but this rate was not, however, fully utilized in 1995 although cuttings increased by 21 per cent to 6.886 million m^3 as compared to 1994.

Of the cuttings in 1995, 69 per cent were exported, and today wood is the main Latvian export product. In 1995 the export value amounted to 360 million USD and in 1994 to 210 million USD or 26.4 per cent of the value of total exports. The main export countries are Sweden, the UK and Germany. Since 1992 rough timber exports have increased most rapidly, and Latvia is lacking a complete cycle in the wood processing sector, so that there is a low rate of utilization of harvested wood. Establishing a pulp factory in Latvia would advance the paper industry and could improve the whole wood processing industry.

Latvia's climate is appropriate for **peat** formation. Peat is a renewable resource, although renewability rates are very slow. The total amount of peat is estimated at approximately 11.3 billion m^3 or 1.7 milliard tons, of which 1.1 milliard tons is fuel peat. The total amount that can be technically utilized for fuel production is estimated at approximately 760 million tons including 40 per cent moisture content, and about 25 per cent of this is estimated as actually available for the energy sector. If peat is used sensibly, sustainability can be achieved. Currently this is the case. The estimated annual increase in peat reserves is about one million tons, well above the current, rapidly increasing, extraction rate at 621 thousand tons in 1994 (cf. Table 10.2). Most of the fuel peat was used by the CHP–1 plant in Rīga owned by Latvenergo, which implies considerable transport expenditures.

Another renewable resource is **fish resources** in the Baltic Sea, more than 10 per cent of which are located in Latvia's economic zone. The fishing quota in Latvian waters in 1994 was 130 000 tons. The fishing of herring, sprat, cod and salmon in the Baltic Sea is regulated by the International Baltic Sea Fishing Commission which was established under the auspices of the Gdansk Convention. Each country is assigned a quota for each type of fish. With respect to other species of fish in Latvia's waters, limits are set out by Latvia's own national regulations. In 1994, the total catch in the Latvian waters of the Baltic Sea was 46 000 tons or 35 per cent of the quota.

Latvia is fairly well supplied with **mineral resources** which are directly or indirectly needed for construction. Over the last five years, mining of useful resources has declined, and the current level is at only 33 per cent of the level in 1991. In 1994, however, the mining of some resources including limestone, gypsum and clay began to increase again.

In the not so distant future **new resources** may become available in Latvia, namely oil, wind power, geothermal energy resources, industrial mineral waters, iron ore and natural underground gas storage facilities. According to geological investigations there are fairly good prospects for discovering oil deposits in the Latvian part of the continental shelf of the Baltic Sea, probably of the magnitude of 125 million tons of oil. It is also possible that there are small oil deposits in south-western Latvia. If the licence agreement, signed in 1995 between the Latvian government and the American oil companies AMOCO and and the Swedish company OPAB, were to be departed from, it has been estimated that Latvia's income from oil extraction could be 1.6 – 1.8 milliard USD in a period of 20–25 years. According to the agreement, oil investigation and extraction can be started only after the determination of a boundary between Latvia and Lithuania in the Baltic Sea, and a boundary has not yet been accepted after the regaining of independence.

In the south-western regions of Latvia, industrial mineral waters have been found. These have high levels of bromine and lithium and could be used for industrial purposes. Magnetite iron ore has been found in central Latvia. The ore is located at a considerable depth, up to one kilometre underground, but it is of very good quality.

Experiments with wind power have started. The Ainazi wind park, with a capacity of 2.600 kW and an expected annual production of 2.5 million kWh, was developed as a joint stock company in 1995 with significant assistance from the German government and the company Preussen Elektra.

There are several subterranean sources of geothermal waters in Latvia which in the future could be used for heating and air conditioning. The reserves of thermal water, situated in the central and south-western part of Latvia, are estimated to be 200 billion m³. At present the area is being geologically prospected, and potential consumers are sought. A pilot demonstration station is also planned (Eikmanis, 1994).

Another underground resource with future development potential are the unique geological formations which provide possibilities for creating new natural gas storage facilities. The potential could be as high as 50–100 milliard m³, of which 2.1 milliard m³ are active in the existing Incukalns storage. This is a tremendous natural resource which would allow Latvia to participate in long-term European large-scale projects of interstate pipelines. For oil and oil products, export facilities exist at the Ventspils port terminal on the Baltic Sea with an estimated capacity of 33.5 million tons annually; in 1995 18 million tons of oil and oil products were transferred, and it would be possible for Latvia to increase her participation in the international oil transport system from Russia to Western Europe.

10.4 Environmental Effects

Most environmental problems in Latvia are concentrated in what is known as hot spots like major industrial centres, transportation networks, and territories previously occupied by the Russian armed forces. Some problems are found throughout the country, notably eutrophication and degradation of water ecosystems, transboundary movements of pollution, and accumulations of household and industrial waste. On the other hand, Latvia can be proud of its relatively unspoilt nature, its vast tracts of forest lands, its untouched sea shores and its relatively low level of overall pollution.

In the 1990s mobile transport has become the main source of **air pollution** causing approximately 65–70 per cent of total emissions. Emissions from vehicles are calculated indirectly by registering fuel consumption or travelled distances and using emission factors from automobiles, ships, aeroplanes and locomotives. It must be noted that in Latvia's case because of smuggling and black market operations, actual fuel consumption is higher than is reflected in the official data. In 1992 pollution from vehicles was calculated at 51 400 tons, of which nitrogen oxides contributed 53 per cent, hydrocarbons 44 per cent and sulphur dioxide 3 per cent. The environmental impact from transport is recognized as one of worst environmental problems. Presently the transport infrastructure and the quality of vehicles do not correspond to environmental norms approved in the advanced industrial countries (Ministry of the Environment, 1995).

Annual emissions from stationary sources of pollution reached a total level of 100 700 tons in 1994, of which sulphur dioxide contributed 52 per cent, carbon oxides 25 per cent, nitrogen oxides 10 percent and particles 13 per cent. Other pollutants contributed an additional 3100 tons. During the 1980s, while economic growth was still taking place although at reduced rates, emissions from stationary sources decreased because of the introduction of new abatement technologies and increased use of natural gas. In the 1990s noxious emissions have been significantly reduced due to economic depression and decreased fuel consumption without taking any special measures. The decline has been particularly pronounced for industrial pollution (cf. Table 10.3). Pollution has decreased less than production, and there is a trend towards increasing emissions of sulphur and particles because heating systems are using more heavy fuel and liquid heating fuel like peat instead of natural gas. Small and medium-sized boiler houses contribute a disproportionately large share of total emissions.

As the number of automobiles in Latvia increases, and as heavy fuel is substituted for natural gas, emissions of sulphur and nitrogen oxides will continue to increase. This may cause Latvia to violate international agreements. Emissions of sulphur dioxide per capita were 20 kg in 1994. Compared to other Eastern European countries where sulphur abatement equipment is not used, this is a low level, but compared to Western Europe it is about average (cf. Tables 1.2 and 1.3). In Switzerland emissions were 9 kg per capita, and in the western parts of Germany 40 kg per capita (ECAT, 1996, p. 149).

Table 10.3 Air pollution from stationary sources in Latvia, 1991–96

	1991	1992	1993	1994	1995	1996
Total emissions (1000 tons)						
Sulphur oxide (SO_2)	58.5	38.3	43.7	52.2	38.1	44.9
Nitrogen oxide (NO_x)	14.6	10.4	8.7	10.3	7.9	8.7
Carbon monoxide (CO)	32.1	23.2	20.9	24.9	23.5	23.8
Particles	27.6	14.0	9.4	13.3	12.5	11.8
Industrial sources (per cent)						
Sulphur oxide (SO_2)	8	-	3	2	-	-
Nitrogen oxide (NO_x)	31	-	23	22	-	-
Carbon monoxide (CO)	28	-	11	12	-	-
Particles	70	-	39	49	-	-

Notes: Besides industrial sources, stationary polluters include power plants and heat boilers; among these, plants owned by Latvenergo contribute much less carbon monoxide and particles than smaller boilers.
Sources: Ministry of the Environment, 1996; Central Statistical Bureau of Latvia, 1997b, p 34.

The total amount of emissions of **greenhouse gases** in 1990 was 27 632 Gg CO_2 equivalent, and the main components were 83 per cent CO_2, 14 per cent CH_4 and 3 per cent N_2O. Other components included NO_2, CO and volatile organic compounds. The major source of CO_2 is the energy sector which contributes 98 per cent. From 1990 to 1994 the amount of CO_2 emissions from stationary sources decreased from 17 to 12.5 million tons. Because 44 per cent of Latvia's territory is covered by forests, the accumulation of CO_2 in the atmosphere was estimated be about 50 per cent of total emissions in 1990. Of the emissions of CH_4, 75 per cent originate from livestock farming, while nearly 25 per cent are emitted by waste storage facilities and a small amount is emitted by the energy sector. The major source of N_2O emissions is the use of mineral fertilizers in agriculture; because the use of such fertilizers has declined over the last four years, N_2O emissions have also been reduced. The major source of other gases is vehicular traffic (ECAT, 1996, p. 153).

Since 1990 **water pollution** has decreased because of reductions in overall volumes of sewage water and improved purification methods. Emissions of polluted sewage waters declined by 27 per cent between 1990 and 1994, and there was a 70 per cent reduction in biologically degradable substances, a 54 per cent reduction in phosphorous compounds, and a 30 per cent reduction in nitrogen compounds (ECAT, 1996, p. 160).

In 1994, 402 million m^3 of sewage water were discharged into Latvia's rivers. Of this volume, 30 per cent could be rated as relatively pure, 60 per cent was purified but still contained certain amounts of pollution, while 10 per cent was not purified at all. In 1996 the total amount dropped to 331 m^3, and purification improved, so that 33 per cent was relatively pure, 58 per cent was partly purified, and 9 per cent not treated (Central Statistical Bureau of Latvia, 1997b, p. 54). Along with the sewage waters, Latvia's water reservoirs received 12 000 tons of biologically degradable substances, 554 tons of phosphorous compounds, and 3200 tons of nitrogen compounds.

Most sewage waters, 216 million m^3, come from household use. Of these waters, 10 per cent are relatively pure, 78 per cent undergo purification, and 12 per cent are not purified at all. The second largest emitter of sewage waters is industry with 72 million m^3, of which 49 per cent is relatively pure, 50 per cent partly purified, and 1 per cent without purification.

The biological purification systems, which are used to clean communal waste water, are in many cases used to treat industrial waste water as well. This increases the risk of inflow of illegally dumped toxic materials, which could halt the operation of purification systems for a considerable period of time. Chemical monitoring and early warning systems are needed to avert this possibility.

Since 1990 some types of **sea pollution** have also declined. Despite the fact that the use of mineral fertilizers in Latvian agriculture has declined considerably, the extensive inflow of nutrients into the Bay of Rīga over the last decade, as well as the accompanying inflow of large amounts of phosphorous, have left the bay as one of the most eutrophic systems in the Baltic Sea. The contents of nitrogen and phosphorus in the Baltic Sea have increased by four to eight times since the turn of the century. The main source of phosphorous in Latvia's rivers is sewage water, while the main source of nitrogen is agriculture. Compared to annual averages in the 1980s, the inflow of nitrates into the Bay of Rīga has decreased by 34 per cent in 1991–94, the inflow of ammonium has decreased by 33 per cent, and the inflow of phosphates has decreased by 19 per cent (ECAT, 1996, p. 160). Eutrophication has been declared the primary environmental problem in Latvia. The target of the government's environmental policy is a 50 per cent reduction of nitrogen inflows from specific sources by the year 2010 (Ministry of the Environment, 1995).

In 1994 Latvia joined the Helsinki convention on the environmental protection of the Baltic Sea. In 1990 Latvia accounted for 7 per cent of the fresh water inflow into the Baltic Sea and for 17 per cent of the total nitrogen and 5 per cent of the total phosphorous inflow. Much of this is, however, transboundary pollution, because 53 per cent of the water which flows into the Baltic sea is transit water. Although many environmental problems in Latvia are local in nature, transboundary aspects of pollution are nevertheless pronounced. The amount of sulphur and nitrogen oxide which was brought into Latvia in 1992, for example, was four times higher than the domestically produced amounts of these pollutants. It is also true, however, that 80 per cent of the sulphur oxides and 90 per cent of the nitrogen oxides which are emitted into the air in Latvia end up in neighbouring countries and in the Baltic Sea (cf. Tables 15.1 and 15.2). Among major foreign industrial sites situated near Latvia causing significant transboundary pollution are the Mazeiki oil processing plant as well as the Naujoji Akmens cement plants in Lithuania.

Latvia's largest rivers have their source in other countries, and 53 per cent of the discharge which enters the Baltic Sea from Latvia originates outside the country. This means that pollution which occurs in neighbouring countries is often transported through Latvia. The largest transboundary river systems in Latvia are the Daugava, the Lielupe and the Venta. The share of the basins of these rivers which are located in Latvia are 29 per cent, 50 per cent and 50 per cent, respectively. The sources of the Daugava are found in Russia, but the most heavy pollution problems originate when the river passes through Belarus. This is the segment of the river which is most susceptible to single-source pollution, because there are many large factories along the river in Belarus, including large chemical plants. In November 1990 an accident in the Novopolock chemical factory caused an inflow of cyanide into the Daugava, and extensive fish kills occurred in the 300 km of the Daugava between the Latvian-Belarussian border and the town of Koknese; water supplies from the Daugava were cut off for seven days along the entire course of the river. From Lithuania's oil processing plants, other industrial enterprises and small-town sewage systems pollution flows into the Venta and Lielupe river basins.

10.5 Resources and Environmental Costs as Constraints of Growth

Although there are numerous environmental protection problems in Latvia, government financing for environmental protection is not very high because of the country's overwhelming current economic tasks and limited economic capabilities. In 1994, only 32.5 million lats or 1.7 per cent of GDP were spent on environmental protection. This corresponds to a per capita rate of 12.7 lats or 23.2 USD. In 1996 expenditures declined further to 13.8 million lats, that is 0.5 per cent of GDP or 10.0 USD per capita (Central Statistical Bureau of Latvia, 1997b, p.7).

There are no exact quantitative data currently at our disposal which could indicate the amount of expenditure that are needed to solve Latvia's largest and most urgent problems in the areas of environmental protection, economy of resources, and economic restructuring. It is clear that the amount will be very large and that efficient projects will require considerable amounts of time. The most important environmental protection needs in Latvia in the near future include replacement of out-dated industrial technologies with modern environmentally efficient and energy-saving equipment, installation of sewage purification plants in Latvia's larger cities, installation of air pollution abatement equipment in major industrial enterprises, radical reconstruction of the storage and processing systems for household and industrial waste, and cleaning of heavily polluted territories.

One of the most severe problems facing the Latvian economy, which has a direct effect on environmental protection, is the large amount of energy resources which must be imported, including oil, oil products, natural gas, coal and electricity. In 1995 energy imports amounted to a total value of 199.8 million lats or 378.4 million USD and constituted 21.6 per cent of all imports. In order to reduce the amount of energy imports it is required to carry out major investment projects such as implementation of energy-saving technologies, broad use of alternative energy resources, and construction of new and efficient electric plants.

The successful implementation of such projects will improve the environmental situation in Latvia as well as her economic prospects. On the other hand it will require huge amounts of investment finance. It has been estimated that the modernization and expansion of the country's electricity generating systems alone will, until the year 2010, require an investment of at least 532 million lats, corresponding to about 1 milliard USD. By way of comparison, one can note that Latvia's total GDP in 1995 was 2361 million lats at current prices.

REFERENCES

Bataraga, A. (1994), 'The Energy Restructuring Programme of Latvia', Paper presented at the World Bank conference on *Public Investment Priorities in Latvia*, Paris 19 May 1994, Rīga: Ministry of Economic Affairs.

Boruks, A. (1995), *Farmers, Land and Farming in Latvia* (in Latvian), Rīga: Grāmatvedis.

Central Statistical Bureau of Latvia (1997), *Statistical Yearbook of Latvia 1997* (in Latvian), Rīga: Central Statistical Bureau of Latvia.(a).

Central Statistical Bureau of Latvia (1997), *Indicators of Environmental Protection in Latvia 1996* (in Latvian), Rīga: Central Statistical Bureau of Latvia.(b).

ECAT, Environmental Consultation and Monitoring Centre (1996), *Environmental Survey of Latvia* (in Latvian), Rīga: ECAT.

Eikmanis, E. (1994), 'Perspectives for Geothermal Energy' (in Latvian), *EnerĢētikas Vēstnesis*, (56).

Environmental Protection Committee (1992), *National Report of Latvia to UNCED*, Rīga: Environmental Protection Committee.

Guļāns, P. (1995), 'Latvia Against the Background of the Global Economy' (in Latvian), pp. 13–21 in *Yearbook of the Institute of Economics*, Rīga: Institute of Economics, Latvian Academy of Sciences.

Institute of Economics (1995), *The Economic Situation and the Prospects for Latvia*, Rīga: Latvian Academy of Sciences.

Ministry of Economic Affairs (1996a), *Report on the Development of the Latvian Economy* (in Latvian), Rīga: Ministry of Economic Affairs.

Ministry of Economic Affairs (1996b), *The National Programme of Development of Power Engineering, Draft* (in Latvian), Rīga: Ministry of Energy.

Ministry of the Environment (1995), 'An Environmental Protection Policy for Latvia' (in Latvian), *Latvijas Vēstnesis*, 11 May 1995, Rīga: Ministry of the Environment.

Ministry of the Environment (1996), *Information about Noxious Emissions in Latvia*, Rīga: Ministry of the Environment.

World Bank (1993), *Latvia: The Transition to a Market Economy*, Washington, D.C.: The World Bank.

Zēbergs, V., N. Zeltiņš and I. Stuits (1992), 'Power Engineering in the Baltic States: The Current State and the Most Urgent Tasks' (in Latvian), pp. 49–54 in *Proceedings of the Latvian Academy of Sciences*, Part B 1992/3, Rīga: Latvian Academy of Sciences.

11. Latvia: The Environmental Policy Plan, Resources, and Public Awareness

Raimonds Ernšteins and Ivars Kudreņickis

11.1 The Environmental Policy Plan and the International Framework

The National Environmental Policy Plan for Latvia, confirmed by government in May 1995, was the result of the interaction of a variety of forces and considerations, including popular environmental movements, co-operation among countries bordering the Baltic Sea, environmental standards in the European Union, the European environmental co-operation conferences in Dobřís in 1991, in Lucerne in 1993 and in Sofia in 1995, the UN Conference for Environment and Development in Rio de Janeiro in 1992, as well as experience from the first seven years of national environmental protection administration and the centuries-long cultural identity in Latvia. The plan was formulated with the assistance of the ministries of the environment of the Netherlands and of Sweden. It represents an attempt to integrate environmental policy into general development and regional policies and to mobilize public participation and support as well as various sources of finance for its realization. For successful implementation of environmental policy three main prerequisites are emphasized, namely a properly functioning information system, environmental policy institutions and organizations, and public awareness. A process of necessary developments is now being actively pursued, but in relation to public environmental awareness policies are in at a problem formulation stage.

Although quality of the environment in Latvia in general could be recognized as high – and even improving due to the 49 per cent production decline from 1989 to 1995 (cf. Table 1.3) – as compared to Western Europe, there are a number of acute environmental problems, first of all in particularly polluted urban areas and sites of former Soviet military bases. Four core problem areas were identified in the national plan: water and waste water treatment; solid and hazardous waste management; sustainable resource use and protection policies; and harmonization with EU environmental policies.

Methods for practical implementation and particular solutions for the priority problems are elaborated in some detail in the Environmental Protection Action Programme worked out during 1995–97 (Ministry of the Environment, 1997). The action programme can be considered as a kind of guidebook for developing sub-programmes and practical projects. Generally, it requires a broadening of the scope of environmental policy, all aspects of which should be subject to negotiations and to co-operation, first of all with other governmental institutions and local authorities in order to incorporate the action programme within all types of public policy, including major development programmes from 1994 and 1995 for the national economy, government investments, energy, transportation, forestry, agriculture and industry. An Environmental Protection Fund was established in 1996 financed by environmental taxes and fines. Environmental policy should support the regional development policy which aims at providing equal conditions for life, work and environmental quality and maintaining the cultural identity of regions by means of a state regional development fund, private investment stimulation and discounts for taxes.

Concerning two of the four core problem areas – water and waste water treatment and solid and hazardous waste management – two sectorial environmental action programmes have been worked out in collaboration with international experts, and implementation is now going on.

International co-operation and compliance with and implementation of the various international agreements signed by the Latvian government are essential elements in the national plan and the action programme. Thus in relation to the UN Framework Convention on Climate Change, which was ratified in February 1995, a national report from Latvia was issued in May 1996 describing basic facts and general policies, particularly in energy and transport sectors. A report on the phasing out of ozone depleting substances under the Montreal protocol was prepared in 1995 and revised in 1997.

New laws originating from the national plan and the action programme as well as existing laws on environmental protection are actively harmonized with corresponding EU laws according to the recent White Paper issued by the EU concerning associated countries. This is coordinated and supervised by the Special Integration Bureau of the Cabinet of Ministers.

International co-ordination also takes place in the Baltic Environmental Forum established in Rīga with financial support from the EU in order to enable the three Baltic States to co-ordinate information, expertise and experience exchange in the field of environmental protection according to the realization of co-operation development agreed by the three governments on 21 July 1995. The Baltic Environmental Forum is part of the Baltic States Regional Environmental Development Project and acts as a facilitator for the implementation of national environmental strategies and action programmes.

It organizes seminars, courses and evaluations for encouraging contacts and co-operation between the Baltic neighbours. Important policy initiatives were formulated and supported by the heads of government from the Baltic Sea Region countries in autumn 1996 when the document 'Baltic 21' as an agenda for Baltic Sea Region sustainable development was signed.

11.2 Energy Policy Developments

The main aims of energy policy in Latvia are to increase energy efficiency which will allow a reduction in the massive dependence upon energy imports, which in 1996 supplied 77 per cent of total primary energy consumption, and to reduce pollution from energy production. It is also considered necessary to increase the share of domestic power generation from the current 50 per cent of electricity demand to about 85 per cent, and this is part of the power supply planning within the 'Baltic Ring' project (Government of Latvia, 1997). Increased use of wood and peat will be the main way to increase domestic energy resources, as the potential for increasing hydropower generation is limited. The specific tasks for energy policy include a conversion of small and medium-sized district heating plants to local fuel, which has economic as well as environmental benefits.

The first inventory of air pollution from stationary sources was done in 1980–82. Emissions decreased in the 1980s because of the introduction of technologies aimed at decreasing the emissions of solid particles and nitrogen oxides and because of increased use of gas. In the 1990s noxious emissions have decreased significantly although no special measures were taken. It happened concurrently with the decline in energy consumption (cf. Table 10.1) caused by the 49 per cent decline in production between 1989 and 1995 and by the sharp increase in energy prices (cf. Table 11.1). Due to relative price changes the share of natural gas in total consumption has decreased from 28 per cent in 1990 to 22 per cent in 1995. It has been replaced by Russian heavy fuel oil containing up to 3 per cent of sulphur used in dual-fuel heat-boiler plants and heat-power co-generation plants (Ministry of the Environment, 1995a).

The energy sector is subject to **regulation** as described in the law on regulation of entrepreneurship in the energy sector adopted in September 1995. It defines the energy producers' duties and rights presuming a natural monopoly and is aimed at protecting the interests of the energy users, stimulating efficiency in production and consumption and separating the control functions of the state from the commercial activities of enterprises. An Energy Supply Regulation Board was established having among its functions licensing of energy suppliers, promoting efficient and rational activities of energy suppliers, and promoting economic use of the energy supplied to consumers.

The Board is responsible for regulating **energy tariffs**. It works out methods for tariffs calculation and confirms the tariffs of energy suppliers. The latter function is also delegated to local governments. Energy prices have moved towards world market prices already, and government policy as updated in 1996 (Ministry of Economic Affairs, 1996) is to promote further the development towards world market prices and competition. Any limitations concerning prices should arise from environmental and supply reliability considerations, and tariffs for heating, power and natural gas should be cost-based. Lower tariffs will be offered to large consumers, and protection of low income consumers should be obtained by social assistance programmes. Generally subsidies have been abandoned by now. However, certain economic incentives, namely favourable power purchasing tariffs up to two times the normal tariff, are offered to small hydro and wind energy producers with a capacity of less than 2 MW. Similar preferential tariffs also apply to heat-power co-generation plants with a capacity of less than 12 MW established before June 1997, but this programme is now subject to intense debate.

Table 11.1 Energy prices in Latvia, 1990–95

Lats per GJ	1990	1993	1994	1995	1995	in actual units
Electricity	.035	5.5	5.6	6.7	0.024	lats per kWh
Gasoline	-	4.6	4.9	5.7	5.7	lats per GJ
Diesel	-	2.8	3.3	3.5	3.5	lats per GJ
Heating	.016	2.8	2.9	3.3	14.5	lats per Gcal
Natural gas	.003	1.9	1.6	1.6	64	lats per 1000 m^3
Heavy fuel oil	.003	1.1	1.1	1.2–1.6	50–65	lats per ton
Coal	.005	0.9	1.4–1.6	1.2–1.8	30–45	lats per ton
Peat	.007	1.1	1.1–2.1	1.1–1.6	10–15	lats per ton
Wood	.004	0.4	0.4	0.5–0.6	6–8	lats per m^3

Notes: Prices are quoted exclusive of VAT. The 1995 price for natural gas applies to households only; large consumers pay 60 lats per ton. The tariff for electricity is for residental consumers; large consumers enjoy a discount, in 1994 amounting to 55 per cent. The figures are comparable to those of Table 9.1, as one GJ equals 0.278 MWh; thus if 1 lats equals 1.81 USD or 1.44 ECU, the price of electricity in USD per MWh becomes 36.1, close to the Estonian price in Table 9.1; the price of natural gas becomes 10.7 USD per MWh or lower than the Estonian price of 15.7.
Sources: Ministry of Economic Affairs, 1996; Harne, 1996, p. 41.

Pollution from energy production will also be regulated by economic means, and a law on natural resources tax from 1995 envisages taxes on air polluting emissions depending on the toxic consequences caused by them, and also on the extraction of domestic energy; thus the tax on exploitation of peat is 0.23 USD per ton. At present there are no special taxes on sulphur or carbon content in the fuel consumed in Latvia. Reduction of the amount of pollutant emissions and residues will be carried out gradually taking into account the existing technological level of energy utilities and the actual economical possibilities, and a socially acceptable tax on energy use will be introduced in order to promote consumption efficiency and improvement of the environment.

The **ownership** structure in the energy sector is currently dominated by large, mainly state owned joint-stock companies. The electricity producing company Latvenergo as well as Latvian Gas and Ventspils Oil enjoy monopolies in their respective business areas, but they are included in the list of enterprises to be privatized. During 1997 the shares of Latvian Gas were partly privatized by strategic investors, namely the German Ruhrgas-Preussen Electra consortium and by the Russian Gazprom. Domestic oil products and coal markets have now been liberalized. Privatization is intended to improve the efficiency of energy utilities by creating competition and by attracting private capital. However, the efficiency of energy utilities will be subject to control both during the privatization process and after its completion.

Modernization of the energy sector requires substantial **investment** expenditure. In 1994–95 a number of projects have been initiated in co-operation with foreign experts supported by foreign assistance. A wood harvesting project, an energy conservation awareness campaign and a rehabilitation project for the Daugava Cascade Hydropower System are all supported by the EBRD. Grants from the Swedish government have been received for the rehabilitation of district heating systems in Rīga and Jelgava. Projects for local district heating boiler conversion are supported by the Swedish and the Danish government, and US AID and US TDA support a regional electricity master plan as well as elaboration of a dispatching system for the Baltic countries. The Latvian government actively promotes international co-operation on energy. Latvia has signed the European Energy Charter on 17 December 1994 and confirmed it by law in September 1995.

Latvia's Public Investment Programme (Latvian Energy Agency, 1996) for the energy sector envisages total investments for the years 1995–97 of 200 million USD, of which 8 million USD will come from the budget, 150 million USD from foreign loans, and 45 million USD from other sources. Thus, in 1996 an agreement between the EBRD and the Ministry of Finance provided a credit of 76 million USD for reconstruction of the Daugava river hydropower plant operated by Latvenergo.

11.3 Policies Concerning Domestic Resources

In Latvia the main domestic natural resource is the forests. Forest resources constitute about 25 per cent of total exports, and the share is increasing (cf. Table 10.2). Other resources like clay, sand, gravel, gypsum and limestone are important for domestic use. Increased use of the domestic fuel resources, namely fuel wood and peat, is very important both from an economic and an ecological perspective and is one of the government policy priorities for the energy sector.

As part of the economic transition, **ownership** of natural resources will change from command and control state ownership to the kind that existed in Latvia before its occupation by the USSR in 1940. However, the law on protected nature areas adopted in 1993 states that property rights cannot be restored to lands included in the list of particularly protected nature areas. They can be state property only. Protected areas, which have not been included in the list, may be the property of local governments, persons or legal entities, provided that they observe the rules on the protection and use of the areas according to the environmental policy plan (Cimdiņš, 1995).

Land reform gives rise to difficult problems of liability concerning past environmental damage. The problem is to distribute the responsibility to pay for cleaning up past damage, and an important case is the polluted areas left by the Soviet army after the withdrawal of the armed forces from Latvia. If the former owner's rights to the polluted area are restored, he will be responsible for its cleaning up, but for obvious reasons will normally be reluctant to accept this responsibility. One possibility would be that local governments assume the responsibility for cleaning up areas left by the Soviet military, but they are very short of financial resources.

Ownership of **forest resources** is a mixture of private and public ownership. According to official statistics 6.9 million m^3 were cut in 1995, of which 5.3 million m^3 were harvested in state forests and 1.6 million m^3 in private forests. The permissible cutting rate, estimated at 8.4 million m^3 for 1995, was fully utilized in state forests but not in private forests. However, forest experts claim that official statistics are incomplete and real harvesting larger: at least 7.5 million m^3. The average stump price in Latvia in 1995 was 3270 USD per thousand m^3, but large differences – up to a factor of four – are found among different regions. The 50 largest forest companies harvested 74 per cent of the total and the remaining 283 companies only 26 per cent. It is evident that Latvia today has a large number of small companies, particularly in state forests, which have no long-term economic viability.

At present wood as a fuel is predominantly used in the household sector and in small and medium-sized district heating boiler houses in rural areas. In 1995 2.36 million m^3 of fuel wood was produced. The potential stock of fuel wood in Latvia, corresponding to the currrent permissible cutting rate, is estimated at an annual 3.6 million m^3.

An environmental impact assessment concerning increased use of domestic peat and wood resources for energy production concluded that this would not only be possible, especially in small and medium-sized district heating plants, but that it would entail beneficial consequences for trade, employment and local enterpreneurship, and for fuel supply reliability. The environmental impact could become favourable as well provided that the government implements a number of measures for monitoring and decreasing environmental impact upon flora and fauna. Although investments in fuel handling and boilers will be higher than in the corresponding fossil fuel facilities, these expenditures are only slightly higher than those required for introducing conventional technology, since most existing plants are old and obsolete and have to be replaced in the near future. An alternative, namely extensive use of fuel wood only, without using domestic peat, would cause too extensive cutting of forests for fuel production at relevant places. A balanced development was recommended, taking into account both economic and environmental aspects, namely a combined expansion of domestic wood and peat fuel use as well as increased consumption of natural gas. Considering the comparatively high price of natural gas, it was recommended to expand the use of natural gas in the largest cities of Latvia where air pollution problems are concentrated (Ozoliņš, 1994).

As a means of regulating the exploitation of domestic resources, **taxation** is expected to assume an increasingly important role. The first law on natural resource taxes was passed in 1990 before Latvia regained independence, and it was amended in 1996. Having the same general objective as the first law – to limit pollution and uneconomic use of natural resources and to collect funds for financing environmental protection activities – the new law states two additional important objectives, namely to prevent production and trade of products harmful for the environment and to support a strategy for sustainable development of the national economy. The concept of natural resources has been broadened to include not only direct natural resources extraction and discharge of polluting substances into the environment, but also consumption of products, including packaging, harmful for the environment.

Revenues from resource taxes are used only for activities and projects which are directly related to environmental protection. Until June 1997 basic tax rate revenues for natural resource use and for environmental pollution were distributed between three public authorities; the State Environmental Protection Fund received 30 per cent, district governments 30 per cent, and municipal governments 40 per cent. From June 1997 this scheme was changed, so that the Environmental Fund receives 40 per cent and municipal governments 60 per cent. In the case of so-called product changes the full revenue accrues to the Environmental Fund. If the natural resource use or release of environment pollutants exceeds permissible limits additional rates up to three times the basic rate apply. These additional tax rates as well as the tax payments for trade or import of harmful products and packaging and fines and delay payments are all paid into the Environmental Fund. Tax relief can be obtained by introducing technology improvements or environment protection activities, recycling of materials and utilization of waste materials.

The principles of the new law have yet to be implemented. By 1997 tax rates are still low. It is remarkable that there are no tax rates included in the law directly depending on sulphur and carbon content in fossil fuels. Such tax rates in relation to sulphur contents were proposed but rejected by Parliament because of economic considerations, and heat boilers and equipment in individual households are not subject to taxation. Examples of 1996 tax rates on emissions of air pollutants classified according to toxicity are as follows: 5.2 USD per ton of non-hazardous particles; 7.8 USD per ton of average hazardous substances including CO; 17.3 USD per ton of hazardous substances like SO_2 and NO_x; and 1400 USD per ton of heavy metals and their compounds. Currently these rates are paid only by industry and energy producing enterprises. It can be concluded that in the period from 1991 to 1995 the law has had mainly educational effects, although it has also provided some finance for environmental protection measures.

11.4 Trends in Environmental Policy

The current state of environmental policy is the outcome of several influences, including a long historical and cultural interaction with nature, the relatively late opportunity for organizing a national environmental administration, and the subsequent urgency of policy initiatives as part of the economic transition. Until the Soviet occupation in 1940 environmental policies followed much the same pattern as in the other European countries. In 1912 the first nature reserve, Moricsala, was established. The Soviet strategy of rapid industrialization, large-scale agriculture and uncontrolled urbanization and immigration was more harmful to the environment than other economic development strategies. However, following the passing of a law on nature protection in 1968 the area of protected areas expanded and now includes about 7 per cent of the territory. Also the policy of extensive agriculture contributed to extending the forest areas which now cover 44 per cent of the territory as compared to 25 per cent in 1923.

Gradually other elements of environmental policy were added, and laws were adopted on water utilization in 1972, on underground resources in 1976, and on air pollution in 1981, all completely based on command and control instruments. Supported by continued public pressure which combined environmental and national aspects, the State Committee for Nature Protection was established in 1988 under the auspices of the Supreme Council. In 1993 the environmental administration was further strengthened and unified by the establishment of the Ministry for Environmental Protection and Regional Development (1993), which became the driving force behind the National Environmental Policy Plan of 1995 (Ministry of the Environment, 1995a).

Environmental and resource policy tasks for short-term and long-term periods of 2–4 and 20–30 years, respectively, are set out in the national plan, based on two main principles, firstly that environmental policy and economic policy should be integrated with historical experience into a general policy for sustainable development, and secondly that policies should be supported by popular participation and responsibility and decisions decentralized by means of voluntary agreements, economic incentives and institutions of control.

For the choice of **policy instruments** this implies extended use of economic methods compatible with the general transition from a command and control economy to a market economy. Economic instruments support the principle of free decision-making for companies subject to general economic conditions. The other important principle for applying economic instruments, the equivalence principle for environmental damage and environmental payments, has not been properly implemented, and therefore normative pollution limits were introduced. Much remains to be done before these principles can be put into practice (Bruņenieks, 1996).

The 1996 law on natural resource taxes is a step towards this end. By means of tax relief it stimulates implementation of environmental protection projects as well as recycling of waste either by producers themselves or by delivery to waste recycling plants. The new taxation law is also a step towards harmonization with European Union legislation and standards.

An important instrument is environmental assessments of government policies, programmes and construction projects. A new law on environmental impact assessment is currently in preparation by a government working group in order to replace the existing law from 1990 (Benders et.al., 1996).

Specific action programmes were worked out in collaboration with international experts in the Environmental Protection Action Programme, namely for water and waste water treatment, and for solid and hazardous waste management – two of the core problems identified in the National Plan – and implementation is now going on.

The action programme for **water** addresses the problems of eutrophication, deterioration of water ecosystems and low quality of drinking water caused by insufficient waste water treatment, including transboundary water protection. The major cause of poor water quality in the Baltic Sea is the discharge of untreated rural and urban waste water. In Rīga a waste water treatment facility has been in operation since the early 1990s, and in other big urban areas, including Daugavpils and Liepāja, the appropriate urgency projects are being implemented at present, and it can thus be concluded that urban waste water treatment in most industrial areas is basically under control now. For small and medium-sized water supply and waste water systems a project is now going on called '800+', as it covers more than 800 separate river basins. Sewage treatment plants and water supply systems are under construction, co-financed by foreign programmes and by governmental funds, but the national plan's long-term objective is the creation of self-supporting water enterprises based on user fees in rural areas also.

For **solid waste**, a national management system has not yet been designed or approved in Latvia. Separate strategies for solid waste and hazardous waste need to be developed. In recent years the amount of waste from packaging materials and glass has increased rapidly, but the amount of organic waste has decreased during the transition. There are very few landfills made for appropriately sanitary solid waste disposal and no legal acts for their construction. Normally, simple open waste dumps, often sand or gravel pits, are used not only for solid waste disposal, but also for sludge and even hazardous waste. So far, no waste separation, registration and weighing systems exist in Latvia. The local authorities being formally in charge of waste management in their territory, do not co-ordinate sufficiently with other public institutions, and they possess neither the material, nor manpower capacities to carry it out. However, recently a special waste management programme, the so-called '500-Programme', has been started with international co-operation (Carl Bro International, 1997), and laws on solid waste and chemical compounds are being drafted (Gaile, 1995).

Table 11.2 Environmental expenditures in Latvia, 1995

1000 lats	Air protec- tion	Water protec- tion	Land use	Other areas	Total
Capital investments	247	5 679	19	305	6 250
budgetary resources	1	2 151	19	37	2 208
enterprises	246	3 528	-	268	4 042
Capital repairs	92	197	-	-	289
Current expenditures	1 740	10 199	325	59	12 323
Total	2 079	16 075	344	364	18 862

Note: 1 ECU = 0.69 lats.
Source: Central Statistical Bureau, 1996.

A crucial precondition for project implementation is **investment finance**, but due to the shortage of public funds and significant deficits, only small amounts are available for investment. In 1995 the Latvian state budget deficit amounted to 4 per cent of GDP, and of the total public expenditure of 890 million USD, only 5 per cent were spent on capital investments (Central Statistical Bureau, 1995). Similarly, local government spent about 17 per cent of the total revenues of 505 million USD on financing economic activity

(Ministry of Economic Affairs, 1997). Public expenditures on environmental protection are particularly low at present (cf. Table 11.2).

Total expenditure on environmental protection and rational use of natural resources in 1995 was 37.8 million USD, of which 4.2 USD was for air protection, 32.1 USD was for water protection, 0.7 USD was for protection and rational use of land, and 0.7 USD was other uses. Total capital investments accounted for 33 per cent, current expenditures for 65 per cent, and expenditures for capital repairs for 2 per cent (Table 11.2). Accumulated capital investments in ongoing projects amounted to 73 million USD of which 13 million USD were invested in 1995. Resources necessary to finish the projects are estimated at 30 million USD. Of total accumulated investments 12 million USD originated from public budgets, almost exclusively owned by local governments, and 61 million USD from enterprises. Most of the enterprises were, however, state owned, namely 77 per cent; 12 per cent had mixed ownership, and 11 per cent other forms of ownership. Most investment expenditures were spent on waste water treatment and on drinking water improvement (Central Statistical Bureau, 1996).

Table 11.3   Forecasts for CO_2 emissions from energy production in Latvia for the year 2000

	1990	2000	2000	2000
GDP (1990=100)	100	75	68	60
Energy production (1990=100)	100	85	82	78
Emissions of CO_2 (million tons)	8.27	8.04	7.78	7.51

Note: The three different forecasts for CO_2 emissions in the year 2000 relate only to energy production and correspond to different assumptions for GDP and energy production as indicated. *Source:* Ministry of the Environment (1995b).

The success of environmental policy depends upon the speed of the expected economic recovery and the availability of investment finance. But important types of pollution will be aggravated concurrently with econmic growth, as in the case of CO_2 shown in Table 11.3, where the amount of pollution is closely connected to the volume of production. Economic transition will not eliminate long-term environmental problems, and the first local Agenda 21 development activities have started. The conclusion seems to be that, for environmental policy too, traditional courses of development are the only feasible ones, for example concerning the order of transition to new policy instruments, from command and control to economic and communicative instruments (Ernšteins, 1996).

11.5 Environmental Policy and Public Opinion

In the 1980s growing public worries concerning environmental problems were still more openly expressed and contributed as an essential force both to environmental and national awakening of society. The successful struggle to stop the construction of the environmentally and economically unreasonable Daugavpils hydropower plant on the river Daugava in autumn 1986 was the first really nation-wide public environmental activity in Latvia and like similar events in other Baltic and Central and Eastern European countries played the role of a 'democracy detonator'. After the declaration of independence on 4 May 1990, the newly elected Parliament passed several environmental protection and management laws and regulations during 1990–93 with the general support of the majority and often initiated by the 3.5 per cent parliamentarian representation of the Green Party of Latvia that was established in January 1990. At that time the Environmental Commission of the Parliament had considerable influence.

Informal groups and organizations, to some extent supported by the mass media, which had limited opportunities for activity during the 1980s, had an enormous influence on the nation's nature protection and culture management. The role of both professional and voluntary non-governmental organizations was crucial not only in promoting environmental concerns and raising public awareness, but also in the development of public environmental policy and even formal environmental education, especially during the period of awakening and regaining of independence. However, since the beginning of the 1990s the influence of the green organizations has suffered under the overwhelming pressure of new social and economical problems. Thus the formerly very popular practical public activities, for example, cleaning up, preservation, restoration and rehabilitation activities and campaigns, have unfortunately lost much of their popular support all around Latvia (Ernšteins, 1996).

In order to enhance the efficiency of environmental policy and to ensure a suitable balance between legal regulations, economic incentives and communication and negotiation as policy instruments, it is of first importance to renew public awareness, participation and support. This is an explicit part of the national environmental policy plan, and its main instruments are environmental education and communication (Ministry of the Environment, 1995a). The law on nature protection provides that members of the public receive accurate and complete information about the actual state of the environment and the exploitation of resources, and it also defines the legal rights of the public and public organizations with respect to the implementation of environmental policies.

Environmental education activities are promoted with the aim of overcoming the political contamination of human minds by the 50 years of Soviet rule and of paving the way for a rational understanding of environmental and economic issues. Much of this work is carried out by non-governmental organizations like the Ecological Centre affiliated to the University of Latvia, the Children's Environmental School, Nature Houses and other out-of-school institutions as well as the Culture Fund of Latvia. In primary schools several teacher-enthusiasts are using the newly acquired room for decentralized decions to integrate environmental education in many subjects, and this is supported by the strategy for environmental education formulated by the Ministry of the Environment in 1995. At the secondary school level there is an increasing number of optional courses in environmental science. At the higher educational institutions there used to be only specialized courses within the traditional disciplines, but recently multi-disciplinary graduate and post-graduate courses on environmental science and management have been organized by various institutions, notably the Centre for Environmental Science and Management Studies (CESAMS) at the University of Latvia. This development was supported by the Environmental Science Council of Latvia during its four years of existence from 1991 to 1994 (Ernšteins and Gulbis, 1994).

During the process of liberation the **mass media** had a crucial role in environmental awareness. There was a rapid increase in the number of new newsletters, magazines, bulletins, and radio and TV stations, but unfortunately their interest in nature protection and global and regional environmental events or even hot spot issues has decreased concerning volume as well as quality of coverage. Although rather reliable, the information in the mass media is not sufficient and too variable. During the last decade several specialized bulletins and newspapers were established in order to raise public awareness and participation in nature and culture protection and in interdisciplinary environ-mental science studies, for example the weekly newspaper Elpa ('Breath'), issued from 1990 to 1994, and the quarterly bulletin Vide ('Environment'), issued from 1991 to 1993. The only environmental periodical still published regularly is the Calendar of Nature and History, published by the Latvian Society for Nature and Monument Protection since 1962. A comprehensive content analysis of main national and local newspapers and TV and radio programmes based in Rīga, carried out by CESAMS for a two month period, January–March 1994, demonstrates very limited opportunities for receiving information on environmental topics. In the national newspapers only 27 articles on environmental issues were found during the period of investigation, corresponding to 4 per cent of the number of articles and 2.6 per cent of the printing space.

In 1995 the Ministry of State Reforms organized a wide **public opinion** survey on governmental information. In a rating of issues, on which the public would like to receive information, environmental protection was rated modestly as number 14. Public opinion about the sufficiency of information on the activities of various ministries places the Ministry of the Environment as number 11 with only 3.1 per cent indicating satisfaction with its information efforts. However, other results show that almost all information circulated to the public by the mass media and other sources actually originates from the ministry although this is not indicated. The results also show that 17 per cent of the population want more information about the activities of this ministry and 29 per cent on environmental issues generally. The social groups exhibiting most interest for more information are students and pupils (25 per cent), civil servants (25 per cent), young people between 15 and 24 years of age (21 per cent), the urban population outside Rīga (19 per cent) and persons with higher education (18 per cent).

CESAMS has carried out several questionnaire surveys on environmental issues, and a large survey in 1995 included respondents from Rīga as well as selected rural towns and districts. The results show that the majority of respondents (56 per cent) assess the environmental conditions in Latvia in general as 'average', whereas opinion about environmental conditions in the biggest cities is generally negative (49 per cent); conditions in rural districts are slightly better evaluated, and even more so in rural towns. Opinions concerning the practical work carried out in the local surroundings are basically negative (42 per cent) and only 14 per cent are very satisfied. Results on the public access to information show that 54 per cent assess the level of information about environmental conditions as 'poor' or 'very poor', but the level of information about environmental policy is even more unsatisfactory, as 66 per cent describe their knowledge on the subject as poor and only 4 per cent consider themselves as well informed. In contrast, the results on public participation confirm that 84 per cent of respondents indicated their readiness to participate in environmental decision making and in practical environmental problem-solving, although most respondents had not taken part in any activities (Blumberga and Linde, 1996; Rutka, 1996).

Similar results were obtained in a survey carried out by the Ecological Centre of the University of Latvia in 1996, and in fact the situation has not changed much since the early years of transition as indicated by a survey from 1992 done by J.D. Gooch (1994), who concluded that public opinion on environmental issues was based on emotions and self-observations rather than on proper information and that the relatively high public interest for environmental issues at that time was ephemeral and populistic.

The general conclusion from several surveys of public opinion on environmental issues (Ernšteins et. al., 1995; Rutka, 1996) are that personal observations and the mass media are the main source of information, that most people are insufficiently informed about environmental problems and about opportunities for participation, and that the public generally confine the· sphere of interest and participation to local environmental issues and specific activities in the neighbourhood and in the family.

REFERENCES

Benders, J., M. Vircavs and V. Segliņš (1996), 'Screening and Quality Control', pp. 48–81 in H. Kristofersson and A.Tesli (eds.), *Environmental Impact Assessment in the Baltic Countries and Poland*, Rīga: NORD Environment.

Blumberga, U. and I. Linde (1996), *Public Participation in Environmental Decision Making*, Rīga: ULEC, VIDE.

Bruņenieks, J. (1996), 'Natural Resource Taxes' (in Latvian), *Zemes Reformas vēstnesis* (2), 36–8.

Carl Bro International (1997), *National Municipal Solid Waste Strategy for Latvia* (Project Report), Copenhagen: Carl Bro International.

Central Statistical Bureau (1995), *Statistical Yearbook of Latvia 1995*, Rīga: Central Statistical Bureau.

Central Statistical Bureau (1996), 'Environmental Protection Indicators in Latvia 1995', *Statistical Bulletin*, Rīga: Central Statistical Bureau.

Cimdiņš, P. (1995), 'Outline to Sustainable Environmental Policy in the Transition Period', pp. 92–124 in *Proceedings from the First Baltic Workshop on Environment and Property Rights*, Līgatne 1994, Rīga: ULEC, VIDE.

Ernšteins, R. (1996), 'Environmental Movement and Education in Latvia as Imperative Developmental Interrelations' (in Latvian), *Acta Universitatis Latviensis* (604), 34–47.

Ernšteins, R. and A. Gulbis (1994), *National Survey of Latvia on Public Awareness and Environmental Education*, HELCOM working paper 7/12/94, Rīga: HELCOM.

Ernšteins, R., Ē. Leitis and D. Brila (1995), 'Cognitive Conditions of Forming Public Environmental Awareness and Access of Information' (in Latvian), *Acta Universitatis Latviensis* (601), 52–3.

Gaile, B. (1995), 'Development of National Solid Waste Management System in Latvia', Report presented at the *G–24 Conference*, 2 May 1995, Rīga: ULEC, VIDE.

Gooch, J.D. (1994), 'Environmental Values and Attitudes in the Baltic States', Paper presented at the *Nordiska Statvetenskapliga Kongressen*, August 1993, Oslo.

Government of Latvia (1997), 'Government Policy in the Energy Sector' (in Latvian), *Enerģētikas Vēstnesis*, **5** (133).

Harne, N.J. (1996), *Energy Tariff Project Latvia. Summary Report*, Roskilde: Risø National Laboratory.

Latvian Energy Agency (1996), *Energy in Latvia 1995*, Rīga: LEA.

Ministry of Economic Affairs (1996), *National Programme of Energy of Latvia: The First draft*, Rīga: Ministry of Economic Affairs.

Ministry of Economic Affairs (1997), *Economic Development of Latvia*, Rīga: Ministry of Economic Affairs.

Ministry of the Environment (1995a), *National Environmental Policy Plan for Latvia*,

Rīga: Ministry of the Environment.

Ministry of the Environment (1995b), *National Report of the Republic of Latvia to the UN Convention About Climate Changes*, Rīga: Ministry of the Environment.

Ministry of the Environment (1996), *Information about Noxious Emissions in Latvia*, Rīga: Ministry of the Environment.

Ministry of the Environment (1997), *Environmental Protection Action Programme*, Rīga: Ministry of the Environment.

Ozoliņš, P. (1994), 'Environmental Problems and Policy Instruments in Latvian Agriculture and Forestry', Chapter 8, pp. 140-165 in K. Eckerberg (ed.), *Comparing Nordic and Baltic Countries – Environmental Problems and Policies in Agriculture and Forestry*, TemaNord 1994:572, Copenhagen: Nordic Council of Ministers.

Rutka, A. (1996), 'Public Awareness and Participation in Environmental Problem-Solving' (in Latvian), *Acta Universitatis Latviensis* (604), 48–56.

12. Lithuania: Nuclear Power, Pollution, and Restructuring

Linas Čekanavičius

12.1 Prospects for Economic Growth and Restructuring

From 1989 to 1995 Lithuania's GDP decreased by 61 per cent, and this dramatic economic recession has caused a significant drop in the rate of exploitation of natural resources and in the amount of environmental pollution (cf. Table 1.3). Under such circumstances questions of economic survival tend to gain priority over problems of environmental sustainability, as is clearly reflected in the relative magnitude of funds allocated for environmental protection. However, the expected economic recovery on the one hand, and rather low rates of energy consumption and production efficiency, combined with the scarcity of domestic resources, on the other, necessitate assessment of domestic resources as well as the state of the environment.

Lithuania has 99 kilometres of coast line and an area of 65 200 square kilometres. The size of the population is 3.7 million. The landscape is predominantly lowland plains, and Lithuania has few natural resources apart from agricultural lands, comprising about two thirds of the country's territory, and forests covering another 28 per cent. Small deposits of oil and gas have been discovered, along with larger amounts of peat and materials like lime, sand, gravel and clay.

Assessment of the economic environmental performance of countries in transition is complicated for several reasons: rapid and comprehensive changes are difficult to monitor; the measuring stick itself changes, and in Lithuania the monetary unit was converted from the Soviet rouble to the provisional 'coupons' and finally in 1993 to a national currency, the litas; a shadow economy has considerable but unknown dimensions; the system of official statistics is itself in a state of disarray and transition. There have been remarkable discrepancies in published data on the performance of the Lithuanian economy in recent years, and the scale of the recession is subject to dispute (IMF, 1992). Presently, it is officially claimed that the economic situation is stabilizing and showing signs of recovery. The privatization process has entered its final stage, and 82 per cent of enterprises are now in private hands. Growth resumed in 1994 with growth rates of 1–2 per cent, and it is expected that economic growth will soon reach at least 4–5 per cent and that the economic structure will change correspondingly (cf. Table 12.3). However, the experience of the last few years shows that official forecasts tend to be too optimistic.

12.2 Energy Consumption and Efficiency

Since the peak in 1991 total energy supply has been cut by more than half, the formerly large amount of energy exports, notably electricity and oil products, have disappeared, and energy prices have soared to world market levels creating social and economic difficulties in transferring price increases to consumers (cf. Tables 12.1, 13.1 and 13.2). Other characteristic features of the Lithuanian energy sector persist: high intensity of energy consumption and production and insufficient energy efficiency; negligible local energy resources; almost complete dependence on fuel imported from Russia and large overdue debts to suppliers; unsolved security and environmental problems of the Ignalina nuclear power plant.

Lithuania has very few primary energy resources, and domestic resources like fire-wood, peat and hydropower at present contribute just about 2 per cent of primary energy inputs. Thus, there is a nearly complete dependence on fuel imports from Russia. Crude oil and natural gas are imported only from Russia. Most coal is brought in from Russia, and some is imported from Poland. Recently some attempts were made to find alternative suppliers of energy, for example some 25 000 tons of orimulsion fuel, a combustible liquid consisting of asphaltens and water, were bought in Venezuela and brought to Lithuania by sea. However, extended use of orimulsion is by no means without problems because of its impact on the environment.

However, the Lithuanian energy transformation capacity considerably exceeds the needs of domestic customers. This striking imbalance of the energy supply potential and the energy consumption demand is a legacy from Soviet times, when Lithuania was intended to be integrated as an energy supplier in the whole north-western region of the former Soviet Union. Even in the peak years around 1990 the capacity of natural gas importation by pipeline was utilized less than 50 per cent, and there was considerable spare capacity concerning oil refining as well as import and export by pipeline. In the years 1988–91 the primary energy supply in Lithuania was twice the level of final consumption, and approximately half of the output of electric energy as well as refined petroleum products were exported. But during 1992–94 both primary energy supply and final consumption decreased by about 50 per cent, from the all-time peaks in 1989 and 1985 – primary supply reached 18 million tons of oil equivalent (TOE) in 1989, and final consumption 9.9 million TOE in 1985 – to 8.3 million TOE and 5.3 million TOE, respectively, in 1994. Most significant was the 65 per cent decrease of the natural gas supply due to the price differential between natural gas and the considerably less expensive heavy fuel oil. Supplies of petroleum products and of nuclear energy decreased by half (cf. Table 12.1).

Table 12.1 Energy supply and efficiency in Lithuania, 1980–94

million TOE	1980	1985	1990	1991	1992	1993	1994
Total primary energy supply	-	16.2	17.3	18.0	11.1	9.1	8.3
Oil products	-	9.0	7.3	8.0	3.8	4.1	3.9
Natural gas	-	3.6	4.7	4.8	2.8	1.5	1.7
Coal	-	0.8	0.8	0.7	0.6	0.4	0.3
Nuclear power	-	2.3	4.1	4.1	3.5	3.2	2.0
Domestic energy resources	-	0.5	0.4	0.4	0.4	0.4	0.5
Final energy consumption	-	9.9	9.1	9.4	6.4	5.4	5.3
per capita	2.6	2.7	2.4	2.5	1.8	1.5	1.4
per unit GDP	2.3	2.1	1.5	1.8	2.0	2.3	2.4

Notes: Final energy consumption per unit GDP is measured in TOE (tons of oil equivalent) per capita and per unit of GDP as expressed in billion of litas in 1992 prices. Domestic energy resources include fire-wood, peat and hydropower.
Sources: Ministry of Energy, 1995.

Energy consumption both per unit of GDP and per unit of capita has decreased since the 1980s (cf. Tables 12.1, 1.2 and 1.3). This was accelerated by the economic recession, but at least part of the decrease was due to increased efficiency in energy consumption. In 1990 primary energy consumption per unit of GDP was approximately three times higher than the Western European average (Lithuanian Energy Institute, 1993), and this excessive and wasteful energy consumption was caused by low and heavily subsidized energy prices, inadequate or missing metering of individual energy consumption, and a general lack of incentives for energy savings and efficiency.

However, starting from 1990, when energy supplies from Russia were temporarily reduced for political reasons, and later on, when imported fuel prices gradually soared to world market levels and when energy subsidies for domestic customers were gradually abolished, the amount of energy consumed both per unit of GDP and per capita came down. Since 1992 there has been a slight increase in energy consumption per unit GDP, while consumption per capita continued its decline. Taking into account that the energy intensive industries were most hard-hit by the energy price rise and so far have not recovered, these trends probably indicate an undervaluation of GDP. Despite the overall decrease in energy consumption, energy efficiency is now no higher than in the 1980s. But the drop in overall energy production has been beneficial for the environment, mostly because of reduced atmospheric pollution from the energy sector.

Domestic resources of fossil fuels in Lithuania are small. There are 19 small deposits of oil containing an estimated 8 million tons, and currently only a few thousand tons are extracted monthly from three oil fields. At most about 1 million tons of oil might be extracted annually, but the quality of this oil is high, and it is expected that it will be used for production of lubricants. The main domestic resources are wood and peat. The extraction of peat can not be increased very much beyond the 1994 level when it increased more than twice due to favourable weather conditions as well as increased export demand; of the 54 peat deposits containing 122 million tons, 20 are utilized. But forests occupy 28 per cent of the country, and with modern efficient equipment they could play an important role in the Lithuanian energy supply. Only 20 per cent of the hydropower potential is currently utilized, and in order to exploit it further small hydropower plants must be introduced. The general potential of hydroelectric generating capacity of the Lithuanian rivers is estimated at 585.1 MW, with a potential energy output of 5.1 million kWh annually. Presently one bigger hydroelectric power plant, one recently built hydroelectric pumped storage power plant and 12 smaller power plants are in operation, while projects of restoring and reconstructing some other small power plants are under consideration. Solar energy should have the same possibilities as in, for example, Denmark, since the average annual energy from the sun is 900 kWh/m^2 compared to about 1000 kWh/m^2 in Denmark (Fenhann, 1994, p. 87). There are some resources of geothermal energy in the western part of the country, which could be used for district heating in the port of Klaipeda.

It is claimed that local energy resources, like hydropower, wood and peat, could contribute a larger share of energy production, especially if used for the production of heat in district heating systems rather than electric power generation. Rational use of local energy resources could probably save about 15–25 per cent of imported fuels (Lithuanian Energy Institute, 1993). Therefore, steps are being taken towards conversion of boilers to local solid fuel.

12.3 Exploitation of Domestic Resources

There are more than 500 deposit fields of **mineral resources** in Lithuania, including 230 million tons of limestone, 105 million tons of dolomite, 34 million tons of silica clay, 82 million tons of anhydrite, 5 million tons of marl, 93 million tons of clay, and 676 million tons of sand and gravel.

Extraction has decreased year by year since 1990 and is at present about 20–30 per cent of the 1989 level. Deposits of anhydrite and chalk marl are not so far exploited. The building industry relies almost exclusively on local resources, and the deceptive abundancy of mineral resources has evoked a rather wasteful attitude towards their utilization.

Surface minerals are extracted by open excavation, usually in quarries, with negative impacts on the environment like destroyed land surfaces, spread of dust, formation of depressive funnels especially at ground water levels. So far 32 thousand ha of land or 0.5 per cent of the territory have been destroyed. Quite often quarries are located in ecologically sensitive areas, namely wooded hills or river valleys with peat-bogs in watersheds.

Surface **waters** consist of lakes, ponds, a dense network of rivers, and the northern part of the Curonian Lagoon. The total length of rivers and streams comes to 29.9 thousand km with an average density of about 1 km per km^2. A significant part of the hydrographic network is composed of 60 thousand km of regulated river stretches and drainage dykes. Natural stretches of rivers and streams in Lithuania amount only to 15 per cent of the total length. The average surface water run-off amounts to 26.1 km^3 (Ministry of Environmental Protection, 1996). The total number of lakes and ponds in Lithuania is about 10 thousand, and their combined surface area is more than 120 thousand ha.

Consumption of surface water is close to 4 billion m^3 per year; almost 90 per cent is consumed by industry, notably the energy industry, 6 per cent by households, about 2 per cent by agriculture and 2 per cent by pond fish production. Industrial and agricultural consumption has decreased during the last few years because of the drop in industrial production levels and due to the partial destruction of previously built irrigation systems. In contrast, consumption of surface water by the energy sector has increased. The Ignalina Nuclear Power Plant presently needs about 3 billion m^3 of surface water annually.

Resources of ground water in Lithuania amount to 750 million m^3 annually of fresh drinking water and 2 million m^3 annually of mineral medicinal water, including 200 thousand m^3 of brine. Potential safe yields of fresh ground water are expected to be much higher: about 1200 million m^3 annually. At present about 400 million m^3 of fresh ground water is extracted. More than half is consumed in the vicinity of the largest cities, Vilnius, Kaunas and Klaipeda. Present extraction of fresh underground water amounts to nearly 30 per cent of the total resources, and in the coastal area even up to 50–70 per cent of local resources. However, compared with the situation in 1989 consumption of ground water has decreased by 22 per cent due to industrial and agricultural production decline and due to price induced water savings by consumers. Less than 30 per cent of surveyed resources of mineral medicinal water is extracted.

The dominant **soils** in the natural soil cover in Lithuania are the turf podzol type, which are characterized by a low podzol process, covering 22 per cent of the area and turf clay-type soils covering 20 per cent. Soil resources have been severely damaged or completely destroyed for an area of about 680 thousand ha or 11.4 per cent of the total territory of Lithuania, most of which, 573 thousand ha, are covered by cities and roads. Water and wind erosion has damaged soils on 96.5 thousand ha, and completely destroyed or excavated soils covering more than 9.8 thousand ha. Recently the intensity of erosion processes has slackened a little due to the sharp drop in agricultural production and construction.

Currently 28 per cent of Lithuania's territory is covered by **forests**, of which 67 per cent are coniferous forests and 29 per cent soft-wood deciduous forests. About 98 per cent of the state-owned forests belong to the forestries and national parks. There are some private forests as well. The total annual increase in timber volume is estimated at 11.9 million m^3, with a yearly cut-out yield of 6.9 million m^3, including 4.3 million m^3 of coniferous wood, 2.4 million m^3 of soft and 0.2 million m^3 of hard deciduous wood (Ministry of Environmental Protection, 1996). Sustainable annual yield quotas were often violated during the pre-war, World War II and early post-war periods, but after 1961 the Lithuanian forests were cut strictly according to quotas. This had a noticeable positive impact on the productivity of the forests. A national forest inventory has been held every five years since 1956.

In the period 1970–90 5 million m^3 of timber were used annually, of which 2.7–3.3 million m^3 were locally produced and the remaining 1–3 million m^3 imported from Russia (Malisauskas, 1993). The situation has changed, and in 1993–94 as much as 4–4.5 million m^3 of timber were produced in Lithuanian forests. This increase was caused partly by extensive damage due to strong winds and extraction of the windbreaks, partly by growing export demand, particularly for carving wood, plywood and paper-wood.

Forests also provide hunting resources, and at present 18 species of mammals and 27 species of birds are considered as hunting game. Seven species are hunted intensively, namely musk rat, fox, racoon dog, wild boar, red deer, roe deer and moose, and two species, beaver and hare, with moderate intensity. Most of the game bird species are abundant or common (Ministry of Environmental Protection, 1996).

Forests are used commercially for harvesting mushrooms and berries, notably blueberry, which covers 57 per cent of the berry fields, that is about 19 300 ha, but also red bilberry, cranberry, raspberry, wild strawberry and forest fruits such as hazelnut and medical herbs like juniper, black alder, bearberry, lycopod and Iceland lichen. The most valuable of the edible mushrooms are chanterelles, white-caps and russules. A single hectare of Lithuanian forest yields about 30 kg of edible mushrooms annually on average, and some areas may yield as much as 70–100 kg. Thus a total volume of 20 000–25 000 tons of edible mushrooms are produced by Lithuanian forests per year.

Commercial **fishing** takes place in the Lithuanian parts of the Baltic Sea and the Curonian Lagoon, as well as in the lakes, reservoirs, rivers and fishery ponds. Most of the major Lithuanian rivers could be used for commercial and sports fishing, and for reproduction of migratory and non-migratory fish species. Fish biomasses in rivers are in the range 200–250 kg per ha. No significant changes in either quantity or quality of fish resources have been recorded in the last few years. Monitoring of fish and fish forage resources have taken place since 1993 in the Baltic Sea, the Curonian Lagoon, and in the Nemunas river delta. So far there is no monitoring of fish and crayfish resources in the inland water bodies. Resources allow safe annual quotas of 40–50 thousand tons of fish in the Lithuanian coastal waters of the Baltic Sea and 3500 tons in the Curonian Lagoon and other inland waters. Fish ponds provide up to 6000 tons of fish annually. However, because of the underdeveloped fish processing industry, during the last few years Lithuania has been using just about 20–25 per cent of the assigned fish catch quotas. Privatization of ownership rights to lakes and fish farms, growing costs of commercial fishing and reduced market demand have caused a significant drop, 25–33 per cent, of fish catches in ponds and rivers as well.

Crayfish is caught in more than 350 lakes and more than 100 streams. Crayfish catching is carried out on a rather small scale and no crayfish breeding programme is currently in place. However, recently some efforts to introduce crayfish breeding technologies used in Nordic countries were undertaken.

Lithuania has considerable potential for the **recreational** use of coastal zones, areas near the lakes, river valleys and suburban recreational zones, that is about 2 million ha or one third of the total area. The total number of visits to these areas are 60 million man-days annually. The most heavily visited territories are located in the coastal zone, eastern Lithuania, and in the vicinity of the largest cities. The Baltic coast zone accounts for only 0.8 per cent of the recreational areas, but receives about 15 per cent of the visits.

12.4 Environmental Effects

The major source of **air pollution** in Lithuania is transport which accounts for most carbon monoxide and nitrogen oxide pollution and for 71 per cent of total air pollution in 1994. Pollution from transport declined up until 1992, but is now increasing, from 402 thousand tons in 1993 to 438 thousand tons in 1994. The lion's share is generated by motor cars, namely 96 per cent or 422 thousand tons in 1994, up from 350 thousand tons in 1993, as their number is growing. The majority of cars, imported from Western Europe, are old, obsolete and very often poorly maintained (Ministry of Environmental Protection, 1995). Emissions from railway vehicles and from aviation is increasing as well, in both cases due partly to better monitoring, partly to growing intensity of traffic.

In contrast to emissions from mobile sources, pollution from stationary sources, first of all the major share of sulphur dioxide emissions, has continued its decline after 1992. Total SO_2 emissions have also declined (cf. Tables 12.2 and 1.3). The largest emission sources are located either in the major cities, namely Vilnius, Kaunas, Klaipeda, Siauliai and Panevezys, or in the major industrial centres, that is Naujoji Akmene, Kedainiai and Jonava. In 1994 point sources produced 560.5 thousand tons of pollutants, of which 68 per cent were collected or neutralized and the remaining 180 thousand tons were emitted into the atmosphere; in 1993 the emissions were 188 thousand tons (Ministry of Environmental Protection, 1995). The reduction of pollution in recent years was caused by the drastic economic recession, which is the price Lithuania had to pay both for the intentional transition to the market economy and for the unintentional environmental improvement.

The most important industrial air pollution sources are the Akmene Cement Factory, The Mazeikiai Oil Refinery – which emitted 35.4 thousand tons of pollutants in 1993 and 10.4 thousand tons in 1994 – and the mineral fertilizer plants in Kedainiai and Jonava. The Lithuanian State Power Plant situated at Elektrenai, which has a total capacity of 1800 MW and burns a combination of heavy fuel oil and natural gas, emitted 8 thousand tons of pollutants in 1993 and 9 thousand tons in 1994; the Mazeikiai State Thermal Power Plant emitted 11 thousand tons in 1993 and 10 thousand tons in 1994 (Ministry of Environmental Protection, 1995). Abatement equipment, cyclones, bag filters or electrostatic precipitators, is generally old, worn-out and inefficient. Power plants and especially small boilers often used for district heating still lack relevant analytical and control equipment for combustion process control. Modification of burners was started in some power stations in order to reduce the emissions of nitrogen oxides but due to the lack of necessary funds this process is virtually at a standstill.

Because the industrial centres in Mazeikiai and in Naujoji Akmene are situated just 10–15 km from the Latvian border, they inevitably have some influence on the air quality in Latvia. Lithuania is a member of the Convention on Long-Range Transboundary Air Pollution which requires that SO_2 emissions must be reduced by 30 per cent of the 1980 level in 1993, and volatile organic components (VOC) emissions by 30 per cent of the 1988 level in 1999. Due to significant industrial production decline, Lithuania is well ahead of those requirements: SO_2 emissions have been reduced by 64 per cent since 1980, nitrogen oxides emissions by 35 per cent since 1987, and

VOC emissions went down from 20 thousand tons in 1990 to 7 thousand tons in 1993.

Emissions of greenhouse gases has also been considerably reduced because of the decline of industrial production and fuel consumption (cf. Table 12.2). In 1992 CO_2 emissions in Lithuania amounted to 285 tons per km^2 as compared to, for instance, 2900 tons per km^2 in Germany. In the late 1980s CO_2 emissions in Lithuania were approximately 11 tons per capita, but in recent years this has been reduced to 4.9 tons per capita. Lithuania's contribution to global carbon dioxide emissions was 0.1 per cent in 1993 (Ministry of Environmental Protection, 1996).

Table 12.2 Pollution of air and water in Lithuania, 1986–94

1000 tons		1986	1990	1991	1992	1993	1994
Regional	SO_2	188	143	175	97	83	84
air	NO_x	73	68	86	47	50	55
pollution	CO	576	580	566	327	334	-
Greenhouse	CO_2	41.1	36.7	38.6	21.3	18.4	-
gases	methane	38	41	43	25	16	-
	nitrogen oxide	4	3	4	2	2	-
Water consumption		-	4285	4132	3578	4232	3831
Waste water discharge		-	4040	3881	3537	3338	3778
Water	phosphorus	-	1249	881	1438	1535	1502
pollution	nitrogen	-	145	177	173	101	166
Solid waste disposal		-	-	-	1987	2325	2191
Nuclear	atmospheric	8.5	9.8	1.1	2.2	1.5	8.2
pollution	Lake Druksiu	-	25.8	3.1	22.6	4.2	7.7

Notes: Emissions of CO_2 are measured in million tons. Water consumption and waste water discharge are both measured in million m^3. Nuclear pollution include long-term radioactive pollution from the Ignalina nuclear power plant measured in GBq discharged into the atmosphere and into Lake Druksiu.
Source: Ministry of Environmental Protection, 1996.

Waste water discharge and **water pollution** has declined slightly in recent years due to the recession (cf. Table 12.2). About 25 per cent of the 4000 million tons of waste water is cleaned sufficiently, and 25 per cent is released without any treatment. The situation, however, remains unsatisfactory for the major cities which lack biological waste water treatment systems of the appropriate capacity. Only the energy industry has maintained the same level of water consumption, about 3.3. billion m^3 or 85–8 per cent of the total water consumption in Lithuania. Furthermore, the Ignalina Nuclear Power Plant is responsible for consumption of about 99 per cent of all the water consumed by the energy sector.

The major share of the waste water volume comes from sewage. After the introduction of mechanical treatment in Kaunas it is estimated that when similar plants are built in Vilnius, Siauliai and Klaipeda, organic pollution of water bodies will be reduced by as much as 70 per cent. Industrial enterprises discharge waste water into the local sewerage system, in some cases after pre-treatment for specific pollutants that are not removed during the regular sewage treatment. Agriculture's share in water pollution comes in the form of the dungwash runaway from the live-stock farms and from the fields, where dungwash is sprinkled on as a fertilizer. Even when the discharging standard of 100 m³ per ha is obeyed, parts of dungwash get into the drainage systems and, eventually, to the water bodies. According to data obtained from joint Danish–Lithuanian research in the Minija river basin, 2–3 kg of nitrogen and 0.7–2.5 of phosphorus are washed away per hectare of fields annually. Other research, conducted by the Academy of Agriculture, indicates higher figures, namely 10–7 kg per ha and 0.6 kg per ha, respectively.

Ground water quality is poor in almost one third of the territory where nitrogen concentrations exceed 45 mg per litre; only in 10 per cent of the territory is the concentration below 10 mg per litre. Permanganate oxidation exceeds 5 mg per litre in 30 per cent of the territory. Ammonium concentration in the ground water exceeds 0.2 mg per litre in 10–5 per cent of the territory. Concentrations of heavy metals are rather low. Surface water quality has, surprisingly, not improved despite the general economic decline. Biochemical oxygen demand (BOD) exceeds the maximum permitted amount by up to 2 times in 60–70 per cent of Lithuanian rivers with concentrations of 2–4 mg O_2 per litre. In 20 per cent of the rivers it is 4.0–6.0 mg O_2 per litre. About 80 per cent of the rivers are heavily polluted by nutrients. The major Lithuanian rivers contain 1–2 mg of nitrogen per litre and 0.05–0.10 mg of phosphorus per litre. Concentrations of nitrogen compounds in the medium-sized rivers in northeastern Lithuania are as high as 40 mg per litre and those of phosphorus up to 0.4 mg per litre. Heavy metal pollution of Lithuanian rivers is not significant.

Water quality in the Curonian Lagoon mostly depends on the quality of water supplied by the Nemunas river, but it also receives about 1.4 km³ of rainfall water annually. In 1985–8 about 45–65 thousand tons of nitrogen and 2.8–3.5 thousand tons of phosphorus were brought to the Curonian Lagoon by rivers annually, but this has decreased to 26 and 1.5 thousand tons, respectively, in 1992. Only 10–20 per cent of these nutrients remain in the Lagoon, the rest are carried out to the Baltic Sea. The state of the Curonian Lagoon is rather poor, and because of biogenic compounds it suffers from intensive eutrophication and recurring death of fish, especially during the algae blooming periods. The impact of the water outflow from the Lagoon is distinctly felt some 10–15 km away, and occasionally in the summer season the adjacent beaches must be closed. Water quality could be substantially improved by efficient sewage treatment in Klaipeda, Kaunas and Vilnius, but it also depends on pollution generated in the Kaliningrad region, primarily by its pulp and paper industry.

Only a very general picture of **soil quality** can be presented due to scarcity of data. Cases of soil contamination are found in 75 town and 260 regional dumps, excluding the illegal ones, and in the 67 thousand ha formerly occupied by 275 Soviet military bases. In 1993–5 Lithuanian and Danish experts compiled inventories of contaminated areas with evaluation of the economic damage, assessment of the decontamination methods and costs as well as recommendations for future management and for solutions of legal disputes over responsibility. They include the legacies of the Soviet army in terms of devastated forests and fields, heaps of bombs and mines, fuel-oil pools, and contaminated soil and ground water (Krueger Consult et. al., 1995).

The amount of solid waste disposal has increased since 1992 (cf. Table 12.2), because of increased amounts of household waste from food packaging and disposable containers, which is practically unsorted and goes entirely to dumps. In contrast, the amount of industrial solid waste has decreased due to the industrial recession, but most of this waste is recycled, and only a small fraction is dumped.

At present there is no specific legislation in Lithuania governing the disposal of hazardous waste. According to the Ministry of Environmental Protection the annual generation of hazardous waste, including plating wastes, pesticides, oily wastes, asbestos, solvents and chemicals, was about 225 thousand tons in 1993 and 130 thousand tons in 1994. Dumping of industrial hazardous wastes in landfills was prohibited in 1990, and industry was obliged to store them on site pending the construction of the appropriate disposal facilities. However, many of these storage arrangements are reported to be of inadequate quality, and by now huge waste quantities are beginning to build up in factory storage areas all over the country. Unfortunately Lithuania has only very limited facilities for disposal of hazardous waste, and incineration, recycling or disposal facilities are virtually non-existent. Earlier most plating sludge, spent oil and some other wastes were disposed of in the production of keramzite, a granulated, porous ceramic material, but this has almost come to an end because of the sharp price increase for fuel which makes up 90 per cent of keramzite production costs.

The disposal of hazardous waste was examined in detail in 1993 by Danish consultants. Their report recommended the establishment of a centralized hazardous waste treatment facility which would incorporate incineration, chemical treatment, oil separation and a secure landfill. This facility would be served by a network of five to six transfer stations around the country. The construction costs were estimated at between 36 and 80 million USD, depending on whether a totally new facility is built or an existing cement kiln is used for incineration treatment. Following that report, the government approved a hazardous waste management programme in February 1993. Although some budgetary funds for its implementation were allocated in 1993 and 1994, the funding ceased in 1995. Apparently in the present economic situation waste management is not considered to be a national priority.

The main source of **radioactive waste** in Lithuania is the Ignalina nuclear power plant. Residues of used radioactive fuel is kept in water pools adjacent to the reactor buildings. The capacities of the pools were designed for 10 years of operation, and they are expected to fill up quite soon. Solid radioactive wastes resulting from plant operation are separated according to radioactivity level and stored in on-ground type vaults. At present, approximately half the waste depository volume is filled up. Liquid radioactive waste is concentrated by evaporation, filtration and ion exchange. Residues are stored in metal tanks. Purified water is recycled for reactor or fuel storage cooling, and some excess purified water is discharged into the lake Druksiai.

Following the Chernobyl accident, concentrations of radionuclides in the air did significantly exceed maximum permitted amounts. However, radioactive pollution originating from the Chernobyl accident is decreasing, and examination of food produced in Lithuania does not reveal any excess concentrations of Chernobyl radionuclides.

The Ignalina plant is obliged to carry out monitoring of its radioactive leakage itself. Thus, the only direct source about the radioactive emissions are monthly and annual reports submitted by the Ignalina plant (cf. Table 12.2). Some radioactive nuclides get into the waste water treatment system. The mud extracted in the treatment system is stored in a special pit. As much as 0.40–0.65 GBq of artificial radionuclides are accumulated annually. Tritium presents a separate problem. An indirect estimate indicates that as much as 1000 GBq of tritium must have been released in Druksiai Lake in 1993 alone (Ministry of Environmental Protection, 1995).

12.5 Resources and Environmental Cost as Constraints on Economic Growth

Although it is officially claimed that the decline of the Lithuanian economy has been stopped, in terms of GNP produced it is still in a deep hole, with GNP at about 40 per cent as compared to the 1989 level. Nevertheless, it is true that in the last years some positive signs have emerged for reform and stabilization. Privatization of former state property is progressing, and 65 per cent of the labour force is employed in the private sector; the currency, the litas, is relatively stable and pegged to the US dollar at the rate of 4 to 1 under the provisions of a Currency Board, established in April 1995; inflation is down from 1163 per cent in 1992 to 13 per cent in 1996; the interest rate is 20–25 per cent as compared to 85–100 per cent two years ago, which made any long- or medium-range investments virtually impossible.

However, stabilization is quite shaky, and the future of the Lithuanian economy is far from secure: unemployment is slowly but inexorably creeping up, officially standing at about 6–7 per cent to which should be added hidden unemployment of probably about 15 per cent; the standard of living has decreased drastically since 1988, pushing a large part of population to the verge of social unrest; partly due to the fixed exchange rate the foreign trade deficit is growing; many Lithuanian firms, especially those that are heavily dependent on the CIS countries either for the steady supply of raw materials or for markets for finished products, are functioning in a stop-go mode; a number of industrial firms, including some of the largest ones, are able to keep on moving only due to governmental support such as soft loans, subsidies, and postponement of tax or energy bill payments. In particular, the strongly increasing energy prices, which are an important element of stabilization, present a major threat to the Lithuanian economy, and in April 1996, the total debt of Lithuanian consumers to the energy suppliers amounted to more than 100 million litas for electricity and more than 200 million litas for heating. Correspondingly, the Lithuanian debt to the fuel suppliers in Russia has reached a peak of more than 60 million USD.

In the current situation environmental and resources problems are not considered very important, either in themselves, or as restraints upon future economic growth. It is usually asserted (UNDP, 1996) that the main assets of Lithuania are its well-qualified and cheap labour force and its geographical position with potential for expanding foreign trade. A major possible constraint on economic development are the social costs imposed by the transition processes. Until now they have not seriously jeopardized the reforms, but social acceptance may diminish with the reduction of resources available to buffer the hardship. However, particularly the energy sector is crucial for the future, because of the strong dependence of Lithuania on energy imports from Russia, and combined with the dangerously mounting debts to the suppliers of gas, oil and nuclear fuel, this makes Lithuania's development plans extremely vulnerable to the availability of energy resources.

It is hard to evaluate the potential social, environmental and economic costs of economic restructuring and transition to a market economy, let alone the costs of achieving environmentally sustainable production. However, in recent years quite a few evaluations of Lithuanian economic prospects for the next 10–15 years have been attempted (Lithuanian Energy Institute, 1995). One such forecast, prepared by the Lithuanian Energy Institute, explores possible long-term development results in two scenarios, assuming 'slow growth' of GDP of 4 per cent and 'fast growth' of GDP of 8 per cent annually, respectively (cf. Table 12.3). In both cases it is expected that the contribution of agriculture to GDP is bound to decrease gradually, mainly because of the significant increase in the relative weight of the service sector, including banking. Moreover, it is expected that the structure of industrial output will change in favour of the fuel and food industries and that the share of machinery production will decrease from the present 15 per cent to approximately 11 per cent.

Table 12.3 Economic structure in Lithuania, 1993–2015

per cent; growth scenario:	1993	1997	2000 slow	2000 fast	2015 slow	2015 fast
Industry	25	26	25	25	24	22
Electricity, gas, water	6	8	8	7	8	5
Agriculture	11	8	8	7	5	4
Transport and communications	11	11	10	11	10	13
Construction	8	9	9	10	9	13
Trade	17	18	18	18	18	18
Banking	7	8	8	9	10	13
Other activities	15	12	14	13	16	12
Total	100	100	100	100	100	100

Note: The slow and fast growth scenarios imply annual overall growth rates of 4 per cent and 8 per cent, respectively.
Source: Lithuanian Energy Institute, 1995.

Similar results were obtained in forecasts by the Ministry of Economic Affairs, where the relative weight of the service sector is predicted to increase in line with the forecasts of the Energy Institute. However, it is expected that at the turn of the century agriculture will play a more significant role than predicted in Table 12.3, and the share of industry is predicted to decrease even more, from 25 per cent in 1993 to 18 per cent in 2005. Yet another forecast of structural changes (Balsys and Maciekus, 1995), based on estimates of sectoral outputs and elasticities of energy consumption, predicts that growth will start in industry, construction and agriculture in about 1996 and that by the year 2000 production levels in these sectors will reach 75 per cent of the level in 1990. The most optimistic forecast is for light industry which is expected to be at 118 per cent of the 1990 level in 2000.

The future role of energy, environment and domestic resources have been analysed in several government reports. A National Energy Strategy was aproved by the government in April 1994 (Lithuanian Energy Institute, 1993). Exploitation of mineral resources is described in the Programme of the Exploitation and Usage of Mineral Resources prepared by the Lithuanian

Geological Service in 1994. Other programmes for the natural resources development and exploitation have been prepared as well, including a National Agriculture Activity Development Programme adopted in September 1993, and a Forestry Sector Development Programme up until the year 2010 adopted in September 1994. An important and comprehensive programme, the Lithuanian National Environmental Strategy, was finalized in 1996 and submitted to the government (Ministry of Environmental Protection, 1996).

REFERENCES

Balsys, O. and V. Maciekus (1995), 'Forecasting of Lithuanian Industry, Construction, and Agricultural Development, and Their Demand for Fuel and Energy Resources' (in Lithuanian), *Ekonomika*, **39** (1), 5–23.

Department of Statistics (1995), *Survey of Lithuanian Economy*, Vilnius: Department of Statistics.

Department of Statistics (1996), *Economic and Social Development in Lithuania*, Vilnius: Department of Statistics.

Fennhan, J. (1994), 'Energy Strategies for the Baltic Countries', in J. Birk Mortensen (ed.), *Environmental Economics and the Baltic Region*, Copenhagen: Copenhagen University, Institute of Economics.

IMF (1992), *Economic Review: Lithuania*, Washington, D.C.: International Monetary Fund.

Krueger Consult and Baltic Consulting Group (1995), *Inventory of Damage and Cost Estimate of Remediation of Former Military Sites in Lithuania*, Vilnius: Baltic Consulting Group.

Lithuanian Energy Institute (1993), *Lithuanian National Energy Strategy*, Kaunas: Lithuanian Energy Institute.

Lithuanian Energy Institute (1995), *Scenarios of Lithuanian Economic Development. First Draft* (in Lithuanian), Kaunas: Lithuanian Energy Institute.

Malisauskas, V. (1993), *Use and Protection of Natural Resources* (in Lithuanian), Vilnius: Academia.

Ministry of Energy (1995), *Balances of Electricity, Heat, Fuel and Energy in Lithuania* (in Lithuanian), Vilnius: Ministry of Energy.

Ministry of Environmental Protection (1992), *Lithuanian National Report for the United Nations' Conference on Environment and Development*, Vilnius: Ministry of Environmental Protection.

Ministry of Environmental Protection (1995), *Lithuania's Environment: Status, Processes, Trends*, Vilnius: Ministry of Environmental Protection.

Ministry of Environmental Protection (1996), *Lithuanian National Environmental Strategy*, Vilnius: Ministry of Environmental Protection.

Simenas, A. (1996), *Economic Reform in Lithuania* (in Lithuanian), Vilnius: Prada.

UNDP (1996), *Lithuania: Human Development Report*, Vilnius: UNDP.

World Bank (1994), *Lithuania: Energy Sector Review*, Report No. 11867-LT, Washington, D.C.: The World Bank.

13. Lithuania: Energy Imports and Exports, and Economic Instruments

Vytautas Snieška

13.1 The Economy, the Environment, and Energy Policy in Transition

The environmental situation as well as energy consumption has changed dramatically in Lithuania since 1991 because of economic depression, price increases of imported raw materials and energy, and restructuring of production. As a consequence the state of the environment has improved, and this has also been supported by some policy responses, for example an increase in the share of GDP spent on investments in the construction of communal sewage water treatment, but attempts to develop and implement a government strategy for environmental protection are still at a preparatory stage.

From 1989 to 1995 the Lithuanian GDP declined by 61 per cent, and for industrial production the decline was even more drastic, namely about 80 per cent. The economic structure also changed profoundly. The share of agriculture in total production decreased from 28 per cent in 1990 to 8 per cent in 1994. In the same period the share of wholesale and retail trade increased from 5 per cent to 24 per cent (Department of Statistics, 1995). In industry the most vulnerable branches were those most intimately integrated into the Russian economy because of imports of raw materials and exports of semi-manufactured articles or finished products. Most severely hit were branches with high intensity of energy and raw materials, the prices of which have soared to world market levels. In the transition period policies have to some extent sheltered consumers against the social consequences of energy price increases, but the burden was felt by industrial enterprises, where the share of energy and fuel in total production increased from 5 per cent in 1990 to 22 per cent in 1993. For production of construction materials the share increased from 13 to 38 per cent. The very low rate of capacity utilization also contributed to the increase in the share of energy costs (Ministry of Energy, 1996).

Various scenarios for future economic growth have been worked out by the government. A slow growth scenario assumes 4 per cent annual GDP growth as in the National Energy programme, and a fast growth scenario with rapid economic reforms and development assumes 5–7 per cent annual growth which exceeds the 5 per cent expected by the World Bank (cf. Table 12.3). The size of GDP in 2005 is expected to be 60 per cent and 95 per cent of the level in 1989, respectively, in the two scenarios (Ministry of Energy, 1996).

13.2 Energy Policy, Imports and Exports

In the 1980s the structure of energy consumption in Lithuania was different from that of other European countries. The major part, about one half, was consumed by industry and transportation. The residential sector consumed less than a quarter (cf. Table 13.1). Among the reasons was the rapid development of the chemical industry and the building materials industry, which are highly energy intensive. Lithuania produced huge amounts of energy intensive products such as cement, 950 kg per capita, and fertilizers, 220 kg per capita, which is more than almost any other European country. From 1991 to 1994 final energy consumption declined by 44 per cent, and industrial consumption declined by 62 per cent.

Household consumption of energy decreased less than that of other sectors, and in 1994 it was back at approximately the same level as in 1990, particularly for heating for which the price elasticity of demand is relatively low. Although there are several examples of waste, when temperatures are kept high in almost empty industrial buildings due to poor management and low flexibility of industrial organization, the share of households in heating consumption has increased from 26 per cent in 1992 to 49 per cent in 1994. The most widespread system of heating is district heating to which about 55 per cent of all buildings in Lithuania are connected, and in large cities the proportion is more than 70 per cent. Heating is supplied by heating power plants and boiler houses which operate mostly on either fuel oil or natural gas. The average amount of heat consumed per square metre is 450 kWh, that is more than twice the amount in, for example, Denmark. This is due to heavy heat losses caused by poor thermal insulation of buildings – a legacy of Soviet times when energy resources were deceptively abundant and available at very low prices – losses in supply networks, and lack of metering and technical means for controlling the level of heating in individual apartments. Energy saving programmes, insulation of houses, improvement of district heating systems and usage of local energy resources are seen as the ways to more efficient energy consumption. For the remaining 45 per cent of buildings, which are not connected to district heating systems, improvements could be obtained by replacing the dominant type of fuel, namely coal, with more efficient and less polluting types of fuel.

According to the National Energy Strategy, the greatest potential for power consumption saving includes reduction of heat losses in industrial enterprises and apartments. The heating season in Lithuania lasts 190–200 days, and it is estimated that 1 per cent of heating saved would amount to 43 kTOE (kiloton of oil equivalent). A centralized district heating system is potentially efficient and has been a success in western countries, but it requires highly efficient networks and the use of heat from the power plants. The question is whether the costs of renovating the old system are less than the cost of constructing small decentralized combined heat and power units. Since Lithuania has a natural gas network, gas units are an obvious possibility.

Table 13.1 Energy supply, exports, and consumption in Lithuania, 1989–94

million TOE	1989	1990	1991	1992	1993	1994
Primary energy supply	18.6	17.3	18.0	11.1	9.1	8.3
Energy exports and losses	8.8	8.2	8.6	4.7	3.7	3.0
Final energy consumption	9.8	9.1	9.4	6.4	5.4	5.3
Industry and construction	3.3	3.1	3.2	1.9	1.4	1.2
Transportation	2.2	1.7	2.1	1.4	1.1	1.1
Agriculture	0.8	0.9	0.8	0.5	0.4	0.2
Households	2.2	1.9	2.1	1.7	1.7	2.0
Other sectors	1.3	1.5	1.2	0.9	0.8	0.8

Notes: Amounts of energy are measured in million tons of oil equivalent (TOE).
Sources: Ministry of Energy, 1995; LEI, 1995.

Electric power plants in Lithuania are fuelled by oil and nuclear fuel. The largest thermal power plant, the Elektrenai power station between Vilnius and Kaunas with 1800 MW capacity, used to burn heavy fuel oil with 3.5 per cent sulphur content. In the 1980s no power plants had cleaning equipment for sulphur and nitrogen oxides. The 2500 MW Ignalina nuclear power plant in the north-eastern part of the country consists of two Chernobyl type reactors. The construction of the third reactor was stopped due to serious public discontent. The plant poses a danger to the environment, but if it had to be closed down Lithuania would lack power supply, as it presently supplies 77 per cent of electricity production; in 1993 it supplied no less than 87 per cent. Near Kaunas a pumped storage hydropower plant was nearly completed in the 1980s. The planned capacity of 1600 MW has been cut by half due to widespread public resistance.

Total electricity production has dropped by almost two thirds from the peak amount of 29.158 GWh in 1989 (cf. Table 13.2). From 1990 to 1994 the production of thermal power plants declined by 85 per cent and that of Ignalina by 55 per cent. Final domestic consumption declined by 45 per cent, primarily industrial and agricultural consumption. The most dramatic change

took place concerning electricity exports. In 1990 42 per cent of total production was exported to other parts of the Soviet Union, but in 1994 the export
surplus had vanished, and in 1994 17 per cent of final consumption was
imported (cf. Table 13.2). In the Soviet period Lithuania also exported oil
products to Latvia, Estonia and the Kaliningrad region. Oil and gas were
imported by pipelines from Russia, and crude oil was processed in Lithuania
at the Mažeikiai refinery which produced 12 million tons of oil products
annually. In 1990 42 per cent of total fuel imports were re-exported. During
the blockade in the months April to June 1990, production at the Mažeikiai
refinery was discontinued. Production resumed afterwards, and gasoline could
be brought without problems into Lithuania.

*Table 13.2 Electricity production, exports, and consumption in Lithuania,
1980–2015*

thousand GWh	1980	1985	1990	1994	2004	2015
Production	11.5	21.0	28.4	9.8	13.0	13.2
Ignalina NPP	-	9.5	17.0	7.7	-	-
Thermal power plants	11.2	11.1	11.0	1.6	-	-
Hydropower plants	0.5	0.4	0.4	0.5	-	-
Exports	0.1	6.2	12.0	−1.1	1.5	0
Final consumption	9.9	11.2	12.0	7.1	8.1	9.9
Industry and construction	4.9	5.5	5.5	2.8	3.3	4.1
Transportation	0.2	0.2	0.2	0.1	0.2	0.2
Agriculture	1.8	2.3	2.7	0.7	0.7	0.7
Households	1.1	1.4	1.8	1.5	1.8	2.1

Notes: Ignalina is the site of Lithuania's nuclear power plant. The parts of production not
accounted for are losses in the transmission system. One GWh equals 85.71 TOE (tons of oil
equivalent).
Sources: LEI, 1993b, 1995; Ministry of Energy, 1994.

Electricity production is expected to recover only slowly. From 1994 to the
year 2015 total production is predicted to increase by 32 per cent and final
consumption by 50 per cent (cf. Table 13.2). These estimates are based upon
the analyses in the National Energy Strategy (LEI, 1993a), a programme for
restructuring energy supply and consumption, which was approved by the
government on 19 April 1994. The principal directions of the National Energy
Strategy include the following: energy consumption efficiency should
increase, so that by 2015 the final energy consumed per unit of GDP will
drop to 50–60 per cent of the present level. Security of the Ignalina nuclear
power plant should be improved; the first block of the plant is going to be
closed down by 2004 and the second block by 2008, and general guidelines

on the future of nuclear energy in Lithuania should be adopted by 1998. At the upper basin of the Kruonis hydroelectric pumped storage power plant a third and fourth power units should be constructed; the third unit was in fact completed in 1995. A larger share of energy should be produced by combined heat and power plants. Domestic extraction of crude oil should be promoted and an oil import and export harbour at the Baltic coast should be constructed. Agreements should be negotiated with the Republic of Latvia on usage of its underground gas storage facilities while simultaneously exploring possibilities for the construction of gas storage facilities in Lithuania as well as the possibilities for supplies of natural and liquified gas from Western Europe. The potential of renewable energy resources including industrial and house-hold wastes should be evaluated and promoted by pilot projects. Contacts with neighbouring countries should be developed in order to improve reliability of fuel and energy supply including export and import of energy during peak load periods. Air pollution should be reduced by substituting natural gas for fuel oil and by other measures in order to meet Lithuania's national and international obligations.

Energy efficiency is being encouraged through increases in energy prices. Nearly two thirds of domestic gas consumers are now individually metered as compared to virtually none in 1994. Metering of hot and cold water in residential apartments is now quite common as well. Metering of gas and water is encouraged by favourable tariffs.

13.3 Environmental Protection in the Short and Medium Terms

The aims of environmental policy as well as relations between environmental policy and economic development, main action programmes, various adminis-trative and economic means, and the division of responsibility between government and other institutions are outlined in the The State Strategy for Environmental Protection prepared by the Ministry of the Environment (1996).

The environmental problems of **energy production** include air pollution by sulphur and greenhouse gases and radioactive pollution. Electric thermal power plants and boilers contributed 57 per cent of emissions of SO_2 in 1993. There are also rather high sulphur contents in residues from the Russian crude oil used in the petroleum industry. Sulphur emissions are a type of pollution which can be reduced substantially as in western countries by means of abatement equipment and more efficient energy production, transmission and consumption (Ministry of the Environment, 1995).

Serious environmental protection problems are connected with the Ignalina nuclear power plant, namely emission of radionuclides into the atmosphere, insufficient depositories for hard and liquid radioactive wastes, thermal influences on lakes, and the risk of accidents. Recently various precautions have been taken to increase the safety of the Ignalina plant in co-operation with Danish and Swedish experts. It is recommended in the State Strategy for Environmental Protection that the Ministry of Energy should be responsible for the construction of storage units for used nuclear fuel and installation of seismic control systems. Both means should be accomplished by the year 2000. In February 1994 an agreement was signed with the European Bank for Reconstruction and Development on a donation of 33 million ECU for improving safety at the Ignalina plant. The project consists of three types of measures, namely service, short-term technical measures for increasing safety, and increase of operational safety. Preliminary analysis, conducted as part of this agreement, showed that it may be profitable to close down the first block of the Ignalina plant in 1998, because large investments in expensive measures for the increase of safety will have too short a period of operation, as the expected service period of the first block will end about the year 2000. But further discussions in the Lithuanian mass media and in research circles were dominated by the opposite opinion and generally more favourable attitudes towards continued production of nuclear energy.

Environmental problems originating in the **extractive industries** mainly take the form of destruction of nature and landscapes caused by pit construction and open excavation mining, by expanding oil extraction, and by using geothermal energy. These problems may become more acute when policies stimulate decreasing imports of raw materials and expanding use of domestic resources as well as exports of products made from local resources or in some cases unprocessed domestic raw materials. Similar damage to the natural environment is caused by the expansion of urbanization, but this is not considered a priority issue. The government strategy concerning extraction of resources attempts to combine maximum economic exploitation with improvements in the quality of the natural environment. The means is first of all development of an efficient system of territorial planning, including documentation and evaluation of potential natural resources and preparation of a cartographic base for territorial planning. But it is also intended to develop a system of taxation on exploitation of resources in order to internalise costs in terms of natural damage into the calculations of enterprises.

Other branches of **industry** present specific environmental problems. Among the most important industrial product groups are food and beverages which contribute 29 per cent of industrial production; oil products account for 27 per cent, textiles and knit-wear for 9 per cent, chemicals and chemical materials for 6 per cent, and machines, electric equipment and processed metals for 6 per cent. It is expected that the food, oil products and light industries will retain their role until the year 2000, but the relative importance of the machine building industry is expected to decline (cf. Table 12.3). Some branches are considered to possess the potential for future expansion, including forestry and wood processing, flax growing and processing, leather and fur processing, dairy production and construction materials production. An environmentally sustainable expansion of industrial production requires that emerging pollution problems are prevented, including emissions of chromium, organic materials and detergents from the leather industry, formaldehyde, hard parts, solvents and lacquer wastes from wood processing, whey and organic materials, detergents and waste heat from dairies, dust and asbestos from the building materials industry, and nitrogen and phosphorus compounds and acid emission from the chemical industry.

The future industrial structure will depend on the relative international competitiveness of various branches, and it is expected that removing trade barriers against other countries by introducing more flexible tax systems and expanding infrastructure and information systems will also contribute to improving environmental responsibility. In recent years several enterprises in various industrial branches have taken part in international co-operation projects for waste treatment. Thus joint ventures have started between the Craft Jacob's Suchard and Lietuva confectionary factories, between the Freda and Klaipėdos Baldai furniture factories, and between the Jonava Achema and Kėdainiai Chemical factories. Another priority area concerning waste treatment is improvement of the total production and consumption cycle of products. The Ministry of the Environment together with the Ministry of Trade and Industry are currently working out analyses of various kinds of packaging, their impact on the environment, their deposition and recuperation as well as related taxation problems.

Many obstacles to efficient industrial waste treatment still have to be overcome, including lack of special knowledge, insufficient contamination control, lack of technical equipment and investment funds, and lack of support from top level management. One of the most acute waste problems remains unsolved, namely the deposition of harmful wastes in the Auštrakiai dump near Šiauliai where a major emergency may happen at any moment.

As part of the State Strategy of Environmental Protection it is proposed to stimulate financially enterprises which invest in efficient waste treatment and pollution abatement equipment. Enterprises will also be supported by technical assistance, education and information. Special educational and teaching programmes are proposed for managers.

Environmental projects and institutions receive **finance** from various sources. In the government investment programme, for the years 1995–97 priority was given to investments in energy production and savings, transportation and environmental protection. Total environmental investments for the years 1995–97 were 916 million litas, corresponding to approximately 225 million ECU, mainly channelled through local management systems for environmental protection. This sum is a combination of direct expenditures from the state budget, foreign loans with low interest and financial resources of municipalities.

In 1995 the major part, 47 per cent, of the 105 million litas state budget expenditures on environmental protection purposes was directed towards construction of sewage water treatment plants in Vilnius, Kaunas, Klaipeda, Šiauliai and Palanga. The remaining part of the total of 257 million litas of investment funds for environment protection purposes envisaged in the invest-ment programme consists of 132 million litas from foreign sources and 20 million litas from local budgets. In 1996 the total of 316 million litas was composed of 162 million litas from the state budget, 118 million litas from foreign sources, and 37 million litas from local budgets.

Table 13.3 Environmental programme expenditures in Lithuania, 1994–96

per cent	Assigned funds 1994	Needed funds 1995	Assigned funds 1995	Needed funds 1996	Assigned funds 1996
Water protection	2	4	6	4	4
Air protection	3	9	4	2	0
Waste processing	0	0	1	1	2
Pesticide processing	-	-	-	45	43
Landscape protection	27	24	16	14	13
Biological variety protection	3	3	10	4	4
Fish protection	14	11	8	4	4
Environmental monitoring	40	29	37	21	25
Ecological education	10	20	13	2	3
Ecological expertise	1	0	5	1	0
Publications	-	-	-	2	2
Total (per cent)	100	100	100	100	100
Total (thousand litas)	1325	3084	1174	4456	3500

Notes: The budget figures include only expenditures for the programme of the Ministry of the Environment. In March 1994 a currency board arrangement was adopted and the litas pegged to the dollar at the rate of 4 litas per dollar.
Source: Ministry of the Environment, 1996.

In addition, the state budget assigns expenditures to other ministries for environmental purposes. State funds for environmental programmes for which the Ministry of the Environment is responsible, including policy formulation, preparation of legal acts, environmental protection territorial planning, monitoring, research and education, are shown in Table 13.3 for the years 1994–96. A characteristic feature is that only a fraction, 38 per cent in 1995 increasing to 79 per cent in 1996, of the funding necessary for carrying out the programme obligations of the ministry was actually assigned.

Several other ministries and institutions receive government finance. The

Ministry of Communication was provided with 135 000 litas in 1994 for a transport and environmental protection programme. The Ministry of Agriculture is responsible for an ecological agriculture development programme in northern Lithuania, and for this purpose the so-called Tatula fund was established which received 3.5 million litas in 1994 and 4 million litas in 1995. The environmental protection activity of the Ministry of Forestry is primarily connected with planting new forests and with the creation of three national parks in Aukštaitija, Dzūkija and Žemaitija which are under the supervision of this ministry. In 1994 4 million litas were assigned from the state's budget to plant forests and 2.7 million litas for national parks. In 1995 assignments were 7.9 and 2.7 million litas, respectively.

Another source of finance, specifically intended for environmental purposes is the Lithuanian State Environment Protection Fund created in 1988. Into this fund is channelled proceeds from fines, paid according to the law on the use of natural resources, the law on environmental taxes, the law on hunting rules, as well as fines for accidental release of pollution into the environment and other fines. In 1994 the fund collected 3.1 million litas and in 1995 about 4 million litas. The proceeds are distributed between several purposes; 30 per cent are designated for repair of environmental damage, for the removal of pollution sources and for other environmental investments; 40 per cent are used for environment research, for ecological education and for information; finally 30 per cent are directed towards encouragement of personnel employed in environment protection and for promotion of public participation.

There are a number of deficiencies in the current system of financing. Resources are very scarce, particularly for activities outside the priority area of sewage water treatment, and planned funds may not be used for environmental purposes because of a lack of resources for other state activities; thus, in 1994 150 million litas were planned for environmental purposes, but only 100 million litas were actually assigned; in Vilnius only 17 per cent of planned environmental investment funds were spent and in Kaunas 90 per cent. The existing centralized financing system does not stimulate effectiveness but rather the construction of too large installations. The financing system could be improved by creating special accounts in each local management institution for the accumulation of environmental funds which could be supplemented by the necessary share of taxes and business contributions. Also the Ministry of the Environment accumulates taxes aimed for environmental purposes as well as payments for sewage water treatment and other environmental services directly into environmental accounts. This would be closer to a polluter pays principle, where the polluter directly covers environment protection costs, in contrast to the current system, where money raised by means of general taxes is used to cover environment protection costs.

However, taking into account the fact that consumers currently are not able to pay taxes covering the costs, government finance should play a decisive role. Concerning the priority area of sewage water treatment it is expected that customer's taxes levied according to water consumption may be increased in the medium term. It is also expected that user payments may be increased, for example for visiting protected territories and for using natural recreational resources. In order to mobilize the participation of enterprises it is suggested in the State Strategy for Environmental Protection that they should be offered loans on preferential terms.

13.4 Administrative Means of Environmental Protection

Environmental protection must in part rely on administrative means. This requires monitoring and law enforcement mechanisms which are currently not very efficient in Lithuania. These problems are partly due to the very complicated structure of the existing legal system of environmental regulation. Legal rights and obligations must be more precisely defined, and this is particularly important in the current situation of ongoing privatization of ownership, where responsibility for damage caused earlier is not juridically well determined.

Therefore, a major goal of legal reform is to create a unified and simple system of laws for environmental protection. Such reform should be started without delay with the help of consultants who know European Union laws, as it is of utmost importance that environmental legislation is compatible with the legal system of the European Union.

Particularly urgent is legal regulation of territorial planning which is a precondition for rational utilization of land, resources and the natural environment, that is for realizing a balanced development where the needs of economic growth are combined with environmental protection interests.

13.5 Economic Means

The aim of economic means is to express size of the harm caused to the environment in terms of market prices and to create economic incentives for environmental protection. Economic means include taxes on pollution, sales of pollution permits, taxes on resource exploitation, customers' payments, as well as tax reductions, subsidies or loans in order to stimulate private environmental investment. They aim to motivate people to reduce the emission of pollution, to implement abatement techniques and to preserve natural resources.

In order to be efficient, economic means should be directed towards a reduction in the source itself. They should be easily executed and managed, and the costs of their implementation and their usage should be easily calculated. They should be socially acceptable and compatible with existing market and institutional structures and provide clear signals. Economic means are more flexible than administrative rules, and they motivate individuals to socially rational decisions while leaving the right to make the decisions to the enterprises themselves. Furthermore, they provide government finance. On the other hand they are difficult to change quickly, and the reactions of economic agents may be difficult to predict. Like administrative means they require extensive monitoring and control.

The system of **pollution taxes and penalties** in Lithuania is now under review, not least because existing taxes are not properly indexed to inflation and do not correspond to the changing economic and political conditions. From 1991 to 1995 indexation covered only 70 per cent of actual inflation which reached 1163 per cent in 1992; from July 1995 charge rates have been fully indexed, and at that time they were also corrected for past inflation. Ambient air and water quality standards exist for about 800 substances, and as in other Eastern European countries the existing system levies taxes on a large number of pollutants, namely 100 types of air polluting and 51 water polluting substances, that is many more than in most Western European and other countries, and monitoring has been insufficient partly due to the large number of pollutants and charge rates.

Charge rates are differentiated between enterprises, and they are set by environmental inspectors after negotiations with enterprises, taking into account the pollution load and ambient standards in the specific region, the type of products and technologies of the enterprise, as well as its financial situation. For each enterprise and for each pollutant a maximum allowable pollution limit is set, but for many polluters they are negotiated and replaced by more generous so-called temporary allowable pollution limits. For pollution of less than half the maximum allowable limit no charge is paid, and then an increasing charge rate is levied up to the limit when the rate equals the so-called base rate. For pollution exceeding the limit the charge rate is increased by 100 per cent for energy producing enterprises, and by 400 per cent for industrial enterprises. The same system of taxation rates applies to enterprises with temporary allowable limits, except that they pay the base rate for all pollution below the limit. Charge rates are rather low as compared to rates in other countries, and furthermore, monitoring and tax collection are not strict and often subject to negotiation with environmental inspectors (Sėmenienė et. al., 1997).

The new tax system will be simplified and hopefully more efficient at motivating enterprises to reduce pollution. It is expected that the new system will tax only the main polluting substances, including sulphur oxides, nitrogen oxides, dust, biological waste, nitrogen and phosphorus in waste water, and some more. Furthermore, tax rates will be reduced, so that initially taxes will be rather low. Later on they will be gradually increased when efficient tax collection is in place.

One of the main aims of **taxation of the usage of natural resources** is to redistribute this wealth to all members of society, not only to buyers and sellers of natural resources in the market. So, tax calculation will be related, not only to type and quantity of resource use, but also to the market price. Resource taxes will include 5 per cent of the market price. This tax rate was chosen because it is similar to other sales taxes for various products and to taxes on natural resources usage in other countries.

In the former tax system tax discounts were applied to stimulate reduction and usage of wastes and investments in resource savings. The discount reduced the profit tax from 29 per cent to 15 per cent, but it was not very effective because the profitability of most industrial enterprises is very low. But gradually this privilege of reduced taxes is expected to play an increasingly important role. In the new tax system juridical and physical persons, who contribute at least 25 per cent towards the costs of environmental protection investment, are to be exempted from taxes according to the main tariff, with the aim of covering environmental expenses, but for no longer than three years. Up to now the effect of this law has been limited, for different economic and institutional reasons. But it stimulates enterprises to reduce pollution and to invest their own funds in environmental protection equipment. It is recommended in the State Strategy for Environmental Protection that a modern tax discount system should be developed along similar lines, enabling tax authorities, for example, to reduce VAT, excise or even profit taxes for enterprises, which implement pollution and waste reducing techniques. This would allow enterprises to fully or partly cover their environmental costs and at the same time stimulate pollution abatement and industrial development. An example is the suggested differentiation of excise taxes on petrol according to the content of lead. A higher tax rate on leaded petrol would force the polluters to cover at least part of the costs connected with the impact on the environment; it is administratively easy to accomplish, as it requires only an order from the government, and it provides a clear signal to drivers to use unleaded petrol and install catalytic converters. Besides, it will contribute to financing the government budget. The burden of this tax will be most heavily felt by those industrial branches which use large amounts of oil products.

Government **subsidies**, including donations and low interest loans, are considered to be an indispensable means of financing public investments for waste treatment and other environmental purposes until citizens become able and willing to cover all real consumption expenses. It is suggested that a so-called Rotational Environmental Protection Fund be established to provide subsidies for enterprises and municipal institutions in order to stimulate investments.

Extended use of **consumer payments** is recommended and expected to gradually cover an increasing part of the costs of water supply to households and enterprises, waste water cleaning, and disposal of solid waste from households and enterprises. Eventually, consumer payments would totally cover costs and stimulate the economical use of water and other resources. The advantage of this policy instrument is that it gives a serious incentive to change behaviour. But social problems could arise, and exceptions should be made for low-income families, for example when the costs of water, sewage and waste disposal are higher than a certain, high percentage of total family income, and this could easily happen for many families in contemporary Lithuania.

A specific type of consumer payment recommended in the State Strategy for Environmental Protection is payment for parking in large city centres. This would reduce motor-car traffic, and the expenses of hiring a payment collector could easily be covered. Perhaps many of the increasing number of drivers in Lithuania will resent this type of environmental taxation, and some of them would probably be able to pass the payment on to their customers.

13.6 Environmental Policy and Public Opinion

The standard of living in Lithuania has decreased drastically since 1988, pushing large parts of the population to the verge of social unrest. Taking this into account, it is no wonder that the general opinion is that environmental problems are not at all the most important. This is evident from a comparison of the sums that were requested by the Ministry of the Environment from the State Budget in 1994–96 for environmental protection purposes and those actually allocated by Parliament (cf. Table 13.3). Thus, the modest amounts requested were 3.1 and 4.5 million litas in 1995 and 1996 respectively, but only 1.2 and 3.5 million litas were assigned, that is about 38 and 79 per cent, respectively (Ministry of the Environment, 1996). Furthermore, the economic recession brought relief to the environment due to the observable decrease in the volume of pollution, especially in regard to pollution of the atmosphere (cf. Table 1.3). So far no qualified and serious research on the environmental sustainability of economic development has ever been conducted in Lithuania. Thus, it could be asserted that at present Lithuania is much more concerned with economic survival than with environmental sustainability.

REFERENCES

Department of Statistics (1994), 'Heat and Fuel Balance 1993' (in Lithuanian), *Statistikos Rinkinys* (1994).
Department of Statistics (1995), *Lithuanian Statistical Chronicle* (in Lithuanian), Vilnius: Department of Statistics.

Fennhan, J. (1994), 'Energy Strategies for the Baltic Countries', in J. Birk Mortensen (ed.), *Environmental Economics and the Baltic Region*, Copenhagen: Copenhagen University, Institute of Economics.

LEI (1993a), *Lithuanian National Energy Strategy*, Kaunas: Lihuanian Energy Institute, 1993.

LEI (1993b), *Energy in Lithuania. Power, Heat and Fuel Balances 1980–1992*, Kaunas: Lithuanian Energy Institute.

LEI (1995), *Programme for the Development of Lithuanian Energetics* (in Lithuanian), Kaunas: Lithuanian Energy Institute.

Lotspeich, R. (1995), 'Strategies for Environmental Policy in Transition Economies, Command versus Market Instruments', *Comparative Economic Studies*, **37** (4), pp. 125–45.

Mališauskas, V. (1993), *The Use of Natural Resources and Their Protection* (in Lithuanian), Vilnius: Ecoslit.

Mikėnas, V. (1996), 'Peculiarities of "Kaunas Waters" Investments Project: A Strange Way to Increase the Price', *Kauno Diena* (24 April 1996), 5.

Ministry of Energy (1995), *The Balances of Lithuania's Electricity, Heat, Fuel and Energy* (in Lithuanian), Vilnius: Ministry of Energy.

Ministry of Energy (1996), *National Programme for Increasing Energy Efficiency* (in Lithuanian), Vilnius: Ministry of Energy.

Ministry of the Environment (1993), *The Programme for Recycling of Wastes and Raw Materials*, Vol. 1, abridged version (in Lithuanian), Vilnius: Ministry of the Environment.

Ministry of the Environment (1995), *Country Programme for Phasing out Ozone Depleting Substances*, Vilnius: Department of Statistics.

Ministry of the Environment (1996), *The State Strategy for Environmental Protection* (in Lithuanian), Vilnius: Ministry of the Environment.

Rutkauskas, A.V. (1995), *Ecological Cost Minimization Strategies* (in Lithuanian), Vilnius: Ecoslit.

Sėmenienė, D., R. Bluffstone and L. Čekanavičius (1997), 'The Lithuanian Charge System: Evaluation and Prospects for the Future', in R. Bluffstone and B.A. Larson (eds.), *Controlling Pollution in Transition Economies: Theories and Methods*, Aldershot: Edward Elgar.

Snieška, V. (1992), 'Economic Externalities and Global Problems' (in Lithuanian), in *Tarptautinių ekonominių santykių bei globalinių problemų ekonomikos pagrindai*, Kaunas: Technologija.

Snieška, V. (1994), 'Environmental Problems of the New Baltic States in a Period of Transition to a Market Economy', pp. 55–61 in J. Birk Mortensen (ed.), *Environmental Economics and the Baltic Region*, Copenhagen: Copenhagen University, Institute of Economics.

Vilemas, J. (1996), 'Perspectives for Lithuanian Energy. Economic, Ecological and Social Aspects' (in Lithuanian), *Mokslas Ir Technika*, **1996** (2), 10–15.

Žukauskas, A., B. Jaskelevičius and A. Stumbras (1996), 'Production and Atmospheric Pollution' (in Lithuanian), *Mokslas Ir Technika*, **1996** (2), 1–2.

PART FOUR

International Co-operation

14. Environmental Co-operation in the Baltic Region

Jesper Jespersen

14.1 International Environmental Problems

The regional character of the environmental problems of the Baltic Sea calls for co-ordinated action by all countries involved. The main sources of pollution are well documented by the work of the Helsinki Commission (HEL-COM), which was established following the signing of the Helsinki Convention by all coastline states as far back as 1974. After the political changes of 1989–90 the willingness to provide data from the East and financial funds from the West have increased considerably. The newly released figures have unveiled that much is still to be done before the Baltic Sea is cleaned up. This could be achieved with intensified and co-ordinated investments and more trans-national financial support.

Environmental issues become an international matter of concern whenever there are consequences which affect a geographical area including several independent states. Then there emerges the problem of identifying these issues as well as possible methods of regional policy co-ordination. Basically, one can distinguish between two kinds of international environmental problems, global problems such as changes of the climate and the ozone layer, and regional problems like air or sea water pollution. The global climate is affected by increasing concentrations of greenhouse gases in the atmosphere. As these gases disperse themselves equally around the globe it becomes unimportant from an environmental point of view where the polluting source is located geographically. The crucial matter is the total emission. Some countries are more endangered than others by these future events, and there will be rather big differences in global environmental concern dependent on the average income per capita. Hence, political attitudes among the participating nations towards global pollution will range from 'free riding' to 'disproportional cleaning up'.

The Baltic Sea has all the qualities of a genuine regional problem. This makes it a possible show case to answer the following three analytical questions:

1. How could it happen that the Baltic Sea nearly died?
2. How to avoid futher pollution?
3. Which decision models and policy proposals are appropriate for cleaning up?

The environmental and economic benefits to be gained from a cost effective policy depend upon co-ordinated decision making and co-operation within the Baltic Region, where the deep rooted differences in income and preferences must be taken into consideration.

Concerning the **global climate changes** and emission of greenhouse gases the case is rather straightforward. As already mentioned the ultimate impact on the change of climate is independent of where the source of exhaustion is located. A reduction in for instance Poland has an equal effect on the Baltic Sea Area as a similar reduction in Denmark, Iceland or Los Angeles (for that matter). Due to a rather huge variation in per capita and per GDP-unit emission from one country to another, the same quantitative reduction of pollution can be obtained at very different costs.

These differences in costs and in attitudes towards global pollution problems create a situation where an economically beneficial arbitrage in pollution abatement between countries may be undertaken. Countries with relatively high costs related to further reduction of emissions could more cheaply pay for extra restrictions on greenhouse gases in countries with lower costs and with lower ambitions on global pollution. The end result would be a cleaner environment at a lower cost. Unfortunately, such a strategy also opens up an endless process of attempts at 'free riding' among countries, which has to be taken into account.

By definition **regional pollution**, from air pollution, waste water and nuclear pollution, depends on what kind of pollution is considered. The impact of air pollution depends upon, first the sensitivity of the area – sulphur is a much bigger problem in an acidic area – and second, the transmission routes and wind and weather conditions.

Waste water pollution depends on the kind of waste which is emitted, the local cleaning arrangements and the kind of transmission channels. One channel of use is the existing rivers. Another is a constructed sewage system where the waste water can be controlled much closer. The first way is quite likely to cross several regions or even countries before reaching the sea. The sewage system collects waste water which is directed either to the sea or to the ground water. In both cases the pollution can be limited by national activity.

Energy conversion and extraction creates regional environmental impacts. Regional problems related to conventional power plants are mainly distributed by air, although for example extraction of oil-shale and brown coal may indeed create waste water problems.

Nuclear power plants endanger the surrounding region with the risk of radioactive fall-out. The case of Chernobyl has demonstrated that a rather extended area can suffer when the nuclear process gets out of control, and this certainly makes any nuclear power station a genuine regional problem. A different kind of pollution problem is related to the deposit of used radioactive material from the nuclear plants. It does not have to be placed in the same region where the power plant is located. In fact, radioactive waste is traded between countries; it is hoped that it is under strict control to prevent any abuses; but still the disposal of nuclear waste is a global environmental problem.

14.2 The Baltic Sea – An Example of International Co-operation

The Baltic Sea is an illustrative case of how to detect sources of pollution and to discuss concrete costs and benefits of environmental policies. One reason for this is the shape of this inland sea. The tributaries from water sources are rather easy to identify, because any transmission to other seas go through the narrow passages between the Danish Islands. Contributors to the regional pollution of the Baltic Sea are much less diffuse than for example the North Sea. Sources of air borne pollution are, of course, also in this case somewhat more difficult to detect and identify. Concentration and size of polluting activities are important especially with regard to regional problems when the natural local cleaning capacity is exceeded.

Until the early 1950s the Baltic Sea was considered as being in a rather healthy condition. Industrial production had made no real impact, power and energy production were still low and not very concentrated, the number of lorries and cars small, and agriculture was not based on the intensive use of fertilizers and pesticides. Forty years later that situation has changed dramatically. Parts of the Baltic Sea are today almost dead. This is so despite the dramatic decline in production in a number of the former communist countries which has temporarily reduced the environmental pressure from a number of the polluting sources. There are at least three reasons for this development. First, all countries in the Baltic Region experienced a period of exceptionally high growth rates in material production. The first 20–25 years after the war showed previously unexperienced growth rates. Second, pollution was considered a costless externality of production, especially the part of pollution which could be sent out of the local area by high chimneys or sewage systems. In that period the sea and the air were considered as endless waste containers. Third, decision making in trans-national questions is in general difficult. Around the Baltic Sea such a process was extra difficult because of the two opposed political systems. Things had to become really bad before the generally antagonistic attitudes could be overcome, and still there were rather suspicious attitudes concerning the real intentions behind the Baltic Sea initiatives, for example whether pollution control monitors were intended rather as posts for military search.

The early 1970s led to a shift in attitudes towards environmental problems. Pollution and exploitation of natural resources were recognized as a threat to future human development. In fact, the United Nations called for a world conference in Stockholm in 1972 on widespread international co-operation on environmental matters. More than 100 countries participated, but only one country from Eastern Europe – Romania. The other communist countries decided to abstain because the German Democratic Republic was not invited.

Principle 21 of the Stockholm Declaration is related to transboundary pollution: 'States have the responsibility to ensure that activities within their jurisdiction or control do not cause damage to the environment of other States or of areas beyond the limits of national jurisdiction' (Bergström, 1992, p. 6).

The energy crisis in 1973–74 made the western energy importing countries much more conscious of the limited resources in general and especially increasingly concerned about energy consumption and supply. In contrast to that the communist countries still considered energy and natural resources as important means of production which should be kept cheap. Measured per unit of GDP the production in the Eastern European countries became increasingly energy intensive and as a result more and more polluting, which accelerated the already existing local and regional environmental problems in the Baltic Sea Area.

Although there was an increasing awareness of the bad state of the environment there was no political pressure which could really resolve this deadlock situation before the drastic political changes in 1989–90. An opinion poll carried out in the autumn of 1990 in Sweden, Finland, Estonia and Leningrad gave the result that a majority considered environmental protection more important than economic growth (Bergström, 1992, p. 8). It is a kind of irony that the main reason why environmental pressure has been lifted somewhat in the Baltic Sea Area since 1990 is a dramatic fall in production. In fact, it never became a choice between growth and environmental protection. This fall in production, which has hit Russia and the three Baltic States severely, has turned national political priorities somewhat away from the transboundary environmental issues. Hence, the need for intraregional and intensified collaboration within the Baltic Sea Area is even stronger today than five years ago.

14.3 The Helsinki Convention

Taking the particular political situation into consideration it is remarkable that in 1974 The Convention on the Protection of the Marine Environment of the Baltic Sea was signed by all independent countries bordering the Baltic Sea. The Convention was not enforced in practice until 1980, when the steering agency, the Helsinki Commission (HELCOM), was set up. It is an intergovernmental organization where each government appoints representatives to the Commission, mainly experts from the national environmental protection agencies. The Commission meets once a year and only occasionally the ministers of environment gather in HELCOM. In addition a small secretariat was set up in Helsinki to serve the Commission and to survey the environmental condition of the Baltic Sea.

As a consequence of the regained sovereignty of the Baltic States and mirroring the changed priorities in environmental considerations, the Convention was revised and later signed by all independent states in the Baltic Sea Area in April 1992. The new Convention covers all water areas of the Baltic Sea, including internal parts, such as for example the Rīga Bay and the Russian part of the Finnish Bay, which were earlier excluded. The new Convention also demands that parties shall apply the precautionary principle in the environmental protection of the Baltic Sea Area.

The Helsinki Convention was the first international agreement that in principle covered all sources of pollution affecting a certain geographical area. This means waste water, air borne material and gases and pollution from ships. As an instrument to obtain some of the intentions of the Convention, the Helsinki Commission (HELCOM) was reinforced. The main activities of HELCOM and the related secretariat were to monitor and survey the environmental conditions and developments in the Baltic Sea. In addition a special Task Force was established to detect main point-sources of pollution, so-called hot spots, and to put forward an action plan on how to reduce the emissions from the different polluting sources. All signatory states are members of HELCOM. The Task Force was enlarged with representatives from more countries and international organizations, including the Czech and Slovak Republics, Norway, EU, EBRD, NIB (The Nordic Investment bank) and some non-government organizations.

In 1993 HELCOM finished the second and enlarged survey of the environmental conditions of the Baltic Sea and the main sources of pollution, the hot spots. The carrying out of this survey had taken five years, and it is certainly a very thorough and competent piece of work (HELCOM, 1993). These investigations made it possible to establish a data base for highly qualified judgements on how to reduce further pollution of the Baltic Sea in an effective way.

The survey focused on the quantities of biologically polluting material (Biological Oxygen Demand, BOD), nitrate, phosphorus and sulphur. Within the regions surrounding the Baltic Sea 132 hot spots were detected, and a short list of the most urgent hot spots to be cleaned up was established. This listing gives a picture of the most urgent action to be taken if further pollution is to be prevented (cf. Table 14.1).

Table 14.1   Geographical distribution of Baltic Sea hot spots, 1993

	Hot spots number	Most severe hot spots number	Required investment million ECU
Denmark	4	0	312
Estonia	13	5	1545
Finland	10	0	424
Belarus	3	0	31
Latvia	10	7	417
Lithuania	16	6	497
Poland	38	20	4023
Russia	18	8	1372
Sweden	12	0	451
Czech and Slovak Republics	3	2	113
Germany	9	1	350
Ukraine	1	1	214
Total	132	47	9749

Notes: The distribution of investment costs by countries is to some extent arbitrary because of some cases of transborder hot spots.
Source: HELCOM (1995).

As can be seen from Table 14.1 the required investment for removing the hot spots from the map was estimated to be approximately 10 milliard ECU. Up until 1995 only a few specific plans of action had been worked out, amounting to just above 1 milliard ECU. Very few of these investment plans have yet been finished. In fact, at the HELCOM meeting in November 1994 only eight hot spots had been removed from the list, namely four Swedish and four Finnish, and they would probably have been cleaned up anyhow (HELCOM, 1994).

14.4 Recent developments in the Baltic Sea Area

Despite the rather low investment in pollution abatement, the opening statement of the annual report on the state of the Baltic Sea from the Danish Environmental Agency pronounced in late 1994: 'Overall there has been very

significant reduction of the pollution load to the Baltic Sea since 1991'
(Danish Environmental Agency, 1994, p. 5). But the following sentence gives
the explanation of this seeming paradox: 'This reduction has to a large extent
happened as a consequence of the falling production in agriculture and
manufacturing in the Baltic Republics and in Poland' (Ibid., p. 5).

The report could have added 'as well as in Sweden, Finland and Russia'
(cf. Jespersen, 1995; Aage, 1994, pp. 26-31). The early 1990s were miserable
years in all these countries from an economic point of view. Due to this
extraordinary development it is difficult to judge the impact of the environmental investments in the Baltic Sea Area. Anyhow, the report from the
Danish Environmental Agency reproduced some preliminary figures showing
the development of pollution from the 47 worst hot spots divided into three
categories (cf. Table 14.2).

Table 14.2 Pollution from the 47 most severe Baltic Sea hot spots, 1991–94

1000 tons per year	1991	1994	HELCOM planned	norm
BOD$_5$	453	68	216	46
Nitrate	245	138	120	102
Phosphorus	23	24	20	7

Note: BOD (Biological Oxygen Demand) measures pollution by organic materials.
Source: Danish Environmental Agency, 1994, Tables 3.1.1 and 3.1.2

One further reason why the improvements are so small is to be found in
the fact that many of the worst hot spots are situated in the economically
weakest countries. A number of these countries have large accumulated
environmental problems from the past of more local character which from a
political point of view are considered most important when scarce financial
resources are decided upon.

In the period 1991–94 investment of only 233 million ECU has been
undertaken in these severe hot spots, equivalent to 7 per cent of the total
requirement. International financial resources only provided 4 million ECU
(HELCOM, 1994, p. 13). Looking at the actual investment plans we find that
they represent approximately one third of the needed investments to clear up
the hot spots entirely. Also the internationally provided financial resources are
very limited here. They are reported not to count for more than 10 per cent
of the total.

A general conclusion of the evaluation report (HELCOM, 1994; cf.
Jespersen et. al., 1994) is that nearly all investment projects need some kind
of international financing if they are to be undertaken within a reasonable

time horizon. This, of course, leads to a strong recommendation of more 'soft loan' facilities, if the threat of further pollution is to be avoided when production starts to pick up again in Central and Eastern Europe. The more one moves towards the East, the more pronounced the financial needs seem to be.

It should be added with regard to international funding of environmental investments that the co-operation within the HELCOM agreement could create a rather high return in kind, namely improvements in the environment. If the funds are earmarked to raise the environmental standard of the Baltic Sea it would pay to transfer some money reserved for national initiatives in the rich countries into international funding. Looked upon as a whole the Baltic Sea Area would get more environmental improvement for less money through this kind of collaboration.

Just after the political change in 1989–90 a number of western countries increased the amount of money which they were willing to use as support to the new states and the changed governments. These funds were supposed to support the democratic transformation process and through that also an increased care for the environment (Ministry of Foreign Affairs, 1994). The latter aspect was especially important for nearby countries like Finland, Sweden and Denmark, but initiatives were also taken by the Nordic Council in order to include the Barents Sea Region as part of the environmental protection area in which all Nordic countries had a common interest.

On the other hand the politically changed situation in Central and Eastern Europe also meant a more positive attitude towards joint projects of cleaning up the Baltic Sea. One aspect is the shortcomings of the past with respect to pollution and energy consumption. Another aspect is how to avoid repetition of these failures in the future. Here new and cleaner technology is of crucial importance. This can be provided through joint ventures between western and eastern companies.

The Nordic countries have also provided some funds for such joint venture investments in cleaner production and cleaner technology. The Nordic Investment Bank (NIB) and especially the Nordic Environment Finance Corporation (NEFCO) are examples of financial support working in co-ordination with HELCOM, and at the same time it may catalyse further funds from the European Investment Bank (EIB), the European Bank for Reconstruction and Development (EBRD) and eventually the World Bank (IBRD). The last mentioned three institutions have as a principle that they always look for local partners for co-operation before giving any financing, and NIB and NEFCO could possibly function in this role.

As a consequence the Nordic ministers of the environment have in a common strategy towards the Baltic Sea Area emphasized the importance of further backing to the work carried out within the framework of HELCOM (Nordic Council of Ministers, 1994). Among many things, the Nordic Council has supported the establishment of one to two integrated environment monitoring posts in each of the Baltic countries. Hereby the collection and investigation of data and the co-ordination of environmental protection should be facilitated in an effective way as recommended by HELCOM.

14.5 International Agreements on Sulphur and Nitrate Reductions

From a wider perspective it is not reasonable to restrict the international agreements only to the Baltic Sea Area. Pollution is trans-national and even trans-regional. On the other hand some regions are more sensitive than others depending on the naturally occurring circumstances. This problem is well known in a number of European Areas, for instance the Alpine regions suffering from transit traffic. Hence, it would be rational to distinguish between global and regional agreements on reductions in environmental damaging activities.

In 1978 the United Nations' Economic Commission for Europe (UN-ECE) initiated a common European Measurement and Evaluation Programme (EMEP) with the purpose of monitoring the quality of air with special regard to sulphur, nitrate and ammonia (Statistics Denmark, 1996). This programme has developed a rather detailed model for diffusion and transportation of these items within Europe. It is calculated how much each participating country exports and imports. Although the data are uncertain this statistical material opens the way for more detailed studies of the distribution of contributions to the pollution of sensitive areas between countries.

Another new set of data are the so-called 'critical loads'. For each sensitive region it is calculated how much pollution can be absorbed without a lasting deterioration of the environment. The absorption capacity differs quite a lot from region to region and from one material to another. The optimal use of this information would call for an agreement among the polluting countries that takes into consideration these differences.

Until now this has not been the case with regard to the very few international agreements which have been settled. In 1985 a protocol was made under the auspices of UN-ECE saying that emissions of sulphur should be reduced by at least 30 per cent before the year 1993 by all signatory states. One adverse observation can be made related to the efficiency of this agreement, namely the weakness that all countries are expected to make the same reduction independently of the scale of damaging effects and costs of reductions.

A second protocol with regard to sulphur emissions was signed in 1994 by 25 European countries and Canada. This agreement differentiates the reduction requirements. The richest countries are expected to reduce emissions from 1980 until 2000 by 80 per cent. The former communist countries are on average expected to limit their emissions by one third, increasing to one half by the year 2010. Although it is a very ambitious agreement which seems to be more realistic than the previous one, it would probably still be more cost efficient if the richer countries made some of the reduction requirements in collaboration with the poorer Central and Eastern European countries.

A nitrate (NO_x) protocol was also established by the UN-ECE in 1988. It was less ambitious than the sulphur agreement, because the goal for each country was only to prevent increases in 1994 as compared to 1987. This protocol was signed by 22 European countries and Canada and USA, and it was agreed to make futher reductions dependent on measurements of critical loads. Those countries especially affected by heavy traffic have also made larger reductions and put restrictions on transit transportation.

14.6 Conclusion

It seems that the organization of the environmental monitoring of the Baltic Sea Area is well established. It is not lack of information, but lack of finance and lack of cost efficient agreements which prevent the investments from being undertaken. It is well documented where the hot spots in regard to the Baltic Sea are situated and how much it will cost to clean them up (HEL-COM, 1995).

It is equally well documented that the Nordic countries and Germany would get more environmental improvement for a given amount of money if they were to invest in the financially weaker countries. It is mainly a political question to explain domestically how to get the greatest improvement in environment for a given amount of money and to find a reasonable formula for sharing the costs – eventually related to the average per capita income and the length of the coastline.

REFERENCES

Aage, H. (1994), 'Sustainable Transition', pp. 15-41 in R.W Campbell (ed.), *The Postcommunist Economic Transformation. Essays in Honor of Gregory Grossman*, Boulder: Westview Press.

Bergström, G.W. (1992), 'Environmental Policy and Co-operation in the Baltic Region', Paper presented at the conference *The Baltic Sea Environment*, Stockholm, Nordic Council of Ministers.

Danish Environmental Agency (1994), *Environmental Support for Eastern and Central Europe. Annual Report 1993*, Copenhagen: Ministry of the Environment.

HELCOM (1993), 'Second Baltic Sea Pollution Load Compilation', *Baltic Sea Environment Proceedings* (45), Helsinki: Helsinki Commission.

HELCOM (1994), 'Hot Spot Review – Executive Summary', *Baltic Sea Environment*

Programme, **1**, Helsinki: Helsinki Commission.

HELCOM (1995), 'Third Activity Inventory. Provisional Version', *Working Paper,* Helsinki: Helsinki Commission.

HELCOM (various issues), *HELCOM – Newsletter,* Helsinki: Helsinki Commission.

Jespersen, J. (1995), 'Case-study: Environmental Protection of the Baltic Sea – An Example of East–West Co-operation' (in Danish), pp. 102-10 in N. Petersen et. al., *Vesteuropas forhold til Central- og Østeuropa,* København: Rådet for Europæisk Politik.

Jespersen, J., Karl-Göran Mäler and Olaf Söterdal (1994), *NEFCO – Evaluation Report,* Copenhagen: Nordic Council of Ministers.

Ministry of Foreign Affairs (1994), *The New Support for Eastern Europe 1994 – Possibilities and Applications* (in Danish), Copenhagen: Ministry of Foreign Affairs.

Nordic Council of Ministers (eds.) (1994), *The Nordic Environmental Strategy, April 1994–March 1996* (TemaNord), Copenhagen: Nordic Council of Ministers.

Statistics Denmark (1996), 'Transboundary Air Pollution 1994' (in Danish), *Statistiske Efterretninger, Miljø,* **11**, Copenhagen: Statistics Denmark.

15. International Assistance and European Integration

Hans Aage

15.1 Introduction

Environmental problems are not generally more severe in the Baltic than in the Nordic countries, but they are more concentrated in certain types and places, and therefore reduction of pollution is often cost-efficient in the Baltic states. Norway and Sweden import pollution, Denmark and the Baltic states export, but the exchange between the two regions is small. The Nordic countries provide 62 per cent of foreign technical assistance to the Baltic states and 18 per cent of investment finance with different geographical and sectoral priorities. An increasing share of investment finance and a higher priority of environmental policies in the Baltic states could be expected.

15.2 Transboundary Pollution

Airborne pollution can travel long distances, several hundreds of kilometres, from the source of emission to the final deposition. This is true particularly for sulphur and nitrogen, but also for ammonia, which all contribute to acidification. Due to the prevailing western winds Norway and Sweden are net importers of pollution, whereas Denmark, Finland, the Baltic states and Poland are net exporters of pollution (cf. Tables 15.1 and 15.2). However, most of the exchange of pollution involves areas other than Scandinavia and the Baltic Area including Poland. About 10 per cent of depositions in Scandinavia originate in the Baltic Area, and an even smaller share of depositions in the Baltic Area originates from emissions in Scandinavia. Finland, Norway and Sweden are importing a small amount of pollution from the Baltic Area, but Denmark is a net exporter to the Baltic states and to Poland (Fenger, 1991, p. 37; Birk Mortensen, 1994, p. 27).

Pollution of the waters of the Baltic Sea is a common concern for the Baltic and the Nordic countries. Poland, the Baltic states and Russia contribute significantly to the total pollution load in the Baltic Sea, although not more than the Nordic countries, and the water from the Baltic Sea entering the inner Danish waters is presumably less polluted than the water it replaces, partly due to the hydrographical conditions, namely that polluted water can be retained in the profound areas of the Baltic Sea. According to data from the late 1980s, Poland contributed 33 per cent of the total nitrogen pollution, the Soviet Union 25 per cent and Denmark, Sweden and Finland together 39 per cent. Concerning phosphorus the contributions were 39 per cent from Poland, 25 per cent from the Soviet Union, and 31 per cent from Denmark, Sweden and Finland. Concerning organic matter (BOD, that is biochemical oxygen demand) the contributions were 19 per cent from Poland, 32 per cent from the Soviet Union, and 49 per cent from Denmark, Sweden and Finland. Corresponding numbers of population are 37.9 million in Poland, about 16 million in the former Soviet coastal areas, including 8 million in the Baltic countries and 5 million in the St. Petersburg area, and 18.6 million in Denmark, Sweden and Finland. This refers to pollution via rivers, from urban areas and from industries. For nitrogen another 25 per cent should be added originating from the air and from the production of algae in the Baltic Sea itself (Ministry of the Environment, 1992, p. 6).

Table 15.1 Emissions and depositions per capita of sulphur, nitrogen, and ammonia in the Scandinavian and Baltic Area, 1990

kg per capita	Sulphur SO_2		Nitrogen NO_x		Ammonia NH_x	
	emission	deposition	emission	deposition	emission	deposition
Norway	20.9	34.5	58.2	19.8	8.1	11.4
Sweden	26.1	28.9	8.6	13.9	7.3	9.3
Finland	57.0	37.6	61.7	14.2	10.5	10.6
Denmark	46.7	12.2	50.6	5.5	16.6	7.3
Estonia	167.5	..	66.3	..	..	..
Latvia	44.4	..	47.0	..	..	..
Lithuania	58.1	..	45.1	..	..	..
Baltic states	75.4	25.4	50.0	8.4	20.0	11.0
Poland	99.4	32.4	35.1	6.5	10.5	7.3

Note: Data refer to 1990 which was the last year of normal production before the economic transition and depression. In the following years emissions in the Baltic states and Poland have decreased by 30–50 per cent (cf. Table 1.3).
Source: Halsnæs and Sørensen, 1993, pp. 31, 37–9.

The relative contribution to the pollution load of the Baltic Sea with heavy metals from Poland, the Baltic states and Russia is probably higher, but reliable data are lacking (Ministry of the Environment, 1992, p. 6; HELCOM, 1993, p. 139). The discharge of chlorines from the paper and pulp industry in Sweden and Finland is also a very harmful type of pollution.

Entirely new ecological disturbances are being actively created by the construction of the connection between Malmö and Copenhagen across the Sound, agreed by Sweden and Denmark in 1990. The chosen project is a combined tunnel and bridge for railway and highway. It was clearly concluded by the joint Swedish–Danish report on the project that this solution would increase air pollution, and besides it is also more expensive than alternative solutions, namely a railway tunnel or a combined tunnel and bridge for a railway (Aage, 1993). But the new problem is that the tunnel–bridge connection, as planned, could disturb the salt water inflow from the Kattegat into the Baltic Sea and thereby reduce the content of salt in the Baltic Sea. The ecological balance is highly vulnerable even to small changes in the water inflow, and several species, for example the Baltic cod, could hardly survive any decreases.

Table 15.2 Atmospheric transport of sulphur, nitrogen, and ammonia between Scandinavia, the Baltic Area, and other areas, 1990

Total emissions in ktons from		Depositions in			
		Scandi-navia	Baltic states and Poland	Other areas	Total emissions
Scandinavia	SO_2	140	16	677	833
	NO_x	51	13	820	884
	NH_x	109	7	117	233
Baltic states and Poland	SO_2	67	713	3643	4423
	NO_x	28	76	1646	1750
	NH_x	21	241	301	563
Other areas	SO_2	434	709	..	..
	NO_x	221	225	..	..
	NH_x	87	120	..	..
Total depositions	SO_2	641	1438	..	..
	NO_x	300	314	..	..
	NH_x	217	368	..	..

Note: Scandinavia includes Norway, Sweden, Denmark and Finland. The Baltic Area includes the Baltic states and Poland.
Source: Halsnæs and Sørensen, 1993, pp. 36–9.

The agreed project, on which on-shore construction started in September 1993, is estimated to reduce the water inflow by 1 per cent, but this has nevertheless caused the Swedish government's advisory board on protection of the environment (Koncessionsnämnden) to clearly advise against the project, and the Swedish Water Court (Vattendomstolen) only accepted the project on the condition that it would be completely environmentally neutral. However, an absolutely environmental neutral solution exists, namely a railway tunnel.

Nuclear pollution is a potential transboundary threat. Due to the prevailing western winds, accidents in Western European nuclear power plants, including the Barsebäck plant in Sweden situated at a distance of 20 km from the city centre of Copenhagen, could have serious effects in the Nordic countries. Taking the different degrees of risk into account the more important sources of transboundary effects might be other more remote plants in Russia, in Central and Eastern Europe, and the Ignalina plant in Lithuania (Nordic Council of Ministers, 1995, pp. 12–14).

Concerning **solid, hazardous waste** the Nordic countries are probably net exporters to Russia, the Baltic states and Eastern Central Europe, but reliable data are not available. Among the first consequences of marketization in Eastern Europe were imports of hazardous waste in Poland and the Soviet Union. After the enforcement of more efficient controls in Poland these exports were diverted towards the Baltic states, Bulgaria, Romania and the former Soviet republics. According to Greenpeace the main suppliers of waste to be dumped like used tyres, radioactive residues, pesticides and dust from steel mills are Germany, Austria and Sweden (Aage, 1993).

The most transboundary type of pollution is contribution to **the greenhouse effect**. The contribution per capita in Eastern Europe is comparable to the Scandinavian contribution. Using an index for 1987 with the contribution from the USA equal to 100, the following corresponding numbers obtain for various countries: GDR 93, Denmark 73, Finland 65, Czechoslovakia 53, Norway 52, Poland 50, Bulgaria 47, Sweden 41, Hungary 31, Romania 30, Yugoslavia 27, Albania 12 (World Resources, 1993, pp. 346–9). However, the relative contribution per unit of GDP produced is much larger in Eastern Europe, as their GDP per capita is only 25–50 per cent of the levels in Western Europe and the USA (cf. Table 1.2).

15.3 International Co-operation

Besides the direct bilateral relations between the Baltic and the Nordic countries, co-operation concerning the environment also takes place within a number of international organizations.

The Helsinki Convention was signed in 1974 by the countries bordering the Baltic Sea, and it went into force in 1980 with the establishment of **HEL-COM** (The Baltic Marine Environment Protection Commission – the Helsinki Commission), an intergovernmental body with ministerial meetings every fourth year. In 1992 the HELCOM-PITF (HELCOM Project Implementation

Task Force) was set up to oversee the improvement of conditions at 132 environmental hot spots around the Baltic Sea, and a Comprehensive Programme to Restore the Baltic Sea to a Sound Ecological Balance was presented in April 1992 with total planned costs until 2012 of 10–17 milliard ECU. In March 1993 a conference was organized in Gdansk on the theme of financing this huge programme, especially through loans from international banks (Aage, 1993; cf. above, Chapter 14).

The ministers of environment from countries within the region of the United Nations' Economic Commission for Europe met in Dobříš at the **Environment for Europe** meeting in 1991 where a major compilation of environmental data for the region was initiated (Dobříš Assessment, 1995). At the meeting in Lucerne in 1993 an Environmental Action Programme for Central and Eastern Europe was carried. The programme stresses cost-efficiency, economic incentives and market mechanisms, the combination of environmental and economic benefits – the so-called win–win policy – and international assistance concerning transboundary environmental problems (Lucerne Conference, 1994). The ministers agreed to a number of specific recommendations at the meeting in Sofia in October 1995, including a 'call upon the international financial institutions to provide their most favorable terms and conditions for qualified environmental investments in both public and private sectors', and a 'commitment to phase out, as soon as possible, unsafe nuclear installations, in particular unsafe nuclear reactors' (Sofia Conference, 1995, pp. 4, 6). The next meeting of the ministers of the environment will take place in Aarhus in June 1998 (cf. European Environmental Agency, 1998).

A number of **international conventions** for improving the environment have been signed. All the countries in Eastern Europe have signed the air pollution convention from 1979, the biodiversity convention, and the climate convention signed in Rio de Janeiro in 1992. Only Hungary and Poland are participating in these conventions to the same degree as the EU countries, whereas other countries in Eastern Europe, and particularly the Baltic countries, have desisted from the ratification of a number of conventions, including conventions concerning dumping of waste at sea, protection of the ozone layer, and transboundary transport of hazardous waste (Ministry of Economic Affairs, 1996, pp. 229–35). These conventions are often worked out in organizations related to the UN, like the UNDP (United Nations Development Programme) and the UNEP (United Nations Environmental Programme).

International financial institutions are increasingly incorporating environmental considerations into their evaluation procedures, and several are operating in the Baltic states. The World Bank (IBRD, International Bank for Reconstruction and Development) includes the IDA (International Development Association) for soft and concessional loans and the IFC (International Finance Corporation) for loans to private firms on market terms.

The EU is involved in a number of institutions. The EIB (European Investment Bank) is an EU institution, and the EU initiated the EBRD (European Bank for Reconstruction and Development) in 1991 with the purpose of supporting reconstruction and marketization in Central and Eastern Europe and in the former Soviet Union. All OECD countries and several other countries are members, but the EU and the EIB together own 57 per cent of the share capital. Technical assistance and increasingly also investment support is provided by the PHARE (Poland and Hungary Assistance to the Reconstruction of the Economy) and TACIS (Technical Assistance to the Commonwealth of Independent States) programmes. Both programmes allocate only minor amounts for environmental purposes; for the PHARE programme, which is targeted towards Central Europe and the Baltic states, the share decreased from 20 per cent to 5 per cent during 1991–4, and in the TACIS programme the share is even smaller as the environment is not even mentioned as a priority area.

The Nordic countries own the NIB (Nordic Investment Bank), established in 1975, which has provided some loans for environmental activities in the Baltic countries, particularly through the BIP (Baltic Investment Programme), a facility of 30 million ECU during 1992–5 for loans with a full government guarantee to small and medium-sized firms in the Baltic countries on the condition that projects are both economically and environmentally viable, and through the NEFCO (Nordic Environment Finance Corporation) established in 1990 for environmental investment loans to Central and Eastern Europe. Other Nordic institutions co-operating with NIB include the NDF (Nordic Development Fund) and NOPEF (Nordic Project Export Fund) (Nordic Council of Ministers, 1995, pp. 15–22, 46–59; Berg, 1995, pp. 7–12).

15.4 Environmental Assistance

Due to methodological problems it is difficult to assess the amount of international environmental assistance to Central and Eastern Europe and to the former Soviet Union. Environmental and other types of assistance, for example for industrial restructuring, are often mixed in the same projects, and the share of assistance differs according to conditionalities for donations and for loans on various terms. Generally, bilateral assistance is mostly pure aid or loans on soft conditions, although these are normally tied to imports from the donor country, whereas multilateral assistance typically consists of loans on market conditions. Bilateral assistance is often used for purely environmental projects, but multilateral assistance more often than not for projects in the energy, industry and transport sectors with a considerable environmental impact. Thus existing data are difficult to compare.

According to data compiled by Manser (1993, p. 89), allocated and anticipated foreign environmental aid to Central and Eastern Europe (excluding the Baltic states and the former Soviet Union) amounted to 2295 million ECU during 1990–2. By far the largest donor was the World Bank which provided 81 per cent of the total, and the largest recipient was Poland which received 45 per cent of the total amount of aid; bilateral assistance amounted to 8 per cent. Nevertheless foreign aid only finances 4–5 per cent of Poland's budget for environmental policy, and for most countries the share is less than 10 per cent (Ministry of Economic Affairs, 1996, pp. 245–6).

Table 15.3   Donors and recipient countries for Nordic and multilateral environmental assistance to Eastern Europe, 1992–94.

million ECU		Esto-nia	Lat-via	Lithu-ania	Baltic area	Other areas	Total
Norway	TA	0.5	0.1	0.5	1.3	13.8	15.1
	IF	..	..	..	..	37.3	37.3
Sweden	TA	3.8	2.9	4.4	11.1	7.9	27.7
	IF	3.7	8.4	17.4	31.2	7.5	38.7
Finland	TA	3.6	0.2	0.2	4.1	7.6	11.6
	IF	8.1	0.1	..	8.2	12.3	20.5
Denmark	TA	3.7	1.6	4.5	11.2	15.2	26.4
	IF	3.2	3.9	6.8	14.0	27.9	41.9
EU	TA	10.6	9.1	12.1	31.7	113.1	144.8
Nordic loans	TA	0.3	0.4	0.4	1.3	1.0	2.6
	IF	5.0	2.3	2.4	9.8	63.3	73.1
Internatio-nal loans	TA	2.9	2.7	9.7	15.3	3.1	18.5
	IF	112.3	33.3	95.2	240.8	737.8	978.5
Total	TA	25.4	16.9	31.9	76.3	161.6	246.7
	IF	132.3	47.5	121.8	303.9	886.1	1190.0

Notes: Assistance data cover the years 1992, 1993 and the first half of 1994. TA denotes technical assistance and IF investment finance. Projects covering more than one country are included in the total only. EU aid includes grants from PHARE and TACIS for environment and energy. Nordic loans include loans from NEFCO, NIB and NOPEF, and international loans include loans from EBRD, EIB, IBRD and IFC. Amounts of assistance shown are committed, but not necessarily disbursed.
Source: Nordic Council of Ministers, 1995, pp. 26–30.

For Nordic and multilateral assistance to Eastern Europe and Russia more detailed data exist: see Tables 15.3 and 15.4 which cover the period from 1992 to the first half of 1994. Also a detailed compilation of projects with an impact upon the environment in the Baltic states, Poland and western Russia during 1990–4 is available (Berg, 1995).

According to Table 15.3 which includes multilateral assistance and Nordic bilateral assistance, but not bilateral assistance from other countries, to Central and Eastern Europe and areas in the former Soviet Union neighbouring Scandinavia, Nordic bilateral asssistance is not insignificant in the Baltic states, particularly concerning technical assistance; it constitutes 62 per cent of technical assistance to the Baltic states and 18 per cent of investment finance. Concerning financial assistance as a percentage of GDP the Nordic countries are topping the list of donors of all types of assistance to Central and Eastern Europe taken together (Ministry of Economic Affairs, 1996, p. 201).

For technical assistance the most important donors are the PHARE and TACIS programmes of the EU. Table 15.3 includes all expenditures for environmental protection and the energy sector from the EU, about 18 per cent of the total, not only energy projects with a significant environmental impact as for the other donors. For investment finance to the Baltic states the most important source is international financial institutions, which provide 82 per cent of the total. The EBRD and the World Bank provide 56 per cent and 18 per cent, respectively, of Baltic assistance, but for Poland and other areas the pattern is different, as the EBRD and the IBRD have given priority to the Baltic states and to Poland and other areas, respectively. Among other areas mentioned in Table 15.3, Poland received the largest amounts, 18 per cent of total technical assistance and 46 per cent of total investment finance. Russian areas neighbouring Scandinavia received 21 per cent of total technical assistance and 4 per cent of total investment finance, both almost exclusively as Nordic bilateral aid.

15.5 Priorities and Instruments

Concerning the **geographical distribution**, there is a marked tendency for the Nordic countries and for other European bilateral donors as well to concentrate their environmental support on their neighbouring areas, presumably mainly because of the interest in reducing transboundary pollution, but possibly also for political reasons. Thus Norway has supported north-western Russia, Finland has invested in projects in the Kola peninsula and in Estonia, and Sweden has supported waste water treatment in the Baltic states.

Denmark is partly an exception; the law on environmental assistance to Eastern Europe from 1991 and supplementary material from the Ministry of the Environment stipulate that countries bordering the Baltic Sea should receive highest priority, and this was further specified as the Baltic countries, Poland, and the Kaliningrad and St. Petersburg regions (Aage, 1993). The reasons for this priority are, firstly, that environmental transboundary effects originating in these countries are considered to be of some importance, and secondly, that the preference for neighbouring countries is a natural one, given the need to limit the scope of Danish activities in order to gather relevant experience concerning the working out of co-operation programmes, because of the relatively minor amounts of Danish financial support.

Table 15.4 Sectoral distribution and recipient countries for Nordic and multilateral environmental support to Eastern Europe, 1992–94

million ECU		Esto- nia	Lat- via	Lithu- ania	Baltic Area	Other areas	Total
Waste	TA	1.1	0.5	1.1	3.0	2.6	5.6
treatment	IF	0.1	0.4	0.8	1.2	5.0	6.2
Water	TA	2.3	1.7	1.9	5.9	8.5	14.4
protection	IF	32.1	7.4	7.5	47.0	67.9	114.9
Nuclear	TA	0.6	0.2	10.7	11.5	7.7	19.2
safety	IF	..	..	44.9	44.9	1.1	46.0
Other	TA	2.6	2.1	1.8	7.2	17.8	25.0
environment	IF	1.6	0.1	..	1.7	177.5	179.3
Energy	TA	7.7	3.2	4.0	15.9	8.4	24.4
	IF	85.8	38.5	68.6	193.5	360.9	554.4
Industry	TA	0.4	0.1	0.3	1.1	2.6	3.7
	IF	12.8	1.0	..	13.8	65.6	79.4
Transport	TA	..	..	..	..	0.9	0.9
	IF	..	..	..	1.7	208.1	209.8
Total	TA	14.8	7.8	19.8	44.6	48.5	93.1
	IF	132.3	47.5	121.8	303.9	886.1	1190.0

Notes: Assistance data cover the years 1992, 1993 and the first half of 1994. TA denotes technical assistance and IF investment finance. Projects covering more than one country are included in the total only. For the energy, industry and transportation sectors projects with considerable environmental significance are included. Nordic loans include loans from NEFCO, NIB and NOPEF, and international loans include loans from EBRD, EIB, IBRD and IFC. Amounts of assistance shown are committed, but not necessarily disbursed.
Source: Nordic Council of Ministers, 1995, pp. 26–30.

There are marked differences between the Nordic countries concerning the relative importance of support to hardware **investment**, often in various types of infrastructure, and **technical assistance**, which includes soft support like feasibility studies, institutional support, training and monitoring. However, investment projects normally include some technical assistance. The rather limited Norwegian support to the Baltic states is exclusively technical assistance. Sweden and Finland have concentrated on investment finance. For

Denmark the share of investment finance is smaller than for Finland and Sweden, but it is increasing from a low level of about one third in 1991–2, and this is a general trend.

There are also differences concerning the choice of supported **sectors** (cf. Table 15.4). Sweden has mainly supported water treatment, energy projects and nuclear safety, particularly in Lithuania. A large share of the assistance from Finland has been for water treatment, industrial restructuring and the reduction of emissions from industries in Estonia. Denmark has mainly supported treatment of waste and hazardous waste, water treatment and the industry and energy sectors, including a number of district heating projects. Norway has not donated investment finance in the Baltic states, but a large donation is committed for industrial restructuring in Murmansk and the Kola peninsula, particularly the nickel smelter Petchenganikel close to the Norwegian border (Berg, 1996, pp. 42, 47–53).

Other types of project have received support, including projects related to agriculture, nature conservation, monitoring and institutional support, particularly support of local and central public administration. Many donors have been involved in this type of assistance, and Poland has received the largest amounts. Among recipient countries there is a tendency to regard the need for institutional support as declining as compared to the initial phases after the collapse of communism (Berg, 1995, p. 50).

15.6 Assessment of International Assistance

An assessment of foreign environmental assistance must take the **motivations** of donor and recipient countries as its point of departure. On the part of the donor countries one type of motivation is the concern for improving the environment, in the recipient countries, in the donor country itself due to local transboundary effects, and in a global perspective. Economic interests are another possible motivation. There is an interest in supporting the domestic industry for anti-pollution equipment and the consultancy industry. For the EU there is an interest in upgrading environmental policy in Central and Eastern European countries in order to prevent 'environmental dumping' from their export sectors.

The main priority of recipient countries is projects with an economic growth potential, as concern for the environment faded after the collapse of communism concurrently with the deepening of the economic recession. Whether one or another of these partly conflicting objectives will prevail depends on the **mechanism** for allocating assistance funds. Thus the PHARE and TACIS programmes rely upon recipient countries to find and choose which projects to negotiate and implement. This is part of the explanation for the small and until recently declining share of environmental projects. Contradictions between the privatization and marketization drive on the one hand and public support of environmental policy on the other could arise. Thus a Danish engineering company specializing in district heating systems met with unexpected difficulties in Poland, Hungary and Czechoslovakia where private heating was considered more in line with the new decentralized economic system and district heating became correspondingly unpopular among the public (Aage, 1993).

For bilateral aid from Denmark, and partly also from Norway, Sweden and other Western European countries, domestic companies are free to find and present projects. It is an explicit objective to create beneficial effects for Danish exports, production and employment (Aage, 1993), and the very indeterminate priorities with several hundred small projects have left the initiative concerning the allocation of financial support to the applications of Danish business firms in collaboration with their chosen partners in recipient countries. This has been subject to criticism in the press, and in a report from the Government Audit Department (1995, p. 109) it was stated, 'that the aid programmes have benefited the Danish business community more than they have supported the development of a liberal market economy in Central and Eastern Europe'. In particular there has been criticism that in 1991–2 only about one third of the funds were used for equipment and hardware and the larger share for 'paper work'. According to the Danish Environmental Agency (1993, p. 20) it is, however, necessary to persuade eastern receivers of 'the need for careful planning' before investment projects are carried out.

Even if the general political priority of upgrading the environment prevails, it is not evident that additional funds for environmental policy should always be allocated to Central and Eastern Europe rather than to domestic uses. Many types of pollution are not more severe in Eastern than in Western Europe (Tables 1.2 and 1.3; cf. European Environmental Agency, 1998). However, it could nevertheless be cost-efficient to invest in Central and Eastern Europe, where pollution is concentrated on particular types and places and therefore relatively inexpensive to reduce, for example waste water outlets and sulphur emissions from a limited number of cities and industries. Pollution of the Baltic Sea is partly due to untreated waste water from urban areas and industries in the eastern countries, which can be remedied at fairly low costs compared to pollution of the sea from for example Denmark which is mainly caused by agricultural fertilizer usage (Ministry of the Environment, 1992, p. 6).

However, it is also repeatedly stated as a motivation for Danish environmental support to Central and Eastern European countries that transboundary pollution from these countries contribute significantly to local environmental problems in Denmark (Aage, 1993), which is – apart from the potential threat of nuclear contamination – contrary to fact, as Denmark is a net exporter of air pollution and is itself the cause of most of the pollution of the inner

Danish waters. The probability that Denmark receives sulphur pollution emitted in Denmark is 50–100 times larger than the probability of receiving pollution emitted in Poland (Fenger, 1991, p. 36). Therefore, from a narrow Danish point of view, if the aim is to improve the environment in Denmark, available funds are more effectively spent in Denmark rather than in, for example, Poland, because costs of pollution control are not so much lower in Poland than in Denmark. Similar considerations apply to the other Nordic countries vis–à–vis the Baltic states, as they only import small amounts of pollution, the most significant being imports of sulphur pollution to Finland from Estonia (Hiltunen, 1994, pp. 9–15).

15.7 Policy Strategies

Despite the methodological and empirical difficulties of assessing the impact of foreign environmental assistance, there emerge some general tendencies and recommendations from the experience of several years of involvement in Central and Eastern Europe and ensuing criticisms which can be summarized as follows (Ministry of the Environment, 1997; EBRD, 1995; OECD, 1995; Berg, 1995, pp. 52–3; Sandberg, 1992; Nordic Council of Ministers, 1995, pp. 60–79; Löfstedt and Sjöstedt, 1996, pp. 215–24; Hiltunen, 1994, pp. 108–15; Aage, 1997):

– A shift of emphasis from planning and sometimes fruitless studies to investment and equipment, or at least to the involvement of more local experts, is recommended and has also taken place.
– There are several possible projects which would at the same time improve the environment and yield an economic return, especially energy savings like district heating; it could be argued, however, that the limited western assistance should not be used for this type of project which is likely to be funded from other sources.
– Because of the concentration of environmental problems in the eastern countries in certain regions and pollution spots, there are large benefits from concentrating environmental investment on these points, especially private heating systems in towns, nuclear power plants and major industrial polluters, whereas general schemes for reducing for example sulphur pollution by the same amount from all sources seem much less useful.
– A higher priority for environmental policies in recipient countries is recommended, and this type of change is probably also materializing.
– Closer international coordination of assistance is recommended and can presumably also be expected.

But the precondition for improving the allocation of funds for environmental support to Central and Eastern Europe is that the funds are available and that environmental policy will be given an increasing priority. According to an EBRD study ministries of the environment in the Central and Eastern European countries have had their budgets cut by about 65% since 1990, and the Baltic states are not an exception (EBRD, 1995, p. 17).

15.8 European Integration

In late 1995 Estonia, Latvia and Lithuania officially applied for membership of the European Union. This was the temporary culmination of a process which began in February and March 1993 when Agreements on Trade and Commercial and Economic Co-operation were signed by the EU and the Baltic states. In July 1994 this was followed by Free Trade Agreements and in June 1995 by Association Agreements (The Europe Agreements), which are designed to establish a close, long-term association between the EU and individual Central and Eastern European countries. Finally, in December 1997, Estonia, but not Latvia and Lithuania, was included in the group of countries which were selected for full membership because they were considered to fulfil the criteria formulated in Copenhagen in June 1993 most closely: stable institutions for democracy, rule of law and human rights; a well functioning market economy; and the ability to take on the obligations of membership.

In May 1995 a White Paper was adopted by the EU Commission (1995) with guidelines for the Central and Eastern European countries concerning approximation of laws and legal institutions to the EU *acquis communautaire*. The White Paper (41 pages) and its Annex (438 pages) cover 23 policy areas, including environment and energy. It guides policy in three ways: by pointing out the most important laws of the internal market, by indicating necessary administrative and technical structures, and by identifying key measures and the best use of technical assistance from the EU.

The main problem of the three Baltic states is their low level of GDP as compared to other Central and Eastern European countries. As regards institutional reform they have done fairly well, although they are lagging slightly behind Poland, Hungary and the Czech Republic. They have made substantial progress concerning price liberalization, even including energy prices, in trade and foreign exchange liberalization, and in privatization, in Estonia even concerning large-scale privatization (Aage, 1997).

Among the admission requirements for new members of the EU, environmental policy does not occupy a central role. The section on the environment in the White Paper of 1995 is mainly concerned with the free circulation of goods, not the whole range of environmental regulations, and it is not legally binding. Also, the Europe Agreements do not require immediate harmonization of environmental regulations, but only more informal forms of co-operation. Furthermore, many EU standards are so far not precise and binding, but rather statements of intent. There are well-known conflicts of interest between members of the EU, with Germany often pressing for more rigorous rules against the resistance of the UK and Southern Europe. On the part of the Central and Eastern European countries environmental problems is only a secondary concern, as Vaclav Klaus put it: 'The environment and the economy are like whipped cream and cake: Whipped cream can be used to decorate the cake, once the cake is ready' (quoted from Bisschop, 1996, p. 43).

Nevertheless, the Baltic states are actively adopting EU environmental regulations as a sort of anticipatory adaptation, which includes the signing of a number of international conventions. Often this means that previously very strict standards – which were not enforced – have been relaxed concurrently with improved enforcement and stronger reliance on economic incentives. For Danish bilateral environmental assistance, contribution towards implementation of EU regulations and standards in recipient countries is now the general guideline, but the necessary investment costs are huge, and a minimum estimate is 75 milliard ECU for the total Central and Eastern European region (Ministry of the Environment, 1997, p. 23–4).

However, environmental policy is – like security policy – an area where the populations of the current EU member countries have a direct interest in EU enlargement towards the east. In other respects, enlargement will entail an economic burden, and admission to the customs union of the EU is a favour at the expense of other exporters to the EU. But due to transboundary pollution, notably potential nuclear pollution, the EU has a strong interest in the environment in the Baltic states, and therefore environmental policy can be expected to be an important element in the European integration process.

REFERENCES

Aage, H. (1993), 'Denmark's Policies towards Environmental Degradation in Russia, the Baltic States and the East Central European Countries', Paper presented at the *Conference on Environmental Assistance to Eastern Europe*, The Finnish Institute of International Affairs, Gustavelund, Tuusula, 19–21 November 1993; cf. the conference summary reports by Hiltunen (1994).

Aage, H. (1997), 'Public Sector Development: Difficulties and Restrictions', pp. 96–118 in T. Haavisto (ed.), *The Transition to a Market Economy. Transformation and Reform in the Baltic States*, Cheltenham: Edward Elgar.

Berg, C. (1995), *The Environmental Support to the Baltic States, Poland and Western Russia*, Stockholm: Swedish Environmental Protection Agency.

Birk Mortensen, J. (ed.) (1994), *Environmental Economics and the Baltic Region*, Copenhagen: Institute of Economics, University of Copenhagen.

Bisschop, G. (1996), 'Optimism Wanes for a Prompt Cleanup', *Transition*, **2** (17 May

1996), 42–5.

Danish Environmental Agency (various years), *Annual Report* (in Danish), Copenhagen: Ministry of the Environment.

Dobříš Assessment (1995), *Europe's Environment, The Dobříš Assessment*, ed. by D. Stanners and P. Bourdeau, Copenhagen: European Environmental Agency.

EBRD (1995), *A Strategy to Enhance Partnership in Project Financing for Environmental Investments in Central and Eastern Europe*, London: EBRD.

EU Commission (1995), *White Paper. Preparation of the Associated Countries of Central and Eastern Europe for Integration into the Internal Market of the Union*, COM(95) 163 final, 3 May, COM(95) 163 final/2, 10 May, Brussels: EU Commission.

European Environmental Agency (1998), *Europe's Environment: The Second Assessment*, Copenhagen: European Environmental Agency.

Fenger, J. (1991), *Fossil Fuels and Air Pollution* (in Danish), Copenhagen: Dansk Gasteknisk Center.

Government Audit Department (1995), *Report on Assistance to Eastern Europe* (in Danish), Copenhagen: Ministry of Economic Affairs.

Halsnæs, K. and L. Sørensen (1993), 'Perspectives of Regional Co-ordinated Energy and Environmental Planning', *Nordiske Seminar- og Arbejdsrapporter* (640), Copenhagen: Nordic Council of Ministers.

HELCOM (1993), 'Second Baltic Sea Pollution Load Compilation', *Baltic Sea Environment Proceedings* (45), Helsinki: Baltic Marine Environment Protection Commission.

Hiltunen, H. (1994), *Finland and Environmental Problems in Russia and Estonia*, Helsinki: The Finnish Institute of International Affairs.

Löfstedt, R.E. and G. Sjöstedt (eds.) (1996), *Environmental Aid Programmes to Eastern Europe*, Aldershot: Avebury.

Lucerne Conference (1994), *Environmental Action Programme for Central and Eastern Europe*, Lucerne: Council of Ministers of the Environment.

Manser, R. (1993), *Failed Transitions: The Eastern European Economy and Environment Since the Fall of Communism*, New York: The New Press.

Ministry of Economic Affairs (1996), *Enlargement of the EU Towards the East – Economic Perspectives* (in Danish), Copenhagen: Ministry of Economic Affairs.

Ministry of the Environment (1992), *Environmental Indicators 1992* (in Danish), Copenhagen: Ministry of the Environment.

Ministry of the Environment (1997), *EU Enlargement Towards the East – Environmental Perspectives* (in Danish), Copenhagen: Ministry of the Environment.

Nordic Council of Ministers (1995), *Report on Environmental Assistance to Neighbouring Countries* (in Swedish), Stockholm: Nordic Council of Ministers.

OECD (1995), *Environmental Funds in Economies in Transition*, Paris: OECD.

Sandberg, M. (ed.) (1992), *Baltic Sea Region Environmental Protection. Eastern Perspectives and International Co-operation*, Stockholm: Almquist and Wiksell International.

Sofia Conference (1995), *Declaration*, Sofia: Council of Ministers of the Environment.

World Resources Institute (1993), *World Resources 1992–93*, Oxford: Oxford University Press.

Index